HISTORICAL LECTURES AND ESSAYS

HISTORICAL LECTURES AND ESSAYS

BY

CHARLES KINGSLEY

GYAN

Published by

Gyan Publishing House
5, Ansari Road
Daryaganj, New Delhi-110002
Phone: 011-47034999, 9811692060
E-mail: books@gyanbooks.com

Distribution Network
gyanbooks.com
India, USA, Canada, UK, Australia, France

ISBN : 978-81-212-6567-6 (PB)
First Published, 1889

2nd Impression 2022

Printed at: Gyan Press, Delhi.

HISTORICAL LECTURES AND ESSAYS
Author: CHARLES KINGSLEY

HISTORICAL

LECTURES AND ESSAYS

BY

CHARLES KINGSLEY

...

1889

CONTENTS.

ALEXANDRIA AND HER SCHOOLS.

(Four Lectures delivered at the Philosophical Institution, Edinburgh.)

Our little systems have their day;
They have their day and cease to be;
They are but broken lights of Thee,
And Thou, O Lord, art more than they.—*Tennyson.*

THE ANCIEN RÉGIME.

(Three Lectures delivered at the Royal Institution.)

ALEXANDRIA AND HER SCHOOLS.

ALEXANDRIA AND HER SCHOOLS.*

PREFACE.

I SHOULD not have presumed to choose for any lectures of mine such a subject as that which I have tried to treat in this book. The subject was chosen for me by the Institution where the lectures were delivered. Still less should I have presumed to print them of my own accord, knowing how fragmentary and crude they are. They were printed at the special request of my audience. Least of all, perhaps, ought I to have presumed to publish them, as I have done, at Cambridge, where any inaccuracy or sciolism (and that such defects exist in these pages, I cannot but fear) would be instantly detected, and severely censured: but nevertheless, it seemed to me that Cambridge was the fittest place in which they could see the light, because to Cambridge I mainly owe what little right method or sound thought may be found in them, or indeed, in anything which I have ever written. In the heyday of youthful greediness and ambition, when the mind, dazzled by the vastness and variety of the universe, must needs know

* These Lectures were delivered at the Philosophical Institution, Edinburgh, in February, 1854, at the commencement of the Crimean War.

everything, or rather know about everything, at once and on the spot, too many are apt, as I have been in past years, to complain of Cambridge studies as too dry and narrow: but as time teaches the student, year by year, what is really required for an understanding of the objects with which he meets, he begins to find that his University, in as far as he has really received her teaching into himself, has given him, in her criticism, her mathematics, above all, in Plato, something which all the popular knowledge, the lectures and institutions of the day, and even good books themselves, cannot give, a boon more precious than learning; namely, the art of learning. That instead of casting into his lazy lap treasures which he would not have known how to use, she has taught him to mine for them himself; and has by her wise refusal to gratify his intellectual greediness, excited his hunger, only that he may be the stronger to hunt and till for his own subsistence; and thus, the deeper he drinks, in after years, at fountains wisely forbidden to him while he was a Cambridge student, and sees his old companions growing up into sound-headed and sound-hearted practical men, liberal and expansive, and yet with a firm standing-ground for thought and action, he learns to complain less and less of Cambridge studies, and more and more of that conceit and haste of his own, which kept him from reaping the full advantage of her training.

These Lectures, as I have said, are altogether crude and fragmentary—how, indeed, could they be otherwise, dealing with so vast a subject, and so long a period of time? They are meant neither as Essays nor as Orations, but simply as a collection of hints to those who may wish to work out the subject for themselves; and, I trust, as giving some glimpses of a central idea, in the light of which the spiritual history of Alexandria, and perhaps of other countries also, may be seen to have in itself a coherence and organic method.

I was of course compelled, by the circumstances under which these Lectures were delivered, to keep clear of all points which are commonly called "controversial." I cannot but feel that this was a gain, rather than a loss; because it forced me, if I wished to give any interpretation at all of Alexandrian thought, any Theodicy at all of her fate, to refer to laws which I cannot but believe to be deeper, wider, more truly eternal than the points which cause most of our modern controversies, either theological or political; laws which will, I cannot but believe also, reassert themselves, and have to be reasserted by all wise teachers, very soon indeed, and it may be under most novel embodiments, but without any change in their eternal spirit.

For I may say, I hope, now (what if said ten years ago would have only excited laughter), that I cannot but subscribe to the opinion of the many wise men who believe that Europe, and England as an integral part thereof, is on the eve of a revolution, spiritual and political, as vast and awful as that which took place at the Reformation; and that, beneficial as that revolution will doubtless be to the destinies of mankind in general, it depends upon the wisdom and courage of each nation individually, whether that great deluge shall issue, as the Reformation did, in a fresh outgrowth of European nobleness and strength or usher in, after pitiable confusions and sorrows, a second Byzantine age of stereotyped effeminacy and imbecility. For I have as little sympathy with those who prate so loudly of the progress of the species, and the advent of I know-not-what Cockaigne of universal peace and plenty, as I have with those who believe on the strength of "unfulfilled prophecy," the downfall of Christianity, and the end of the human race to be at hand. Nevertheless, one may well believe that prophecy will be fulfilled in this great crisis, as it is in every great crisis, although one be unable to conceive by what method of symbolism the drying up of the Euphrates can be twisted to signify the fall of Constantinople: and one can well believe that a day of judgment is at hand, in which for every nation and institution, the wheat will be sifted out and gathered into God's garner, for the use of future generations, and the chaff burnt up with that fire unquenchable which will try every man's work, without being of opinion that after a few more years are over, the great majority of the human race will be consigned hopelessly to never-ending torments.

If prophecy be indeed a divine message to man; if it be anything but a cabbala, useless either to the simple-minded or to the logical, intended only for the plaything of a few devout fancies, it must declare the unchangeable laws by which the unchangeable God is governing, and has always governed, the human race; and therefore only by understanding what has happened, can we understand what will happen; only by understanding history, can we understand prophecy; and that not merely by picking out—too often arbitrarily and unfairly—a few names and dates from the records of all the ages, but by trying to discover its organic laws, and the causes which produce in nations, creeds, and systems, health and disease, growth, change, decay and death. If, in one small corner of this vast field, I shall have thrown a single ray of light upon these subjects—if I shall have done anything in these pages towards illustrating the pathology of a single people, I shall believe that I have done better service to the Catholic Faith and the Scriptures, than if I did really "know the times and the seasons, which the Father has kept in His own hand." For by the former act I may have helped to make some one man more prudent and brave to see and to do what God requires of him; by the latter I could only add to that paralysis of superstitious fear, which is already but too common among us, and but too likely to hinder us from doing our duty manfully against our real foes, whether it be pestilence at home or tyranny abroad.

These last words lead me to another subject, on which I am bound to say a few words. I have, at the end of these Lectures, made some allusion to the present war. To have entered further into political questions would have been improper in the place where those Lectures were delivered: but I cannot refrain from saying here something more on this matter; and that, first, because all political questions have their real root in moral and spiritual ones, and not (as too many fancy) in questions merely relating to the balance of power or commercial economy, and are (the world being under the guidance of a spiritual, and not a physical Being) finally decided on those spiritual grounds, and according to the just laws of the kingdom of God; and, therefore, the future political horoscope of the East depends entirely on the present spiritual state of its inhabitants, and of us who have (and rightly) taken up their cause; in short, on many of those questions on which I have touched in these Lectures: and next, because I feel bound, in justice to myself, to guard against any mistake about my meaning or supposition that I consider the Turkish empire a righteous thing, or one likely to stand much longer on the face of God's earth.

The Turkish empire, as it now exists, seems to me an altogether unrighteous and worthless thing. It stands no longer upon the assertion of the great truth of Islam, but on the merest brute force and oppression. It has long since lost the only excuse which one race can have for holding another in subjection; that which we have for taking on ourselves the tutelage of the Hindoos, and which Rome had for its tutelage of the Syrians and Egyptians; namely, the governing with tolerable justice those who cannot govern themselves, and making them better and more prosperous people, by compelling them to submit to law. I do not know when this excuse is a sufficient one. God showed that it was so for several centuries in the case of the Romans; God will show whether it is in the case of our Indian empire: but this I say, that the Turkish empire has not even that excuse to plead; as is proved by the patent fact that the whole East, the very garden of the old world, has become a desert and a ruin under the upas-blight of their government.

As for the regeneration of Turkey, it is a question whether the regeneration of any nation which has sunk, not into mere valiant savagery, but into effete and profligate luxury, is possible. Still more is it a question whether a regeneration can be effected, not by the rise of a new spiritual idea (as in the case of the Koreish), but simply by more perfect material appliances, and commercial prudence. History gives no instance, it seems to me, of either case; and if our attempt to regenerate Greece by freeing it has been an utter failure, much more, it seems to me, would any such attempt fail in the case of the Turkish race. For what can be done with a people which has lost the one great quality which was the tenure of its existence, its military skill? Let any one read the accounts of the Turkish armies in the fifteenth, sixteenth, and seventeenth centuries, when they were the tutors and models of all Europe in the art of war, and then consider the fact that those very armies require now to be officered by foreign adventurers, in order to make them capable of even keeping together, and let him ask himself seriously, whether such a fall can ever be recovered. When, in the age of Theodosius, and again in that of Justinian, the Roman armies had fallen into the same state; when tho Italian legions required to be led by Stilicho the Vandal, and the Byzantine by Belisar the Sclav and Narses the Persian, the end of all things was at hand, and came; as it will come soon to Turkey.

But if Turkey deserves to fall, and must fall, it must not fall by our treachery. Its sins will surely be avenged upon it: but wrong must not avenge wrong, or the penalty is only passed on from one sinner to another. Whatsoever element of good is left in the Turk, to that we must appeal as our only means, if not of saving him, still of helping him to a quiet euthanasia, and absorption into a worthier race of successors. He is said (I know not how truly) to have one virtue left; that of faithfulness to his word. Only by showing him that we too abhor treachery and bad faith, can we either do him good, or take a safe standing-ground in our own peril. And this we have done; and for this we shall be rewarded. But this is surely not all our duty. Even if we should be able to make the civil and religious freedom of the Eastern Christians the price of our assistance to the Mussulman, the struggle will not be over; for Russia will still be what she has always been, and the northern Anarch will be checked, only to return to the contest with fiercer lust of aggrandisement, to enact the part of a new Macedon, against a new Greece, divided, not united, by the treacherous bond of that balance of power, which is but war under the guise of peace. Europe needs a holier and more spiritual, and therefore a stronger union, than can be given by armed neutralities, and the so-called cause of order. She needs such a bond as in the Elizabethan age united the free states of Europe against the Anarch of Spain, and delivered the Western nations from a rising world-tyranny, which promised to be even more hideous than the elder one of Rome. If, as then, England shall proclaim herself the champion of freedom by acts, and not by words and paper, she may, as she did then, defy the rulers of the darkness of this world, for the God of Light will be with her. But, as yet, it is impossible to look without sad forebodings upon the destiny of a war, begun upon the express understanding that evil shall be left triumphant throughout Europe, wheresoever that evil does not seem, to our own selfish shortsightedness, to threaten us with immediate danger; with promises, that under the hollow name of the Cause of Order—and that promise made by a revolutionary Anarch—the wrongs of Italy, Hungary, Poland, Sweden, shall remain unredressed, and that Prussia and Austria, two tyrannies, the one far more false and hypocritical, the other even more rotten than that of Turkey, shall, if they will but observe a hollow and uncertain neutrality (for who can trust the liar and the oppressor?)—be allowed not only to keep their ill-gotten spoils, but even now to play into the hands of our foe, by guarding his Polish frontier for him, and keeping down the victims of his cruelty, under pretence of keeping down those of their own.

It is true, the alternative is an awful one; one from which statesmen and nations may well shrink: but it is a question, whether that alternative may not be forced upon us sooner or later, whether we must not from the first look it boldly in the face, as that which must be some day, and for which we must prepare, not cowardly, and with cries about God's wrath and judgments against us—which would be abject, were they not expressed in such second-hand stock-phrases as to make one altogether doubt their sincerity, but chivalrously, and with awful joy, as a noble calling, an honour put upon us by the God of Nations, who demands of us, as some small return for all His free bounties, that we should be, in this great crisis, the champions of Freedom and of Justice, which are the cause of God. At all events, we shall not escape our duty by being afraid of it; we shall not escape our duty by inventing to ourselves some other duty, and calling it "Order." Elizabeth did so at first. She tried to keep the peace with Spain; she shrank from injuring the cause of Order (then a nobler one than now, because it was the cause of Loyalty, and not merely of Mammon) by assisting the Scotch and the Netherlanders: but her duty was forced upon her; and she did it at last, cheerfully, boldly, utterly, like a hero; she put herself at the head of the battle for the freedom of the world, and she conquered, for God was with her; and so that seemingly most fearful of all England's perils, when the real meaning of it was seen, and God's will in it obeyed manfully, became the foundation of England's naval and colonial empire, and laid the foundation of all her future glories. So it was then, so it is now; so it will be for ever: he who seeks to save his life will lose it: he who willingly throws away his life for the cause of mankind, which is the cause of God, the Father of mankind, he shall save it, and be rewarded a hundred-fold. That God may grant us, the children of the Elizabethan heroes, all wisdom to see our duty, and courage to do it, even to the death, should be our earnest prayer. Our statesmen have done wisely and well in refusing, in spite of hot-headed clamours, to appeal to the sword as long as there was any chance of a peaceful settlement even of a single evil. They are doing wisely and well now in declining to throw away the scabbard as long as there is hope that a determined front will awe the offender into submission: but the day may come when the scabbard must be thrown away; and God grant that they may have the courage to do it.

It is reported that our rulers have said, that English diplomacy can no longer recognise "nationalities," but only existing "governments." God grant that they may see in time that the assertion of national life, as a spiritual and indefeasible existence, was for centuries the central idea of English policy; the idea by faith in which she delivered first herself, and then the Protestant nations of the Continent, successively from the yokes of Rome, of Spain, of France; and that they may reassert that most English of all truths again, let the apparent cost be what it may.

It is true, that this end will not be attained without what is called nowadays "a destruction of human life." But we have yet to learn (at least if the doctrines which I have tried to illustrate in this little book have any truth in them) whether shot or shell has the power of taking away human life; and to believe, if we believe our Bibles, that human life can only be destroyed by sin, and that all which is lost in battle is that animal life of which it is written, "Fear not those who can kill the body, and after that have no more that they can do: but I will forewarn you whom you shall fear; him who, after he has killed, has power to destroy both body and soul in hell." Let a man fear him, the destroying devil, and fear therefore cowardice, disloyalty, selfishness, sluggishness, which are his works, and to be utterly afraid of which is to be truly brave. God grant that we of the clergy may remember this during the coming war, and instead of weakening the righteous courage and honour of our countrymen by instilling into them selfish and superstitious fears, and a theory of the future state which represents God, not as a saviour, but a tormentor, may boldly tell them that "He is not the God of the dead but of the living; for all live unto Him;" and that he who renders up his animal life as a worthless thing, in the cause of duty, commits his real and human life, his very soul and self, into the hands of a just and merciful Father, who has promised to leave no good deed unrewarded, and least of all that most noble deed, the dying like a man for the sake not merely of this land of England, but of the freedom and national life of half the world.

LECTURE I.

THE PTOLEMAIC ERA.

BEFORE I begin to lecture upon the Physical and Metaphysical schools of Alexandria, it may be better, perhaps, to define the meaning of these two epithets. Physical, we shall all agree, means that which belongs to φύσις; *natura*; nature, that which φύεται, *nascitur*, grows, by an organic life, and therefore decays again; which has a beginning, and therefore, I presume, an end. And Metaphysical means that which we learn to think of after we think of nature; that which is supernatural, in fact, having neither beginning nor end, imperishable, immovable, and eternal, which does not become, but always is. These, at least, are the wisest definitions of these two terms for us just now; for they are those which were received by the whole Alexandrian school, even by those commentators who say that Aristotle, the inventor of the term Metaphysics, named his treatise so only on account of its following in philosophic sequence his book on Physics.

But, according to these definitions, the whole history of Alexandria might be to us, from one point of view, a physical school; for Alexandria, its society and its philosophy, were born, and grew, and fed, and reached their vigour, and had their old age, their death, even as a plant or an animal has; and after they were dead and dissolved, the atoms of them formed food for new creations, entered into new organisations, just as the atoms of a dead plant or animal might do. Was Alexandria then, from beginning to end, merely a natural and physical phenomenon?

It may have been. And yet we cannot deny that Alexandria was also a metaphysical phenomenon, vast and deep enough; seeing that it held for some eighteen hundred years a population of several hundred thousand souls; each of whom, at least according to the Alexandrian philosophy, stood in a very intimate relation to those metaphysic things which are imperishable and immovable and eternal, and indeed, contained them more or less, each man, woman, and child of them in themselves; having wills, reasons, consciences, affections, relations to each other; being parents, children, helpmates, bound together by laws concerning right and wrong, and numberless other unseen and spiritual relations.

Surely such a body was not merely natural, any more than any other nation, society, or scientific school, made up of men and of the spirits, thoughts, affections of men. It, like them, was surely spiritual; and could be only living and healthy, in as far as it was in harmony with certain spiritual, unseen, and everlasting laws of God; perhaps, as certain Alexandrian philosophers would have held, in as far as it was a pattern of that ideal constitution and polity after which man was created, the city of God which is eternal in the Heavens. If so, may we not suspect of this Alexandria that it was its own fault if it became a merely physical phenomenon; and that it stooped to become a part of nature, and took its place among the things which are born to die, only by breaking the law which God had appointed for it; so fulfilling, in its own case, St. Paul's great words, that death entered into the world by sin, and that sin is the transgression of the law?

Be that as it may, there must have been metaphysic enough to be learnt in that, or any city of three hundred thousand inhabitants, even though it had never contained lecture-room or philosopher's chair, and had never heard the names of Aristotle and Plato. Metaphysic enough, indeed, to be learnt there, could we but enter into the heart of even the most brutish negro slave who ever was brought down the Nile out of the desert by Nubian merchants, to build piers and docks in whose commerce he did not share, temples whose worship he did not comprehend, libraries and theatres whose learning and civilisation were to him as much a sealed book as they were to his countryman, and fellow-slave, and only friend, the ape. There was metaphysic enough in him truly, and things eternal and immutable, though his dark-skinned descendants were three hundred years in discovering the fact, and in proving it satisfactorily to all mankind for ever. You must pardon me if I seem obscure; I cannot help looking at the question with a somewhat Alexandrian eye, and talking of the poor negro dock-worker as certain Alexandrian philosophers would have talked, of whom I shall have to speak hereafter.

I should have been glad, therefore, had time permitted me, instead of confining myself strictly to what are now called "the physic and metaphysic schools" of Alexandria, to have tried as well as I could to make you understand how the whole vast phenomenon grew up, and supported a peculiar life of its own, for fifteen hundred years and more, and was felt to be the third, perhaps the second city of the known world, and one so important to the great world-tyrant, the Cæsar of Rome, that no Roman of distinction was ever sent there as prefect, but the Alexandrian national vanity and pride of race was allowed to the last to pet itself by having its tyrant chosen from its own people.

But, though this cannot be, we may find human elements enough in the schools of Alexandria, strictly so called, to interest us for a few evenings; for these schools were schools of men; what was discovered and taught was discovered and taught by men, and not by thinking-machines; and whether they would have been inclined to confess it or not, their own personal characters, likes and dislikes, hopes and fears, strength and weakness, beliefs and disbeliefs, determined their metaphysics and their physics for them, quite enough to enable us to feel for them as men of like passions with ourselves; and for that reason only, men whose thoughts and speculations are worthy of a moment's attention from us. For what is really interesting to man, save men, and God, the Father of men?

In the year 331 B.C. one of the greatest intellects whose influence the world has ever felt, saw, with his eagle glance, the unrivalled advantage of the spot which is now Alexandria; and conceived the mighty project of making it the point of union of two, or rather of three worlds. In a new city, named after himself, Europe, Asia, and Africa were to meet and to hold communion. A glance at the map will show you what an ὀμφαλὸς γῆς, a centre of the world, this Alexandria is, and perhaps arouse in your minds, as it has often done in mine, the suspicion that it has not yet fulfilled its whole destiny, but may become at any time a prize for contending nations, or the centre of some world-wide empire to come. Communicating with Europe and the Levant by the Mediterranean, with India by the Red Sea, certain of boundless supplies of food from the desert-guarded valley of the Nile, to which it formed the only key, thus keeping all Egypt, as it were, for its own private farm, it was weak only on one side, that of Judea. That small strip of fertile mountain land, containing innumerable military positions from which an enemy might annoy Egypt, being, in fact, one natural chain of fortresses, was the key to Phœnicia and Syria. It was an eagle's eyrie by the side of a pen of fowls. It must not be left defenceless for a single year. Tyre and Gaza had been taken; so no danger was to be apprehended from the seaboard: but to subdue the Judean mountaineers, a race whose past sufferings had hardened them in a dogged fanaticism of courage and endurance, would be a long and sanguinary task. It was better to make terms with them; to employ them as friendly warders of their own mountain walls. Their very fanaticism and isolation made them sure allies. There was no fear of their fraternising with the Eastern invaders. If the country was left in their hands, they would hold it against all comers. Terms were made with them; and for several centuries they fulfilled their trust.

This I apprehend to be the explanation of that conciliatory policy of Alexander's toward the Jews, which was pursued steadily by the Ptolemies, by Pompey, and by the Romans, as long as these same Jews continued to be endurable upon the face of the land. At least, we shall find the history of Alexandria and that of Judea inextricably united for more than three hundred years.

So arose, at the command of the great conqueror, a mighty city, around those two harbours, of which the western one only is now in use. The Pharos was then an island. It was connected with the mainland by a great mole, furnished with forts and drawbridges. On the ruins of that mole now stands the greater part of the modern city; the vast site of the ancient one is a wilderness.

But Alexander was not destined to carry out his own magnificent project. That was left for the general whom he most esteemed, and to whose personal prowess he had once owed his life; a man than whom history knows few greater, Ptolemy, the son of Lagus. He was an adventurer, the son of an adventurer, his mother a cast-off concubine of Philip of Macedon. There were those who said that he was in reality a son of Philip himself. However, he rose at court, became a private friend of young Alexander, and at last his Somatophylax, some sort of Colonel of the Life Guards. And from thence he rose rapidly, till after his great master's death he found himself despot of Egypt.

His face, as it appears on his coins, is of the loftiest and most Jove-like type of Greek beauty. There is a possibility about it, as about most old Greek faces, of boundless cunning; a lofty irony too, and a contemptuousness, especially about the mouth, which puts one in mind of Goethe's expression; the face, altogether, of one who knew men too well to respect them. At least, he was a man of clear enough vision. He saw what was needed in those strange times, and he went straight to the thing which he saw. It was his wisdom which perceived that the huge amorphous empire of Alexander could not be kept together, and advised its partition among the generals, taking care to obtain himself the lion's share; not in size, indeed, but in capability. He saw, too (what every man does not see), that the only way to keep what he had got was to make it better, and not worse, than he found it. His first Egyptian act was to put to death Cleomenes, Alexander's lieutenant, who had amassed vast treasures by extortion; and who was, moreover, (for Ptolemy was a prudent man) a dangerous partisan of his great enemy, Perdiccas. We do not read that he refunded the treasures: but the Egyptians surnamed him Soter, the Saviour; and on the whole he deserved the title. Instead of the wretched misrule and slavery of the conquering Persian dynasty, they had at least law and order, reviving commerce, and a system of administration, we are told (I confess to speaking here quite at second-hand), especially adapted to the peculiar caste-society, and the religious prejudices of Egypt. But Ptolemy's political genius went beyond such merely material and Warburtonian care for the conservation of body and goods of his subjects. He effected with complete success a feat which has been attempted, before and since, by very many princes and potentates, but has always, except in Ptolemy's case, proved somewhat of a failure, namely, the making a new deity. Mythology in general was in a rusty state. The old Egyptian gods had grown in his dominions very unfashionable, under the summary iconoclasm to which they had been subjected by the Monotheist Persians—the Puritans of the old world, as they have been well called. Indeed, all the dolls, and the treasure of the dolls' temples too, had been carried off by Cambyses to Babylon. And as for the Greek gods, philosophers had sublimed them away sadly during the last century: not to mention that Alexander's Macedonians, during their wanderings over the world, had probably become rather remiss in their religious exercises, and had possibly given up mentioning the Unseen world, except for those hortatory purposes for which it used to be employed by Nelson's veterans. But, as Ptolemy felt, people (women especially) must have something wherein to believe. The "Religious Sentiment" in man must be satisfied. But, how to do it? How to find a deity who would meet the aspirations of conquerors as well as conquered—of his most irreligious Macedonians, as well as of his most religious Egyptians? It was a great problem: but Ptolemy solved it. He seems to have taken the same method which Brindley the engineer used in his perplexities, for he went to bed. And there he had a dream: How the foreign god Serapis, of Pontus (somewhere near this present hapless Sinope), appeared to him, and expressed his wish to come to Alexandria, and there try his influence on the Religious Sentiment. So Serapis was sent for, and came—at least the idol of him, and—accommodating personage!—he actually fitted. After he had been there awhile, he was found to be quite an old acquaintance—to be, in fact, the Greek Jove, and two or three other Greek gods, and also two or three Egyptian gods beside—indeed, to be no other than the bull Apis, after his death and deification. I can tell you no more. I never could find that anything more was known. You may see him among Greek and Roman statues as a young man, with a sort of high basket-shaped Persian turban on his head. But, at least, he was found so pleasant and accommodating a conscience-keeper, that he spread, with Isis, his newly-found mother, or wife, over the whole East, and even to Rome. The Consuls there—50 years B.C.—found the pair not too respectable, and pulled down their temples. But, so popular were they, in spite of their bad fame, that seven years after, the Triumvirs had to build the temples up again elsewhere; and from that time forth, Isis and Serapis, in spite, poor things, of much persecution, were the fashionable deities of the Roman world. Surely this Ptolemy was a man of genius!

But Ptolemy had even more important work to do than making gods. He had to make men; for he had few or none ready made among his old veterans from Issus and Arbela. He had no hereditary aristocracy: and he wanted none. No aristocracy of wealth; that might grow of itself, only too fast for his despotic power. But as a despot, he must have a knot of men round him who would do his work. And here came out his deep insight into fact. It had not escaped that man, what was the secret of Greek supremacy. How had he come there? How had his great master conquered half the world? How had the little semi-barbarous mountain tribe up there in Pella, risen under Philip to be the master-race of the globe? How, indeed, had Xenophon and his Ten Thousand, how had the handfuls of Salamis and Marathon, held out triumphantly century after century, against the vast weight of the barbarian? The simple answer was: Because the Greek has mind, the barbarian mere brute force. Because mind is the lord of matter;

because the Greek being the cultivated man, is the only true man; the rest are βάρβαροι, mere things, clods, tools for the wise Greeks' use, in spite of all their material phantom-strength of elephants, and treasures, and tributaries by the million. Mind was the secret of Greek power; and for that Ptolemy would work. He would have an aristocracy of intellect; he would gather round him the wise men of the world (glad enough most of them to leave that miserable Greece, where every man's life was in his hand from hour to hour), and he would develop to its highest the conception of Philip, when he made Aristotle the tutor of his son Alexander. The consequences of that attempt were written in letters of blood, over half the world; Ptolemy would attempt it once more, with gentler results. For though he fought long, and often, and well, as Despot of Egypt, no less than as general of Alexander, he was not at heart a man of blood, and made peace the end of all his wars.

So he begins. Aristotle is gone: but in Aristotle's place Philetas the sweet singer of Cos, and Zenodotus the grammarian of Ephesus, shall educate his favourite son, and he will have a literary court, and a literary age. Demetrius Phalcreus, the Admirable Crichton of his time, the last of Attic orators, statesman, philosopher, poet, warrior, and each of them in the most graceful, insinuating, courtly way, migrates to Alexandria, after having had the three hundred and sixty statues, which the Athenians had too hastily erected to his honour, as hastily pulled down again. Here was a prize for Ptolemy! The charming man became his bosom friend and fellow, even revised the laws of his kingdom, and fired him, if report says true, with a mighty thought —no less a one than the great public Library of

Alexandria; the first such institution, it is said, which the world had ever seen.

So a library is begun by Soter, and organised and completed by Philadelphus; or rather two libraries, for while one part was kept at the Serapeium, that vast temple on the inland rising ground, of which, as far as we can discover, Pompey's Pillar alone remains, one column out of four hundred, the rest was in the Brucheion adjoining the Palace and the Museum. Philadelphus buys Aristotle's collection to add to the stock, and Euergetes cheats the Athenians out of the original MSS. of Æschylus, Sophocles, and Euripides, and adds largely to it by more honest methods. Eumenes, King of Pergamus in Asia Minor, fired with emulation, commences a similar collection, and is so successful, that the reigning Ptolemy has to cut off his rival's supplies by prohibiting the exportation of papyrus; and the Pergamenian books are henceforth transcribed on parchment, parchemin, Pergamene, which thus has its name to this day, from Pergamus. That collection, too, found its way at last to Alexandria. For Antony having become possessor of it by right of the stronger, gave it to Cleopatra; and it remained at Alexandria for seven hundred years. But we must not anticipate events.

Then there must be besides a Mouseion, a Temple of the Muses, with all due appliances, in a vast building adjoining the palace itself, under the very wing of royalty; and it must have porticos, wherein sages may converse; lecture-rooms, where they may display themselves at their will to their rapt scholars, each like a turkey-cock before his brood; and a large dining-hall, where they may enjoy themselves in moderation, as befits sages, not without puns and repartees, epigrams, anagrams, and Attic salt, to be fatal, alas, to poor Diodorus the dialectician. For Stilpo, prince of sophists, having silenced him by some quibbling puzzle of logic, Ptolemy surnamed him Chronos the Slow. Poor Diodorus went home, took pen and ink, wrote a treatise on the awful nothing, and died in despair, leaving five "dialectical daughters" behind him, to be thorns in the sides of some five hapless men of Macedonia, as "emancipated women;" a class but too common in the later days of Greece, as they will always be, perhaps, in civilisations which are decaying and crumbling to pieces, leaving their members to seek in bewilderment what they are, and what bonds connect them with their fellow-beings. But to return: funds shall be provided for the Museum from the treasury; a priest of rank, appointed by royalty, shall be curator; botanical and zoological gardens shall be attached; collections of wonders made. In all things the presiding genius of Aristotle shall be worshipped; for these, like Alexander, were his pupils. Had he not mapped out all heaven and earth, things seen and unseen, with his entelechies, and energies, and dunameis, and put every created and uncreated thing henceforth into its proper place, from the ascidians and polypes of the sea to the virtues and the vices—yea, to that Great Deity and Prime Cause (which indeed was all things), *Noesis Noeseon*, "the Thought of Thoughts," whom he discovered by irrefragable processes of logic, and in whom the philosophers believe privately, leaving Serapis to the women and the sailors? All they had to do was to follow in his steps; to take each of them a branch, of science or literature, or as many branches as one man conveniently can; and working them out on the approved methods, end in a few years, as Alexander did, by weeping on the utmost shore of creation that there are no more worlds left to conquer.

Alas! the Muses are shy and wild; and though they will haunt, like skylarks, on the bleakest northern moor as cheerfully as on the sunny hills of Greece, and rise thence singing into the heaven of heavens, yet they are hard to tempt into a gilded cage, however amusingly made and plentifully stored with comforts. Royal societies, associations of savants, and the like, are good for many things, but not for the breeding of art and genius: for they are things which cannot be bred. Such institutions are excellent for physical science, when, as among us now, physical science is going on the right method: but where, as in Alexandria, it was going on an utterly wrong method, they stereotype the errors of the age, and invest them with the prestige of authority, and produce mere Sorbonnes, and schools of pedants. To literature, too, they do some good, that is, in a literary age—an age of reflection rather than of production, of antiquarian research, criticism, imitation, when book-making has become an easy and respectable pursuit for the many who cannot dig, and are ashamed to beg. And yet, by adding that same prestige of authority, not to mention of good society and Court favour, to the popular mania for literature, they help on the growing evil, and increase the multitude of prophets who prophesy out of their own heart and have seen nothing.

And this was, it must be said, the outcome of all the Ptolemæan appliances.

In Physics they did little. In Art nothing. In Metaphysics less than nothing.

We will first examine, as the more pleasant spectacle of the two, that branch of thought in which some progress was really made, and in which the Ptolemaic schools helped forward the development of men who have become world-famous, and will remain so, I suppose, until the end of time.

Four names at once attract us: Euclid, Aristarchus, Eratosthenes, Hipparchus. Archimedes, also, should be included in the list, for he was a pupil of the Alexandrian school, having studied (if Proclus is to be trusted) in Egypt, under Conon the Samian, during the reigns of two Ptolemies, Philadelphus and Euergetes.

Of Euclid, as the founder (according to Proclus) of the Alexandrian Mathematical school, I must of course speak first. Those who wish to attain to a juster conception of the man and his work than they can do from any other source, will do well to read Professor De Morgan's admirable article on him in "Smith's Classical Dictionary;" which includes, also, a valuable little sketch of the rise of Geometric science, from Pythagoras and Plato, of whose school Euclid was, to the great master himself.

I shall confine myself to one observation on Euclid's genius, and on the immense influence which it exerted on after generations. It seems to me, speaking under correction, that it exerted this, because it was so complete a type of the general tendency of the Greek mind, deductive, rather than inductive; of unrivalled subtlety in obtaining results from principles, and results again from them *ad infinitum*: deficient in that sturdy moral patience which is required for the examination of facts, and which has made Britain at once a land of practical craftsmen, and of earnest scientific discoverers.

Volatile, restless, "always children longing for something new," as the Egyptian priest said of them, they were too ready to believe that they had attained laws, and then, tired with their toy, throw away those hastily assumed laws, and wander off in search of others. Gifted, beyond all the sons of men, with the most exquisite perception of form, both physical and metaphysical, they could become geometers and logicians as they became sculptors and artists; beyond that they could hardly rise. They were conscious of their power to build; and it made them ashamed to dig.

Four men only among them seem, as far as I can judge, to have had a great inductive power: Socrates and Plato in Metaphysics; Archimedes and Hipparchus in Physics. But these men ran so far counter to the national genius, that their examples were not followed. As you will hear presently, the discoveries of Archimedes and Hipparchus were allowed to remain where they were for centuries. The Dialectic of Plato and Socrates was degraded into a mere art for making anything appear alternately true and false, and among the Megaric school, for undermining the ground of all science, and paving the way for scepticism, by denying the natural world to be the object of certain knowledge. The only element of Plato's thought to which they clung was, as we shall find from the Neoplatonists, his physical speculations; in which, deserting his inductive method, he has fallen below himself into the popular cacoëthes, and Pythagorean deductive dreams about the mysterious powers of numbers, and of the regular solids.

Such a people, when they took to studying physical science, would be, and in fact were, incapable of

Chemistry, Geognosy, Comparative Anatomy, or any of that noble choir of sister sciences, which are now building up the material as well as the intellectual glory of Britain.

To Astronomy, on the other hand, the pupils of Euclid turned naturally, as to the science which required the greatest amount of their favourite geometry: but even that they were content to let pass from its inductive to its deductive stage—not as we have done now, after two centuries of inductive search for the true laws, and their final discovery by Kepler and Newton: but as soon as Hipparchus had propounded any theory which would do instead of the true laws, content there to stop their experiments, and return to their favourite work of commenting, deducing, spinning notion out of notion, *ad infinitum.*

Still, they were not all of this temper. Had they been, they would have discovered, not merely a little, but absolutely nothing. For after all, if we will consider, induction being the right path to knowledge, every man, whether he knows it or not, uses induction, more or less, by the mere fact of his having a human reason, and knowing anything at all; as M. Jourdain talked prose all his life without being aware of it.

Aristarchus is principally famous for his attempt to discover the distance of the sun as compared with that of the moon. His method was ingenious enough, but too rough for success, as it depended principally on the belief that the line bounding the bright part of the moon was an exact straight line. The result was of course erroneous. He concluded that the sun was 18 times as far as the moon, and not, as we now know, 400; but his conclusion, like his conception of the vast extent of the sphere of the fixed stars, was far enough in advance of the popular doctrine to subject him, according to Plutarch, to a charge of impiety.

Eratosthenes, again, contributed his mite to the treasure of human science—his one mite; and yet by that he is better known than by all the volumes which he seems to have poured out, on Ethics, Chronology, Criticism on the Old Attic Comedy, and what not, spun out of his weary brain during a long life of research and meditation. They have all perished,—like ninety-nine hundredths of the labours of that great literary age; and perhaps the world is no poorer for the loss. But one thing, which he attempted on a sound and practical philosophic method, stands, and will stand for ever. And after all, is not that enough to have lived for? to have found out one true thing, and, therefore, one imperishable thing, in one's life? If each one of us could but say when he died: "This one thing I have found out; this one thing I have proved to be possible; this one eternal fact I have rescued from Hela, the realm of the formless and unknown," how rich one such generation might make the world for ever!

But such is not the appointed method. The finders are few and far between, because the true seekers are few and far between; and a whole generation has often nothing to show for its existence but one solitary gem which some one man—often unnoticed in his time—has picked up for them, and so given them "a local habitation and a name."

Eratosthenes had heard that in Syene, in Upper Egypt, deep wells were enlightened to the bottom on the day of the summer solstice, and that vertical objects cast no shadows.

He had before suggested, as is supposed, to Ptolemy Euergetes, to make him the two great copper armillæ, or circles for determining the equinox, which stood for centuries in "that which is called the Square Porch"—probably somewhere in the Museum. By these he had calculated the obliquity of the ecliptic, closely enough to serve for a thousand years after. That was one work done. But what had the Syene shadows to do with that? Syene must be under that ecliptic. On the edge of it. In short, just under the tropic. Now he had ascertained exactly the latitude of one place on the earth's surface. He had his known point from whence to start on a world-journey, and he would use it; he would calculate the circumference of the earth—and he did it. By observations made at Alexandria, he ascertained its latitude compared with that of Syene; and so ascertained what proportion to the whole circumference was borne by the 5000 stadia between Alexandria and Syene. He fell into an error, by supposing Alexandria and Syene to be under the same meridians of longitude: but that did not prevent his arriving at a fair rough result of 252,000 stadia—31,500 Roman miles; considerably too much; but still, before him, I suppose, none knew whether it was 10,000, or 10,000,000. The right method having once been found, nothing remained but to employ it more accurately.

One other great merit of Eratosthenes is, that he first raised Geography to the rank of a science. His Geographica were an organic collection, the first the world had ever seen, of all the travels and books of earth-description heaped together in the Great Library, of which he was for many years the keeper. He began with a geognostic book, touched on the traces of

Cataclysms and Change visible on the earth's surface; followed by two books, one a mathematical book, the other on political geography, and completed by a map —which one would like to see: but——not a trace of all remains, save a few quoted fragments—

> We are such stuff
> As dreams are made of.

But if Eratosthenes had hold of eternal fact and law on one point, there was a contemporary who had hold of it in more than one. I mean Archimedes; of whom, as I have said, we must speak as of an Alexandrian. It was as a mechanician, rather than as an astronomer, that he gained his reputation. The stories of his Hydraulic Screw, the Great Ship which he built for Hiero, and launched by means of machinery, his crane, his war-engines, above all his somewhat mythical arrangement of mirrors, by which he set fire to ships in the harbour—all these, like the story of his detecting the alloy in Hiero's crown, while he himself was in the bath, and running home undressed shouting *εὕρηκα*—all these are schoolboys' tales. To the thoughtful person it is the method of the man which constitutes his real greatness, that power of insight by which he solved the two great problems of the nature of the lever and of hydrostatic pressure, which form the basis of all static and hydrostatic science to this day. And yet on that very question of the lever the great mind of Aristotle babbles—neither sees the thing itself, nor the way towards seeing it. But since Archimedes spoke, the thing seems self-evident to every schoolboy. There is something to me very solemn in such a fact as this. It brings us down to some of the very deepest questions of metaphysic. This mental insight of which we boast so much, what is it? Is it altogether a process of our own brain and will? If it be, why have so few the power, even among men of power, and they so seldom? If brain alone were what was wanted, what could not Aristotle have discovered? Or is it that no man can see a thing unless God shows it him? Is it that in each separate act of induction, that mysterious and transcendental process which cannot, let logicians try as they will, be expressed by any merely logical formula, Aristotelian or other—is it, I say, that in each separate act of induction we do not find the law, but the law is shown to us, by Him who made the law? Bacon thought so. Of that you may find clear proof in his writings. May not Bacon be right? May it not be true that God does in science, as well as in ethics, hide things from the wise and prudent, from the proud, complete, self-contained systematiser like Aristotle, who must needs explain all things in heaven and earth by his own formulæ, and his entelechies and energies, and the rest of the notions which he has made for himself out of his own brain, and then pack each thing away in its proper niche in his great cloud-universe of conceptions? Is it that God hides things from such men many a time, and reveals them to babes, to gentle, affectionate, simple-hearted men, such as we know Archimedes to have been, who do not try to give an explanation for a fact, but feel how awful and divine it is, and wrestle reverently and stedfastly with it, as Jacob with the Angel, and will not let it go, until it bless them? Sure I am, from what I have seen of scientific men, that there is an intimate connection between the health of the moral faculties and the health of the inductive ones; and that the proud, self-conceited, and passionate man will see nothing: perhaps because nothing will be shown him.

But we must leave Archimedes for a man not perhaps so well known, but to whom we owe as much as to the great Syracusan—Hipparchus the astronomer. To his case much which I have just said applies. In him astronomic science seemed to awaken suddenly to a true inductive method, and after him to fall into its old slumber for 300 years. In the meantime Timocharis, Aristyllus, and Conon had each added their mites to the discoveries of Eratosthenes: but to Hipparchus we owe that theory of the heavens, commonly called the Ptolemaic system, which, starting from the assumption that the earth was the centre of the universe, attempted to explain the motions of the heavenly bodies by a complex system of supposed eccentrics and epicycles. This has of course now vanished before modern discoveries. But its value as a scientific attempt lies in this: that the method being a correct one, correct results were obtained, though starting from a false assumption; and Hipparchus and his successors were enabled by it to calculate and predict the changes of the heavens, in spite of their clumsy instruments, with almost as much accuracy as we do now.

For the purpose of working out this theory he required a science of trigonometry, plane and spherical: and this he accordingly seems to have invented. To him also we owe the discovery of that vast gradual change in the position of the fixed stars, in fact, of the whole celestial system, now known by the name of the precession of the equinoxes; the first great catalogue of fixed stars, to the number of 1080; attempts to ascertain whether the length of years and days were constant; with which, with his characteristic love of truth, he seems to have been hardly satisfied. He too invented the planisphere, or mode of representing the starry heavens upon a plane, and is the father of true geography, having formed the happy notion of mapping out the earth, as well as the heavens, by degrees of latitude and longitude.

Strange it is, and somewhat sad, that we should know nothing of this great man, should be hardly able to distinguish him from others of the same name, but through the works of a commentator, who wrote and observed in Alexandria 300 years after, during the age of the Antonines. I mean, of course, the famous Ptolemy, whose name so long bore the honour of that system which really belonged to Hipparchus.

This single fact speaks volumes for the real weakness of the great artificial school of literature and science founded by the kings of Egypt. From the father of Astronomy, as Delambre calls him, to Ptolemy, the first man who seems really to have appreciated him, we have not a discovery, hardly an observation or a name, to fill the gap. Physical sages there were; but they were geometers and mathematicians, rather than astronomic observers and inquirers. And in spite of all the huge appliances and advantages of that great Museum, its inhabitants were content, in physical science, as in all other branches of thought, to comment, to expound, to do everything but open their eyes and observe facts, and learn from them, as the predecessors whom they pretended to honour had done. But so it is always. A genius, an original man appears. He puts himself boldly in contact with facts, asks them what they mean, and writes down their answer for the world's use. And then his disciples must needs form a school, and a system; and fancy that they do honour to their master by refusing to follow in his steps; by making his book a fixed dogmatic canon; attaching to it some magical infallibility; declaring the very lie which he disproved by his whole existence, that discovery is henceforth impossible, and the sum of knowledge complete: instead of going on to discover as he discovered before them, and by following his method, show that they honour him, not in the letter, but in spirit and in truth.

For this, if you will consider, is the true meaning of that great command, "Honour thy father and mother, that thy days may be long in the land." On reverence for the authority of bygone generations depends the permanence of every form of thought or belief, as much as of all social, national, and family life: but on reverence of the spirit, not merely of the letter; of the methods of our ancestors, not merely of their conclusions. Ay, and we shall not be able to preserve their conclusions, not even to understand them; they will die away on our lips into skeleton notions, and soulless phrases, unless we see that the greatness of the mighty dead has always consisted in this, that they were seekers, improvers, inventors, endued with that divine power and right of discovery which has been bestowed on us, even as on them; unless we become such men as they were, and go on to cultivate and develop the precious heritage which they have bequeathed to us, instead of hiding their talent in a napkin and burying it in the earth; making their greatness an excuse for our own littleness, their industry for our laziness, their faith for our despair; and prating about the old paths, while we forget that paths were made that men might walk in them, and not stand still, and try in vain to stop the way.

It may be said, certainly, as an excuse for these Alexandrian Greeks, that they were a people in a state of old age and decay; and that they only exhibited the common and natural faults of old age. For as with individuals, so with races, nations, societies, schools of thought—youth is the time of free fancy and poetry; manhood of calm and strong induction; old age of deduction, when men settle down upon their lees, and content themselves with re-affirming and verifying the conclusions of their earlier years, and too often, alas! with denying and anathematising all conclusions which have been arrived at since their own meridian. It is sad: but it is patent and common. It is sad to think that the day may come to each of us, when we shall have ceased to hope for discovery and for progress; when a thing will seem *à priori* false to us, simply because it is new; and we shall be saying querulously to the Divine Light which lightens every man who comes into the world: "Hitherto shalt thou come, and no further. Thou hast taught men enough; yea rather, thou hast exhausted thine own infinitude, and hast no more to teach them." Surely such a temper is to be fought against, prayed against, both in ourselves, and in the generation in which we live. Surely there is no reason why such a temper should overtake old age. There may be reason enough, "in the nature of things." For that which is of nature is born only to decay and die. But in man there is more than dying nature; there is spirit, and a capability of spiritual and everlasting life, which renews its youth like the eagle's, and goes on from strength to strength, and which, if it have its autumns and its winters, has no less its ever-recurring springs and summers; if it has its Sabbaths, finds in them only rest and refreshment for coming labour. And why not in nations, societies, scientific schools? These too are not merely natural: they are spiritual, and are only living and healthy in as far as they are in harmony with spiritual, unseen, and everlasting laws of God. May not they, too, have a capability of everlasting life, as long as they obey those laws in faith, and patience, and humility? We cannot deny the analogy between the individual man and these societies of men. We cannot, at least, deny the analogy between them in growth, decay, and death. May we not have hope that it holds good also for that which can never die; and that if they do die, as this old Greek society did, it is by no brute natural necessity, but by their own unfaithfulness to that which they knew, to that which they ought to have known? It is always more hopeful, always, as I think, more philosophic, to throw the blame of failure on man, on our own selves, rather than on God, and the perfect law of His universe. At least let us be sure for ourselves, that such an old age as befell this Greek society, as befalls many a man nowadays, need not be our lot. Let us be sure that earth shows no fairer sight than the old man, whose worn-out brain and nerves make it painful, and perhaps impossible, to produce fresh thought himself: but who can yet welcome smilingly and joyfully the fresh thoughts of others; who keeps unwearied his faith in God's government of the universe, in God's continual education of the human race; who draws around him the young and the sanguine, not merely to check their rashness by his wise cautions, but to inspirit their sloth by the memories of his own past victories; who hands over, without envy or repining, the lamp of truth to younger runners than himself, and sits contented by, bidding the new generation God speed along the paths untrodden by him, but seen afar off by faith. A few such old persons have I seen, both men and women; in whom the young heart beat pure and fresh, beneath the cautious and practised brain of age, and gray hairs which were indeed a crown of glory. A few such have I seen; and from them I seemed to learn what was the likeness of our Father who is in heaven. To such an old age may He bring you and me, and all for whom we are bound to pray.

LECTURE II.

THE PTOLEMAIC ERA.

(Continued.)

I SAID in my first Lecture, that even if royal influence be profitable for the prosecution of physical science, it cannot be profitable for art. It can only produce a literary age, as it did in the Ptolemaic era; a generation of innumerable court-poets, artificial epigrammatists, artificial idyllists, artificial dramatists and epicists; above all, a generation of critics. Or rather shall we say, that the dynasty was not the cause of a literary age, but only its correlative? That when the old Greeks lost the power of being free, of being anything but the slaves of oriental despots, as the Ptolemies in reality were, they lost also the power of producing true works of art; because they had lost that youthful vigour of mind from which both art and freedom sprang? Let the case be as it will, Alexandrian literature need not detain us long—though, alas! it has detained every boy who ever trembled over his Greek grammar, for many a weary year; and, I cannot help suspecting, has been the main cause that so many young men who have spent seven years in learning

Greek, know nothing about it at the end of the seven. For I must say, that as far as we can see, these Alexandrian pedants were thorough pedants; very polished and learned gentlemen, no doubt, and, like Callimachus, the pets of princes: but after all, men who thought that they could make up for not writing great works themselves, by showing, with careful analysis and commentation, how men used to write them of old, or rather how they fancied men used to write them; for, consider, if they had really known how the thing was done, they must needs have been able to do it themselves. Thus Callimachus, the favourite of Ptolemy Philadelphus, and librarian of his Museum, is the most distinguished grammarian, critic, and poet of his day, and has for pupils Eratosthenes, Apollonius Rhodius, Aristophanes of Byzantium, and a goodly list more. He is an encyclopædia in himself. There is nothing the man does not know, or probably, if we spoke more correctly, nothing he does not know about. He writes on history, on the Museum, on barbarous names, on the wonders of the world, on public games, on colonisation, on winds, on birds, on the rivers of the world, and—ominous subject—a sort of comprehensive history of Greek literature, with a careful classification of all authors, each under his own heading. Greek literature was rather in the sere and yellow leaf, be sure, when men thought of writing that sort of thing about it. But still, he is an encyclopædic man, and, moreover, a poet. He writes an epic, "Aitia," in four books, on the causes of the myths, religious ceremonies, and so forth—an ominous sign for the myths also, and the belief in them; also a Hecate, Galatæa, Glaucus—four epics, besides comedies, tragedies, iambics, choriambics, elegies, hymns, epigrams seventy-three—and of these last alone can we say that they are in any degree readable; and they are courtly, far-fetched, neat, and that is all. Six hymns remain, and a few fragments of the elegies: but the most famous elegy, on Berenice's hair, is preserved to us only in a Latin paraphrase of Catullus. It is curious, as the earliest instance we have of genuinely ungenuine Court poetry, and of the complimentary lie which does not even pretend to be true; the flattery which will not take the trouble to prevent your seeing that it is laughing in your face.

Berenice the queen, on Ptolemy's departure to the wars, vows her beautiful tresses to her favourite goddess, as the price of her husband's safe return; and duly pays her vow. The hair is hung up in the temple: in a day or two after it has vanished. Dire is the wrath of Ptolemy, the consternation of the priests, the scandal to religion; when Conon, the court-astronomer, luckily searching the heavens, finds the missing tresses in an utterly unexpected place—as a new constellation of stars, which to this day bears the title of Coma Berenices. It is so convenient to believe the fact, that everybody believes it accordingly; and Callimachus writes an elegy thereon, in which the constellified, or indeed deified tresses, address in most melodious and highly-finished Greek, bedizened with concetto on concetto, that fair and sacred head whereon they grew, to be shorn from which is so dire a sorrow, that apotheosis itself can hardly reconcile them to the parting.

Worthy, was not all this, of the descendants of the men who fought at Marathon and Thermopylæ? The old Greek civilisation was rotting swiftly down; while a fire of God was preparing, slowly and dimly, in that unnoticed Italian town of Rome, which was destined to burn up that dead world, and all its works.

Callimachus's hymns, those may read who list. They are highly finished enough; the work of a man who knew thoroughly what sort of article he intended to make, and what were the most approved methods of making it. Curious and cumbrous mythological lore comes out in every other line. The smartness, the fine epithets, the recondite conceits, the bits of effect, are beyond all praise; but as for one spark of life, of poetry, of real belief, you will find none; not even in that famous Lavacrum Palladis which Angelo Poliziano thought worth translating into Latin elegiacs, about the same time that the learned Florentine, Antonio Maria Salviano, found Berenice's Hair worthy to be paraphrased back from Catullus' Latin into Greek, to give the world some faint notion of the inestimable and incomparable original. They must have had much time on their hands. But at the Revival of Letters, as was to be expected, all works of the ancients, good and bad, were devoured alike with youthful eagerness by the Medicis and the Popes; and it was not, we shall see, for more than one century after, that men's taste got sufficiently matured to distinguish between Callimachus and the Homeric hymns, or between Plato and Proclus. Yet Callimachus and his fellows had an effect on the world. His writings, as well as those of Philetas, were the model on which Ovid, Propertius, Tibullus, formed themselves.

And so I leave him, with two hints. If any one wishes to see the justice of my censure, let him read one of the Alexandrian hymns, and immediately after it, one of those glorious old Homeric hymns to the very same deities; let him contrast the insincere and fulsome idolatry of Callimachus with the reverent, simple and manful anthropomorphism of the Homerist —and let him form his own judgment.

The other hint is this. If Callimachus, the founder of Alexandrian literature, be such as he is, what are his pupils likely to become, at least without some infusion of healthier blood, such as in the case of his Roman imitators produced a new and not altogether ignoble school?

Of Lycophron, the fellow-grammarian and poet of Callimachus, we have nothing left but the Cassandra, a long iambic poem, stuffed with traditionary learning, and so obscure, that it obtained for him the surname of σκοτεινός, the dark one. I have tried in vain to read it: you, if you will, may do the same.

Philetas, the remaining member of the Alexandrian Triad, seems to have been a more simple, genial, and graceful spirit than the other two, to whom he was accordingly esteemed inferior. Only a few fragments are left; but he was not altogether without his influence, for he was, as I have just said, one of the models on which Propertius and Ovid formed themselves; and some, indeed, call him the Father of the Latin elegy, with its terseness, grace, and clear epigrammatic form of thought, and, therefore, in a great degree, of our modern eighteenth century poets; not a useless excellence, seeing that it is, on the whole, good for him who writes to see clearly what he wants to say, and to be able to make his readers see it clearly also. And yet one natural strain is heard amid all this artificial jingle—that of Theocritus. It is not altogether Alexandrian. Its sweetest notes were learnt amid the chestnut groves and orchards, the volcanic glens and sunny pastures of Sicily; but the intercourse between the courts of Hiero and the Ptolemies seems to have been continual. Poets and philosophers moved freely from one to the other, and found a like atmosphere in both; and in one of Theocritus' idyls, two Sicilian gentlemen, crossed in love, agree to sail for Alexandria, and volunteer into the army of the great and good king Ptolemy, of whom a sketch is given worth reading; as a man noble, generous, and stately, "knowing well who loves him, and still better who loves him not." He has another encomium on Ptolemy, more laboured, though not less interesting: but the real value of Theocritus lies in his power of landscape-painting.

One can well conceive the delight which his idyls must have given to those dusty Alexandrians, pent up forever between sea and sand-hills, drinking the tank-water, and never hearing the sound of a running stream —whirling, too, forever, in all the bustle and intrigue of a great commercial and literary city. Refreshing indeed it must have been to them to hear of those simple joys and simple sorrows of the Sicilian shepherd, in a land where toil was but exercise, and mere existence was enjoyment. To them, and to us also. I believe Theocritus is one of the poets who will never die. He sees men and things, in his own light way, truly; and he describes them simply, honestly, with little careless touches of pathos and humour, while he floods his whole scene with that gorgeous Sicilian air, like one of Titian's pictures; with still sunshine, whispering pines, the lizard sleeping on the wall, and the sunburnt cicala shrieking on the spray, the pears and apples dropping from the orchard bough, the goats clambering from crag to crag after the cistus and the thyme, the brown youths and wanton lasses singing under the dark chestnut boughs, or by the leafy arch of some

> Grot nymph-haunted,
> Garlanded over with vine, and acanthus, and clambering roses,
> Cool in the fierce still noon, where the streams glance clear in the moss-beds;

and here and there, beyond the braes and meads, blue glimpses of the far-off summer sea; and all this told in a language and a metre which shapes itself almost unconsciously, wave after wave, into the most luscious song. Doubt not that many a soul then, was the simpler, and purer, and better, for reading the sweet singer of Syracuse. He has his immoralities; but they are the immoralities of his age: his naturalness, his sunny calm and cheerfulness, are all his own.

And now, to leave the poets, and speak of those grammarians to whose corrections we owe, I suppose, the texts of the Greek poets as they now stand. They seem to have set to work at their task methodically enough, under the direction of their most literary monarch, Ptolemy Philadelphus. Alexander the Ætolian collected and revised the tragedies, Lycophron the comedies, Zenodotus the poems of Homer, and the other poets of the Epic cycle, now lost to us. Whether Homer prospered under all his expungings, alterations, and transpositions—whether, in fact, he did not treat Homer very much as Bentley wanted to treat Milton, is a suspicion which one has a right to entertain, though it is long past the possibility of proof. Let that be as it may, the critical business grew and prospered. Aristophanes of Byzantium wrote glossaries and grammars, collected editions of Plato and Aristotle, æsthetic disquisitions on Homer—one wishes they were preserved, for the sake of the jest, that one might have seen an Alexandrian cockney's views of Achilles and Ulysses! Moreover, in a hapless moment, at least for us moderns, he invented Greek accents; thereby, I fear, so complicating and confusing our notions of Greek rhythm, that we shall never, to the end of time, be able to guess what any Greek verse, saving the old Homeric Hexameter, sounded like. After a while, too, the pedants, according to their wont, began quarrelling about their accents and their recensions. Moreover, there was a rival school at Pergamus where the fame of Crates all but equalled the Egyptian fame of Aristarchus. Insolent! What right had an Asiatic to know anything? So Aristarchus flew furiously on Crates, being a man of plain common sense, who felt a correct reading a far more important thing than any of Crates's illustrations, æsthetic, historical, or mythological; a preference not yet quite extinct, in one, at least, of our Universities. "Sir," said a clever Cambridge Tutor to a philosophically inclined freshman, "remember, that our business is to translate Plato correctly, not to discover his meaning." And, paradoxical as it may seem, he was right. Let us first have accuracy, the merest mechanical accuracy, in every branch of knowledge. Let us know what the thing is which we are looking at. Let us know the exact words an author uses. Let us get at the exact value of each word by that severe induction of which Buttmann and the great Germans have set such noble examples; and then, and not till then, we may begin to talk about philosophy, and æsthetics, and the rest. Very probably Aristarchus was right in his dislike of Crates's preference of what he called criticism, to grammar. Very probably he connected it with the other object of his especial hatred, that fashion of interpreting Homer allegorically, which was springing up in his time, and which afterwards under the Neoplatonists rose to a frantic height, and helped to destroy in them, not only their power of sound judgment, and of asking each thing patiently what it was, but also any real reverence for, or understanding of, the very authors over whom they declaimed and sentimentalised.

Yes—the Cambridge Tutor was right. Before you can tell what a man means, you must have patience to find out what he says. So far from wishing our grammatical and philological education to be less severe than it is, I think it is not severe enough. In an age like this—an age of lectures, and of popular literature, and of self-culture, too often random and capricious, however earnest, we cannot be too careful in asking ourselves, in compelling others to ask themselves, the meaning of every word which they use, of every word which they read; in assuring them, whether they will believe us or not, that the moral, as well as the intellectual culture, acquired by translating accurately one dialogue of Plato, by making out thoroughly the sense of one chapter of a standard author, is greater than they will get from skimming whole folios of Schlegelian æsthetics, résumés, histories of philosophy, and the like second-hand information, or attending seven lectures a-week till their lives' end. *It is better to know one thing, than to know about ten thousand things.* I cannot help feeling painfully, after reading those most interesting Memoirs of Margaret Fuller Ossoli, that the especial danger of this time is intellectual sciolism, vagueness, sentimental eclecticism—and feeling, too, as Socrates of old believed, that intellectual vagueness and shallowness, however glib, and grand, and eloquent it may seem, is inevitably the parent of a moral vagueness and shallowness, which may leave our age as it left the later Greeks, without an absolute standard of right or of truth, till it tries to escape from its own scepticism, as the later Neoplatonists did, by plunging desperately into any fetish-worshipping superstition which holds out to its wearied and yet impatient intellect, the bait of decisions already made for it, of objects of admiration already formed and systematised.

Therefore let us honour the grammarian in his place; and, among others, these old grammarians of Alexandria; only being sure that as soon as any man begins, as they did, displaying himself peacock-fashion, boasting of his science as the great pursuit of humanity, and insulting his fellow-craftsmen, he becomes, *ipso facto,* unable to discover any more truth for us, having put on a habit of mind to which induction is impossible; and is thenceforth to be passed by with a kindly but a pitying smile. And so, indeed, it happened with these quarrelsome Alexandrian grammarians, as it did with the Casaubons and Scaligers and Daciers of the last two centuries. As soon as they began quarrelling they lost the power of discovering. The want of the inductive faculty in their attempts at philology is utterly ludicrous. Most of their derivations of words are about on a par with Jacob Böhmen's etymology of sulphur, wherein he makes *sul,* if I recollect right, signify some active principle of combustion, and *phur* the passive one. It was left for more patient and less noisy men, like Grimm, Bopp, and Buttmann, to found a science of philology, to discover for us those great laws which connect modern philology with history, ethnology, physiology, and with the very deepest questions of theology itself. And in the meanwhile, these Alexandrians' worthless criticism has been utterly swept away; while their real work, their accurate editions of the classics, remain to us as a precious heritage. So it is throughout history: nothing dies which is worthy to live. The wheat is surely gathered into the garner, the chaff is burnt up by that eternal fire which, happily for this universe, cannot be quenched by any art of man, but goes on forever, devouring without indulgence all the folly and the falsehood of the world.

As yet you have heard nothing of the metaphysical schools of Alexandria; for as yet none have existed, in the modern acceptation of that word. Indeed, I am not sure that I must not tell you frankly, that none ever existed at all in Alexandria, in that same modern acceptation. Ritter, I think, it is who complains naïvely enough, that the Alexandrian Neoplatonists had a bad habit, which grew on them more and more as the years rolled on, of mixing up philosophy with theology, and so defiling, or at all events colouring, its pure transparency. There is no denying the imputation, as I shall show at greater length in my next Lecture. But one would have thought, looking back through history, that the Alexandrians were not the only philosophers guilty of this shameful act of syncretism. Plato, one would have thought, was as great a sinner as they. So were the Hindoos. In spite of all their logical and metaphysical acuteness, they were, you will find, unable to get rid of the notion that theological inquiries concerning Brahma, Atma, Creeshna, were indissolubly mixed up with that same logic and metaphysic. The Parsees could not separate questions about Ahriman and Ormuzd from Kant's three great philosophic problems: What is Man?—What may be known?—What should be done? Neither, indeed, could the earlier Greek sages. Not one of them, of any school whatsoever—from the semi-mythic Seven Sages to Plato and Aristotle—but finds it necessary to consider not in passing, but as the great object of research, questions concerning the gods:—whether they are real or not; one or many; personal or impersonal; cosmic, and parts of the universe, or organisers and rulers of it; in relation to man, or without relation to him. Even in those who flatly deny the existence of the gods, even in Lucretius himself, these questions have to be considered, before the question, What is man? can get any solution at all. On the answer given to them is found to depend intimately the answer to the question, What is the immaterial part of man? Is it a part of nature, or of something above nature? Has he an immaterial part at all?—in one word, Is a human metaphysic possible at all? So it was with the Greek philosophers of old, even, as Asclepius and Ammonius say, with Aristotle himself. "The object of Aristotle's metaphysic," one of them says, "is theological. Herein Aristotle theologises." And there is no denying the assertion. We must not then be hard on the Neoplatonists, as if they were the first to mix things separate from the foundation of the world. I do not say that theology and metaphysic are separate studies. That is to be ascertained only by seeing some one separate them. And when I see them separated, I shall believe them separable. Only the separation must not be produced by the simple expedient of denying the existence of either one of them, or at least of ignoring the existence of one steadily during the study of the other. If they can be parted without injury to each other, let them be parted; and till then let us suspend hard judgments on the Alexandrian school of metaphysic, and also on the schools of that curious people the Jews, who had at this period a steadily increasing influence on the thought, as well as on the commercial prosperity, of Alexandria.

You must not suppose, in the meanwhile, that the philosophers whom the Ptolemies collected (as they would have any other marketable article) by liberal offers of pay and patronage, were such men as the old Seven Sages of Greece, or as Socrates, Plato, and Aristotle. In these three last indeed, Greek thought reached not merely its greatest height, but the edge of a precipice, down which it rolled headlong after their decease. The intellectual defects of the Greek mind, of which I have already spoken, were doubtless one great cause of this decay: but, to my mind, moral causes had still more to do with it. The more cultivated Greek states, to judge from the writings of Plato, had not been an over-righteous people during the generation in which he lived. And in the generations which followed, they became an altogether wicked people; immoral, unbelieving, hating good, and delighting in all which was evil. And it was in consequence of these very sins of theirs, as I think, that the old Hellenic race began to die out physically, and population throughout Greece to decrease with frightful rapidity, after the time of the Achæan league. The facts are well known; and foul enough they are. When the Romans destroyed Greece, God was just and merciful. The eagles were gathered together only because the carrion needed to be removed from the face of God's earth. And at the time of which I now speak, the signs of approaching death were fearfully apparent. Hapless and hopeless enough were the clique of men out of whom the first two Ptolemies hoped to form a school of philosophy; men certainly clever enough, and amusing withal, who might give the kings of Egypt many a shrewd lesson in king-craft, and the ways of this world, and the art of profiting by the folly of fools, and the selfishness of the selfish; or who might amuse them, in default of fighting-cocks, by puns and repartees, and battles of logic; "how one thing cannot be predicated of another," or "how the wise man is not only to overcome every misfortune, but not even to feel it," and other such mighty questions, which in those days hid that deep unbelief in any truth whatsoever which was spreading fast over the minds of men. Such word-splitters were Stilpo and Diodorus, the slayer and the slain. They were of the Megaran school, and were named Dialectics; and also, with more truth, Eristics, or quarrellers. Their clique had professed to follow Zeno and Socrates in declaring the instability of sensible presumptions and conclusions, in preaching an absolute and eternal Being. But there was this deep gulf between them and Socrates; that while Socrates professed to be seeking for the Absolute and Eternal, for that which is, they were content with affirming that it exists. With him, as with the older sages, philosophy was a search for truth. With them it was a scheme of doctrines to be defended. And the dialectic on which they prided themselves so much, differed from his accordingly. He used it inductively, to seek out, under the notions and conceptions of the mind, certain absolute truths and laws of which they were only the embodiment. Words and thought were to him a field for careful and reverent induction, as the phenomena of nature are to us the disciples of Bacon. But with these hapless Megarans, who thought that they had found that for which Socrates professed only to seek dimly and afar off, and had got it safe in a dogma, preserved as it were in spirits, and put by in a museum, the great use of dialectic was to confute opponents. Delight in their own subtlety grew on them, the worship not of objective truth, but of the forms of the intellect whereby it may be demonstrated; till they became the veriest word-splitters, rivals of the old sophists whom their master had attacked, and justified too often Aristophanes' calumny, which confounded Socrates with his opponents, as a man whose aim was to make the worse appear the better reason.

We have here, in both parties, all the marks of an age of exhaustion, of scepticism, of despair about finding any real truth. No wonder that they were superseded by the Pyrrhonists, who doubted all things, and by the Academy, which prided itself on setting up each thing to knock it down again; and so by prudent and well-bred and tolerant qualifying of every assertion, neither affirming too much, nor denying too much, keep their minds in a wholesome—or unwholesome—state of equilibrium, as stagnant pools are kept, that everything may have free toleration to rot undisturbed.

These hapless caricaturists of the dialectic of Plato, and the logic of Aristotle, careless of any vital principles or real results, ready enough to use fallacies each for their own party, and openly proud of their success in doing so, were assisted by worthy compeers of an outwardly opposite tone of thought, the Cyrenaics, Theodorus and Hegesias. With their clique, as with their master Aristippus, the senses were the only avenues to knowledge; man was the measure of all things; and "happiness our being's end and aim." Theodorus was surnamed the Atheist; and, it seems, not without good reason; for he taught that there was no absolute or eternal difference between good and evil; nothing really disgraceful in crimes; no divine ground for laws, which according to him had been invented by men to prevent fools from making themselves disagreeable; on which theory, laws must be confessed to have been in all ages somewhat of a failure. He seems to have been, like his master, an impudent light-hearted fellow, who took life easily enough, laughed at patriotism, and all other high-flown notions, boasted that the world was his country, and was no doubt excellent after-dinner company for the great king. Hegesias, his fellow Cyrenaic, was a man of a darker and more melancholic temperament; and while Theodorus contented himself with preaching a comfortable selfishness, and obtaining pleasure, made it rather his study to avoid pain. Doubtless both their theories were popular enough at Alexandria, as they were in France during the analogous period, the Siècle Louis Quinze. The "Contrat Social," and the rest of their doctrines, moral and metaphysical, will always have their admirers on earth, as long as that variety of the human species exists for whose especial behoof Theodorus held that laws were made; and the whole form of thought met with great approbation in after years at Rome, where Epicurus carried it to its highest perfection. After that, under the pressure of a train of rather severe lessons, which Gibbon has detailed in his "Decline and Fall of the Roman Empire," little or nothing was heard of it, save *sotto voce*, perhaps, at the Papal courts of the sixteenth century. To revive it publicly, or at least as much of it as could be borne by a world now for seventeen centuries Christian, was the glory of the eighteenth century. The moral scheme of Theodorus has now nearly vanished among us, at least as a confessed creed; and, in spite of the authority of Mr. Locke's great and good name, his metaphysical scheme is showing signs of a like approaching disappearance. Let us hope that it may be a speedy one; for if the senses be the only avenues to knowledge; if man be the measure of all things; and if law have not, as Hooker says, her fount and home in the very bosom of God himself, then was Homer's Zeus right in declaring man to be "the most wretched of all the beasts of the field."

And yet one cannot help looking with a sort of awe (I dare not call it respect) at that melancholic faithless Hegesias. Doubtless he, like his compeers, and indeed all Alexandria for three hundred years, cultivated philosophy with no more real purpose than it was cultivated by the graceless *beaux-esprits* of Louis XV.'s court, and with as little practical effect on morality; but of this Hegesias alone it stands written, that his teaching actually made men do something; and moreover, do the most solemn and important thing which any man can do, excepting always doing right. I must confess, however, that the result of his teaching took so unexpected a form, that the reigning Ptolemy, apparently Philadelphus, had to interfere with the sacred right of every man to talk as much nonsense as he likes, and forbade Hegesias to teach at Alexandria. For Hegesias, a Cyrenaic like Theodorus, but a rather more morose pedant than that saucy and happy scoffer, having discovered that the great end of man was to avoid pain, also discovered (his digestion being probably in a disordered state) that there was so much more pain than pleasure in the world, as to make it a thoroughly disagreeable place, of which man was well rid at any price. Whereon he wrote a book called Ἀποκαρτερῶν, in which a man who had determined to starve himself, preached the miseries of human life, and the blessings of death, with such overpowering force, that the book actually drove many persons to commit suicide, and escape from a world which was not fit to dwell in. A fearful proof of how rotten the state of society was becoming, how desperate the minds of men, during those frightful centuries which immediately preceded the Christian era, and how fast was approaching that dark chaos of unbelief and unrighteousness, which Paul of Tarsus so analyses and describes in the first chapter of his Epistle to the Romans—when the old light was lost, the old faiths extinct, the old reverence for the laws of family and national life, destroyed, yea even the natural instincts themselves perverted; that chaos whose darkness Juvenal, and Petronius, and Tacitus have proved, in their fearful pages, not to have been exaggerated by the more compassionate though more righteous Jew.

And now observe, that this selfishness—this whole some state of equilibrium—this philosophic calm, which is really only a lazy pride, was, as far as we can tell, the main object of all the schools from the time of Alexander to the Christian era. We know very little of those Sceptics, Cynics, Epicureans, Academics, Peripatetics, Stoics, of whom there has been so much talk, except at second-hand, through the Romans, from whom Stoicism in after ages received a new and not ignoble life. But this we do know of the later sects, that they gradually gave up the search for truth, and propounded to themselves as the great type for a philosopher, How shall a man save his own soul from this evil world? They may have been right; it may have been the best thing to think about in those exhausted and decaying times: but it was a question of ethics, not of philosophy, in the sense which the old Greek sages put on that latter word. Their object was, not to get at the laws of all things, but to fortify themselves against all things, each according to his scheme, and so to be self-sufficient and alone. Even in the Stoics, who boldly and righteously asserted an immutable morality, this was the leading conception. As has been well said of them:

"If we reflect how deeply the feeling of an intercourse between men and a divine race superior to themselves had worked itself into the Greek character—what a number of fables, some beautiful, some impure, it had impregnated and procured credence for—how it sustained every form of polity and every system of laws, we may imagine what the effects must have been of its disappearance. If it is possible for any man, it was not, certainly, possible for a Greek, to feel himself connected by any real bonds with his fellow-creatures around him, while he felt himself utterly separated from any being above his fellow-creatures. But the sense of that isolation would affect different minds very differently. It drove the Epicurean to consider how he might make a world in which he should live comfortably, without distracting visions of the past and future, and the dread of those upper powers who no longer awakened in him any feelings of sympathy. It drove Zeno the Stoic to consider whether a man may not find enough in himself to satisfy him, though what is beyond him be ever so unfriendly. . . . We may trace in the productions which are attributed to Zeno a very clear indication of the feeling which was at work in his mind. He undertook, for instance, among other tasks, to answer Plato's 'Republic.' The truth that a man is a political being, which informs and pervades that book, was one which must have been particularly harassing to his mind, and which he felt must be got rid of, before he could hope to assert his doctrine of a man's solitary dignity."

Woe to the nation or the society in which this individualising and separating process is going on in the human mind! Whether it take the form of a religion or of a philosophy, it is at once the sign and the cause of senility, decay, and death. If man begins to forget that he is a social being, a member of a body, and that the only truths which can avail him anything, the only truths which are worthy objects of his philosophical search, are those which are equally true for every man, which will equally avail every man, which he must proclaim, as far as he can, to every man, from the proudest sage to the meanest outcast, he enters, I believe, into a lie, and helps forward the dissolution of that society of which he is a member. I care little whether what he holds be true or not. If it be true, he has made it a lie by appropriating it proudly and selfishly to himself, and by excluding others from it. He has darkened his own power of vision by that act of self-appropriation, so that even if he sees a truth, he can only see it refractedly, discoloured by the medium of his own private likes and dislikes, and fulfils that great and truly philosophic law, that he who loveth not his brother is in darkness, and knoweth not whither he goeth. And so it befell those old Greek schools. It is out of our path to follow them to Italy, where sturdy old Roman patriots cursed them, and with good reason, as corrupting the morals of the young. Our business is with Alexandria; and there, certainly, they did nothing for the elevation of humanity. What culture they may have given, probably helped to make the Alexandrians, what Cæsar calls them, the most ingenious of all nations: but righteous or valiant men it did not make them. When, after the three great reigns of Soter, Philadelphus, and Euergetes, the race of the Ptolemies began to wear itself out, Alexandria fell morally, as its sovereigns fell; and during a miserable and shameful decline of a hundred and eighty years, sophists wrangled, pedants fought over accents and readings with the true *odium grammaticum*, and kings plunged deeper and deeper into the abysses of luxury and incest, laziness and cruelty, till the flood came, and swept them all away. Cleopatra, the Helen of Egypt, betrayed her country to the Roman; and thenceforth the Alexandrians became slaves in all but name.

And now that Alexandria has become a tributary province, is it to share the usual lot of enslaved countries and lose all originality and vigour of thought? Not so. From this point, strangely enough, it begins to have a philosophy of its own. Hitherto it has been importing Greek thought into Egypt and Syria, even to the furthest boundaries of Persia; and the whole East has become Greek: but it has received little in return. The Indian Gymnosophists, or Brahmins, had little or no effect on Greek philosophy, except in the case of Pyrrho: the Persian Dualism still less. The Egyptian symbolic nature-worship had been too gross to be regarded by the cultivated Alexandrian as anything but a barbaric superstition. One eastern nation had intermingled closely with the Macedonian race, and from it Alexandrian thought received a new impulse.

I mentioned in my first lecture the conciliatory policy which the Ptolemies had pursued toward the Jews. Soter had not only allowed but encouraged them to settle in Alexandria and Egypt, granting them the same political privileges with the Macedonians and other Greeks. Soon they built themselves a temple there, in obedience to some supposed prophecy in their sacred writings, which seems most probably to have been a wilful interpolation. Whatsoever value we may attach to the various myths concerning the translation of their Scriptures into Greek, there can be no doubt that they were translated in the reign of Soter, and that the exceedingly valuable Septuagint version is the work of that period. Moreover, their numbers in Alexandria were very great. When Amrou took Constantinople in A.D. 640, there were 40,000 Jews in it; and their numbers during the Ptolemaic and Roman periods, before their temporary expulsion by Cyril about 412, were probably greater; and Egypt altogether is said to have contained 200,000 Jews. They had schools there, which were so esteemed by their whole nation throughout the East, that the Alexandrian Rabbis, the Light of Israel, as they were called, may be fairly considered as the centre of Jewish thought and learning for several centuries.

We are accustomed, and not without reason, to think with some contempt of these old Rabbis. Rabbinism, Cabbalism, are become by-words in the mouths of men. It may be instructive for us—it is certainly necessary for us, if we wish to understand Alexandria—to examine a little how they became so fallen.

Their philosophy took its stand, as you all know,

on certain ancient books of their people; histories, laws, poems, philosophical treatises, which all have one element peculiar to themselves, namely, the assertion of a living personal Ruler and Teacher, not merely of the Jewish race, but of all the nations of the earth. After the return of their race from Babylon, their own records give abundant evidence that this strange people became the most exclusive and sectarian which the world ever saw. Into the causes of that exclusiveness I will not now enter; suffice it to say, that it was pardonable enough in a people asserting Monotheism in the midst of idolatrous nations, and who knew, from experience even more bitter than that which taught Plato and Socrates, how directly all those popular idolatries led to every form of baseness and immorality. But we may trace in them, from the date of their return from Babylon, especially from their settlement in Alexandria, a singular change of opinion. In proportion as they began to deny that their unseen personal Ruler had anything to do with the Gentiles—the nations of the earth, as they called them—in proportion as they considered themselves as His only subjects—or rather, Him and His guidance as their own private property—exactly in that proportion they began to lose all living or practical belief that He did guide them. He became a being of the past; one who had taught and governed their forefathers in old times: not one who was teaching and governing them now. I beg you to pay attention to this curious result; because you will see, I think, the very same thing occurring in two other Alexandrian schools, of which I shall speak hereafter.

The result to these Rabbis was, that the inspired books which spoke of this Divine guidance and government became objects of superstitious reverence, just in proportion as they lost all understanding of their real value and meaning. Nevertheless, this too produced good results; for the greatest possible care was taken to fix the Canon of these books; to settle, as far as possible, the exact time at which the Divine guidance was supposed to have ceased; after which it was impious to claim a Divine teaching; when their sages were left to themselves, as they fancied, with a complete body of knowledge, on which they were henceforth only to comment. Thus, whether or not they were right in supposing that the Divine Teacher had ceased to teach and inspire them, they did infinite service by marking out for us certain writers whom He had certainly taught and inspired. No doubt they were right in their sense of the awful change which had passed over their nation. There was an infinite difference between them and the old Hebrew writers. They had lost something which those old prophets possessed. I invite you to ponder, each for himself, on the causes of this strange loss; bearing in mind that they lost their forefathers' heirloom, exactly in proportion as they began to believe it to be their exclusive possession, and to deny other human beings any right to or share in it. It may have been that the light given to their forefathers had, as they thought, really departed. It may have been, also, that the light was there all around them still, as bright as ever, but that they would not open their eyes and behold it; or rather, could not open them, because selfishness and pride had sealed them. It may have been, that inspiration was still very near *them* too, if their spirits had been willing to receive it. But of the fact of the change there was no doubt. For the old Hebrew seers were men dealing with the loftiest and deepest laws: the Rabbis were shallow pedants. The old Hebrew seers were righteous and virtuous men: the Rabbis became, in due time, some of the worst and wickedest men who ever trod this earth.

Thus they too had their share in that downward career of pedantry which we have seen characterise the whole past Alexandrine age. They, like Zenodotus and Aristarchus, were commentators, grammarians, sectarian disputers: they were not thinkers or actors. Their inspired books were to them no more the words of living human beings who had sought for the Absolute Wisdom, and found it after many sins and doubts and sorrows. The human writers became in their eyes the puppets and mouthpieces of some magical influence, not the disciples of a living and loving person. The book itself was, in their belief, not in any true sense inspired, but magically dictated—by what power they cared not to define. His character was unimportant to them, provided He had inspired no nation but their own. But, thought they, if the words were dictated, each of them must have some mysterious value. And if each word had a mysterious value, why not each letter? And how could they set limits to that mysterious value? Might not these words, even rearrangements of the letters of them, be useful in protecting them against the sorceries of the heathen, in driving away those evil spirits, or evoking those good spirits, who, though seldom mentioned in their early records, had after their return from Babylon begun to form an important part of their unseen world? For as they had lost faith in the One Preserver of their race, they had filled up the void by a ponderous demonology of innumerable preservers. This process of thought was not confined to Alexandria. Dr. Layard, in his last book on Nineveh, gives some curious instances of its prevalence among them at an earlier period, well worth your careful study. But it was at Alexandria that the Jewish Cabbalism formed itself into a system. It was there that the Jews learnt to become the jugglers and magic-mongers of the whole Roman world, till Claudius had to expel them from Rome, as pests to rational and moral society.

And yet, among these hapless pedants there lingered nobler thoughts and hopes. They could not read the glorious heirlooms of their race without finding in them records of antique greatness and virtue, of old deliverances worked for their forefathers; and what seemed promises, too, that that greatness should return. The notion that those promises were conditional; that they expressed eternal moral laws, and declared the consequences of obeying those laws, they had lost long ago. By looking on themselves as exclusively and arbitrarily favoured by Heaven, they were ruining their own moral sense. Things were not right or wrong to them because Right was eternal and divine, and Wrong the transgression of that eternal right. How could that be? For then the right things the Gentiles seemed to do would be right and divine; —and that supposition in their eyes was all but impious. None could do right but themselves, for they only knew the law of God. So, right with them had no absolute or universal ground, but was reduced in their minds to the performance of certain acts commanded exclusively to them—a form of ethics which rapidly sank into the most petty and frivolous casuistry as to the outward performance of those acts. The sequel of those ethics is known to all the world, in the spectacle of the most unrivalled religiosity, and scrupulous respectability, combined with a more utter absence of moral sense, in their most cultivated and learned men, than the world has ever beheld before or since.

In such a state of mind it was impossible for them to look on their old prophets as true seers, beholding and applying eternal moral laws, and, therefore, seeing the future in the present and in the past. They must be the mere utterers of an irreversible arbitrary fate; and that fate must, of course, be favourable to their nation. So now arose a school who picked out from their old prophets every passage which could be made to predict their future glory, and a science which settled when that glory was to return. By the arbitrary rules of criticism a prophetic day was defined to mean a year; a week, seven years. The most simple and human utterances were found to have recondite meanings relative to their future triumph over the heathens whom they cursed and hated. If any of you ever come across the popular Jewish interpretations of The Song of Solomon, you will there see the folly in which acute and learned men can indulge themselves when they have lost hold of the belief in anything really absolute and eternal and moral, and have made Fate, and Time, and Self, their real deities. But this dream of a future restoration was in no wise ennobled, as far as we can see, with any desire for a moral restoration. They believed that a person would appear some day or other to deliver them. Even they were happily preserved by their sacred books from the notion that deliverance was to be found for them, or for any man, in an abstraction or notion ending in -ation or -ality. In justice to them it must be said, that they were too wise to believe that personal qualities, such as power, will, love, righteousness, could reside in any but in a person, or be manifested except by a person. And among the earlier of them the belief may have been, that the ancient unseen Teacher of their race would be their deliverer: but as they lost the thought of Him, the expected Deliverer became a mere human being: or rather not a human being; for as they lost their moral sense, they lost in the very deepest meaning their humanity, and forgot what man was like till they learned to look only for a conqueror; a manifestation of power, and not of goodness; a destroyer of the hated heathen, who was to establish them as the tyrant race of the whole earth. On that fearful day on which, for a moment, they cast away even that last dream, and cried, "We have no king but Cæsar," they spoke the secret of their hearts. It was a Cæsar, a Jewish Cæsar, for whom they had been longing for centuries. And if they could not have such a deliverer, they would have none: they would take up with the best embodiment of brute Titanic power which they could find, and crucify the embodiment of Righteousness and Love. Amid all the metaphysical schools of Alexandria, I know none so deeply instructive as that school of the Rabbis, "the glory of Israel."

But you will say: "This does not look like a school likely to regenerate Alexandrian thought." True: and yet it did regenerate it, both for good and for evil; for these men had among them and preserved faithfully enough for all practical purposes, the old literature of their race; a literature which I firmly believe, if I am to trust the experience of 1900 years, is destined to explain all other literatures; because it has firm hold of the one eternal root-idea which gives life, meaning,

Divine sanction, to every germ or fragment of human truth which is in any of them. It did so, at least, in Alexandria for the Greek literature. About the Christian era, a cultivated Alexandrian Jew, a disciple of Plato and of Aristotle, did seem to himself to find in the sacred books of his nation that which agreed with the deepest discoveries of Greek philosophy; which explained and corroborated them. And his announcement of this fact, weak and defective as it was, had the most enormous and unexpected results. The father of New Platonism was Philo the Jew.

LECTURE III.

NEOPLATONISM.

We now approach the period in which Alexandria began to have a philosophy of its own—to be, indeed, the leader of human thought for several centuries.

I shall enter on this branch of my subject with some fear and trembling; not only on account of my own ignorance, but on account of the great difficulty of handling it without trenching on certain controversial subjects which are rightly and wisely forbidden here. For there was not one school of Metaphysic at Alexandria: there were two; which, during the whole period of their existence, were in internecine struggle with each other, and yet mutually borrowing from each other; the Heathen, namely, and the Christian. And you cannot contemplate, still less can you understand, the one without the other. Some of late years have become all but unaware of the existence of that Christian school; and the word Philosophy, on the authority of Gibbon, who, however excellent an authority for facts, knew nothing about Philosophy, and cared less, has been used exclusively to express heathen thought; a misnomer which in Alexandria would have astonished Plotinus or Hypatia as much as it would Clement or Origen. I do not say that there is, or ought to be, a Christian Metaphysic. I am speaking, as you know, merely as a historian, dealing with facts; and I say that there was one; as profound, as scientific, as severe, as that of the Pagan Neoplatonists; starting indeed, as I shall show hereafter, on many points from common ground with theirs. One can hardly doubt, I should fancy, that many parts of St. John's Gospel and Epistles, whatever view we may take of them, if they are to be called anything, are to be called metaphysic and philosophic. And one can no more doubt that before writing them he had studied Philo, and was expanding Philo's thought in the direction which seemed fit to him, than we can doubt it of the earlier Neoplatonists. The technical language is often identical; so are the primary ideas from which he starts, howsoever widely the conclusions may differ. If Plotinus considered himself an intellectual disciple of Plato, so did Origen and Clemens. And I must, as I said before, speak of both, or of neither. My only hope of escaping delicate ground lies in the curious fact, that rightly or wrongly, the form in which Christianity presented itself to the old Alexandrian thinkers was so utterly different from the popular conception of it in modern England, that one may very likely be able to tell what little one knows about it, almost without mentioning a single doctrine which now influences the religious world.

But far greater is my fear, that to a modern British auditory, trained in the school of Locke, much of ancient thought, heathen as well as Christian, may seem so utterly the product of the imagination, so utterly without any corresponding reality in the universe, as to look like mere unintelligible madness. Still, I must try; only entreating my hearers to consider, that how much soever we may honour Locke and his great Scotch followers, we are not bound to believe them either infallible, or altogether world-embracing; that there have been other methods than theirs of conceiving the Unseen; that the common ground from which both Christian and heathen Alexandrians start, is not merely a private vagary of their own, but one which has been accepted undoubtingly, under so many various forms, by so many different races, as to give something of an inductive probability that it is not a mere dream, but may be a right and true instinct of the human mind. I mean the belief that the things which we see—nature and all her phenomena—are temporal, and born only to die; mere shadows of some unseen realities, from whom their laws and life are derived; while the eternal things which subsist without growth, decay, or change, the only real, only truly existing things, in short, are certain things which are not seen; inappreciable by sense, or understanding, or imagination, perceived only by the conscience and the reason. And that, again, the problem of philosophy, the highest good for man, that for the sake of which death were a gain, without which life is worthless, a drudgery, a degradation, a failure, and a ruin, is to discover what those unseen eternal things are, to know them, possess them, be in harmony with them, and thereby alone to rise to any real and solid power, or safety, or nobleness. It is a strange dream. But you will see that it is one which does not bear much upon "points of controversy," any more than on "Locke's philosophy;" nevertheless, when we find this same strange dream arising, apparently without intercommunion of thought, among the old Hindoos, among the Greeks, among the Jews; and lastly, when we see it springing again in the Middle Age, in the mind of the almost forgotten author of the "Deutsche Theologie," and so becoming the parent, not merely of Luther's deepest belief, or of the German mystic schools of the seventeenth and eighteenth centuries, but of the great German Philosophy itself as developed by Kant, and Fichte, and Schelling, and Hegel, we must at least confess it to be a popular delusion, if nothing better, vast enough and common enough to be worth a little patient investigation, wheresoever we may find it stirring the human mind.

But I have hope, still, that I may find sympathy and comprehension among some, at least, of my audience, as I proceed to examine the ancient realist schools of Alexandria, on account of their knowledge of the modern realist schools of Germany. For I cannot but see, that a revulsion is taking place in the thoughts of our nation upon metaphysic subjects, and that Scotland, as usual, is taking the lead therein. That most illustrious Scotchman, Mr. Thomas Carlyle, first vindicated the great German Realists from the vulgar misconceptions about them which were so common at the beginning of this century, and brought the minds of studious men to a more just appreciation of the philosophic severity, the moral grandeur, of such thinkers as Emmanuel Kant, and Gottlieb Fichte. To another Scotch gentleman, who, I believe, has honoured me by his presence here to-night, we owe most valuable translations of some of Fichte's works; to be followed, I trust, by more. And though, as a humble disciple of Bacon, I cannot but think that the method both of Kant and Fichte possesses somewhat of the same inherent defect as the method of the Neoplatonist school, yet I should be most unfair did I not express my deep obligations to them, and advise all those to study them carefully, who wish to gain a clear conception either of the old Alexandrian schools, or of those intellectual movements which are agitating the modern mind, and which will, I doubt not, issue in a clearer light, and in a nobler life, if not for us, yet still for our children's children for ever.

The name of Philo the Jew is now all but forgotten among us. He was laughed out of sight during the last century, as a dreamer and an allegorist, who tried eclectically to patch together Plato and Moses. The present age, however, is rapidly beginning to suspect that all who thought before the eighteenth century were not altogether either fools or impostors; old wisdom is obtaining a fairer hearing day by day, and is found not to be so contradictory to new wisdom as was supposed. We are beginning, too, to be more inclined to justify Providence, by believing that lies are by their very nature impotent and doomed to die; that everything which has had any great or permanent influence on the human mind, must have in it some germ of eternal truth; and setting ourselves to separate that germ of truth from the mistakes which may have distorted and overlaid it. Let us believe, or at least hope, the same for a few minutes, of Philo, and try to find out what was the secret of his power, what the secret of his weakness.

First: I cannot think that he had to treat his own sacred books unfairly, to make them agree with the root-idea of Socrates and Plato. Socrates and Plato acknowledged a Divine teacher of the human spirit; that was the ground of their philosophy. So did the literature of the Jews. Socrates and Plato, with all the Greek sages till the Sophistic era, held that the object of philosophy was the search after that which truly exists: that he who found that, found wisdom: Philo's books taught him the same truth: but they taught him also, that the search for wisdom was not merely the search for that which is, but for Him who is; not for a thing, but for a person. I do not mean that Plato and the elder Greeks had not that object also in view; for I have said already that Theology was with them the ultimate object of all metaphysic science: but I do think that they saw it infinitely less clearly than the old Jewish sages. Those sages were utterly unable to conceive of an absolute truth, except as residing in an absolutely true person; of absolute wisdom, except in an absolutely wise person; of an absolute order and law, except in a lawgiver; of an absolute good, except in an absolutely good person: any more than either they or we can conceive of an absolute love, except in an absolutely loving person. I say boldly, that I think them right, on all grounds of Baconian induction. For all these qualities are only known to us as exhibited in persons; and if we believe them to have any absolute and eternal existence at all, to be objective, and independent of us, and the momentary moods and sentiments of our own mind, they must exist in some absolute and eternal person, or they are mere notions, abstractions, words, which have no counterparts.

But here arose a puzzle in the mind of Philo, as it in reality had, we may see, in the minds of Socrates and Plato. How could he reconcile the idea of that absolute and eternal one Being, that Zeus, Father of Gods and men, self-perfect, self-contained, without change or motion, in whom, as a Jew, he believed even more firmly than the Platonists, with the Dæmon of Socrates, the Divine Teacher whom both Plato and Solomon confessed? Or how, again, could he reconcile the idea of Him with the creative and providential energy, working in space and time, working on matter, and apparently affected and limited, if not baffled, by the imperfection of the minds which he taught, by the imperfection of the matter which he moulded? This, as all students of philosophy must know, was one of the great puzzles of old Greek philosophy, as long as it was earnest and cared to have any puzzles at all: it has been, since the days of Spinoza, the great puzzle of all earnest modern philosophers. Philo offered a solution in that idea of a Logos, or Word of God, Divinity articulate, speaking and acting in time and space, and therefore by successive acts; and so doing, in time and space, the will of the timeless and spaceless Father, the Abysmal and Eternal Being, of whom he was the perfect likeness. In calling this person the Logos, and making him the source of all human reason, and knowledge of eternal laws, he only translated from Hebrew into Greek the name which he found in his sacred books, "The Word of God." As yet we have found no unfair allegorising of Moses, or twisting of Plato. How then has he incurred this accusation?

I cannot think, again, that he was unfair in supposing that he might hold at the same time the Jewish belief concerning Creation, and the Platonic doctrine of the real existence of Archetypal ideas, both of moral and of physical phenomena. I do not mean that such a conception was present consciously to the mind of the old Jews, as it was most certainly to the mind of St. Paul, a practised Platonic dialectician; but it seems to me, as to Philo, to be a fair, perhaps a necessary, corollary from the Genetic Philosophy, both of Moses and of Solomon.

But in one thing he was unfair; namely, in his allegorising. But unfair to whom? To Socrates and Plato, I believe, as much as to Moses and to Samuel. For what is the part of the old Jewish books which he evaporates away into mere mystic symbols of the private experiences of the devout philosopher? Its practical everyday histories, which deal with the common human facts of family and national life, of man's outward and physical labour and craft. These to him have no meaning, except an allegoric one. But has he thrown them away for the sake of getting a step nearer to Socrates, or Plato, or Aristotle? Surely not. To them, as to the old Jewish sages, man is most important when regarded not merely as a soul, but as a man, a social being of flesh and blood. Aristotle declares politics to be the architectonical science, the family and social relations to be the eternal master-facts of humanity. Plato, in his Republic, sets before himself the Constitution of a State, as the crowning problem of his philosophy. Every work of his, like every saying of his master Socrates, deals with the common, outward, vulgar facts of human life, and asserts that there is a divine meaning in them, and that reverent induction from them is the way to obtain the deepest truths. Socrates and Plato were as little inclined to separate the man and the philosopher as Moses, Solomon, or Isaiah were. When Philo, by allegorising away the simple human parts of his books, is untrue to Moses's teaching, he becomes untrue to Plato's. He becomes untrue, I believe, to a higher teaching than Plato's. He loses sight of an eternal truth, which even old Homer might have taught him, when he treats Moses as one section of his disciples in after years treated Homer.

For what is the secret of the eternal freshness, the eternal beauty, ay, I may say boldly, in spite of all their absurdities and immoralities, the eternal righteousness of those old Greek myths? What is it which made Socrates and Plato cling lovingly and reverently to them, they scarce knew why, while they deplored the immoralities to which they had given rise? What is it which made those myths, alone of all old mythologies, the parents of truly beautiful sculpture, painting, poetry? What is it which makes us love them still; find, even at times against our consciences, new meaning, new beauty in them; and brings home the story of Perseus or of Hercules, alike to the practised reason of Niebuhr, and the untutored instincts of Niebuhr's little child, for whom he threw them into simplest forms? Why is it that in spite of our disagreeing with their creed and their morality, we still persist—and long may we persist, or rather be compelled—as it were by blind instinct, to train our boys upon those old Greek dreams; and confess, whenever we try to find a substitute for them in our educational schemes, that we have as yet none? Because those old Greek stories do represent the Deities as the archetypes, the kinsmen, the teachers, the friends, the inspirers of men. Because while the schoolboy reads how the Gods were like to men, only better, wiser, greater; how the Heroes are the children of the Gods, and the slayers of the monsters which devour the earth; how Athene taught men weaving, and Phœbus music, and Vulcan the cunning of the stithy; how the Gods took pity on the noble-hearted son of Danae, and lent him celestial arms and guided him over desert and ocean to fulfil his vow—that boy is learning deep lessons of metaphysic, more in accordance with the *reine vernunft,* the pure reason whereby man perceives that which is moral, and spiritual, and eternal, than he would from all disquisitions about being and becoming, about actualities and potentialities, which ever tormented the weary brain of man.

Let us not despise the gem because it has been broken to fragments, obscured by silt and mud. Still less let us fancy that one least fragment of it is not more precious than the most brilliant paste jewel of our own compounding, though it be polished and faceted never so completely. For what are all these myths but fragments of that great metaphysic idea, which, I boldly say, I believe to be at once the justifier and the harmoniser of all philosophic truth which man has ever discovered, or will discover; which Philo saw partially, and yet clearly; which the Hebrew sages perceived far more deeply, because more humanly and practically; which Saint Paul the Platonist, and yet the Apostle, raised to its highest power, when he declared that the immutable and self-existent Being, for whom the Greek sages sought, and did not altogether seek in vain, has gathered together all things both in heaven and in earth in one inspiring and creating Logos, who is both God and Man?

Be this as it may, we find that from the time of Philo, the deepest thought of the heathen world began to flow in a theologic channel. All the great heathen thinkers henceforth are theologians. In the times of Nero, for instance, Epictetus the slave, the regenerator of Stoicism, is no mere speculator concerning entities and quiddities, correct or incorrect. He is a slave searching for the secret of freedom, and finding that it consists in escaping not from a master, but from self: not to wealth and power, but to Jove. He discovers that Jove is, in some most mysterious, but most real sense, the Father of men; he learns to look up to that Father as his guide and friend.

Numenius, again, in the second century, was a man who had evidently studied Philo. He perceived so deeply, I may say so exaggeratedly, the analogy between the Jewish and the Platonic assertions of an Absolute and Eternal Being, side by side with the assertion of a Divine Teacher of man, that he is said to have uttered the startling saying: "What is Plato but Moses talking Attic?" Doubtless Plato is not that: but the expression is remarkable, as showing the tendency of the age. He too looks up to God with prayers for the guidance of his reason. He too enters into speculation concerning God in His absoluteness, and in His connection with the universe. "The Primary God," he says, "must be free from works and a King; but the Demiurgus must exercise government, going through the heavens. Through Him comes this our condition; through Him Reason being sent down in efflux, holds communion with all who are prepared for it: God then looking down, and turning Himself to each of us, it comes to pass that our bodies live and are nourished, receiving strength from the outer rays which come from Him. But when God turns us to the contemplation of Himself, it comes to pass that these things are worn out and consumed, but that the reason lives, being partaker of a blessed life."

This passage is exceedingly interesting, as containing both the marrow of old Hebrew metaphysic, and also certain notional elements, of which we find no trace in the Scripture, and which may lead—as we shall find they afterwards did lead—to confusing the moral with the notional, and finally the notional with the material; in plain words, to Pantheism.

You find this tendency, in short, in all the philosophers who flourished between the age of Augustus and the rise of Alexandrian Neoplatonism. Gibbon, while he gives an approving pat on the back to his pet "Philosophic Emperor," Marcus Aurelius, blinks the fact that Marcus's philosophy, like that of Plutarch, contains as an integral element, a belief which to him would have been, I fear, simply ludicrous, from its strange analogy with the belief of John, the Christian Apostle. What is Marcus Aurelius's cardinal doctrine? That there is a God within him, a Word, a Logos, which "has hold of him," and who is his teacher and guardian; that over and above his body and his soul, he has a Reason which is capable of "hearing that Divine Word, and obeying the monitions of that God." What is Plutarch's cardinal doctrine? That the same Word, the Dæmon who spoke to the heart of Socrates, is speaking to him and to every philosopher; "coming into contact," he says, "with him in some wonderful manner; addressing the reason of those who, like Socrates, keep their reason pure, not under the dominion of passion, nor mixing itself greatly with the body, and therefore quick and sensitive in responding to that which encountered it.

You see from these two extracts what questions

were arising in the minds of men, and how they touched on ethical and theological questions. I say arising in their minds: I believe that I ought to say rather, stirred up in their minds by One greater than they. At all events, there they appeared, utterly independent of any Christian teaching. The belief in this Logos or Dæmon speaking to the Reason of man, was one which neither Plutarch nor Marcus, neither Numenius nor Ammonius, as far as we can see, learnt from the Christians; it was the common ground which they held with them; the common battlefield which they disputed with them.

Neither have we any reason to suppose that they learnt it from the Hindoos. That much Hindoo thought mixed with Neoplatonist speculation we cannot doubt; but there is not a jot more evidence to prove that Alexandrians borrowed this conception from the Mahabharavata, than that George Fox the Quaker, or the author of the "Deutsche Theologie," did so. They may have gone to Hindoo philosophy, or rather, to second and third hand traditions thereof, for corroborations of the belief; but be sure, it must have existed in their own hearts first, or they would never have gone thither. Believe it; be sure of it. No earnest thinker is a plagiarist pure and simple. He will never borrow from others that which he has not already, more or less, thought out for himself. When once a great idea, instinctive, inductive (for the two expressions are nearer akin than most fancy), has dawned on his soul, he will welcome lovingly, awfully, any corroboration from foreign schools, and cry with joy: "Behold, this is not altogether a dream: for others have found it also. Surely it must be real, universal, eternal." No; be sure there is far more originality (in the common sense of the word), and far less (in the true sense of the word), than we fancy; and that it is a paltry and shallow doctrine which represents each succeeding school as merely the puppets and dupes of the preceding. More originality, because each earnest man seems to think out for himself the deepest grounds of his creed. Less originality, because, as I believe, one common Logos, Word, Reason, reveals and unveils the same eternal truth to all who seek and hunger for it.

Therefore we can, as the Christian philosophers of Alexandria did, rejoice over every truth which their heathen adversaries beheld, and attribute them, as Clement does, to the highest source, to the inspiration of the one and universal Logos. With Clement, philosophy is only hurtful when it is untrue to itself, and philosophy falsely so called; true philosophy is an image of the truth, a divine gift bestowed on the Greeks. The Bible, in his eyes, asserts that all forms of art and wisdom are from God. The wise in mind have no doubt some peculiar endowment of nature, but when they have offered themselves for their work, they receive a spirit of perception from the Highest Wisdom, giving them a new fitness for it. All severe study, all cultivation of sympathy, are exercises of this spiritual endowment. The whole intellectual discipline of the Greeks, with their philosophy, came down from God to men. Philosophy, he concludes in one place, carries on "an inquiry concerning Truth and the nature of Being; and this Truth is that concerning which the Lord Himself said: 'I am the Truth.' And when the initiated find, or rather receive, the true philosophy, they have it from the Truth itself; that is from Him who is true."

While, then, these two schools had so many grounds

in common, where was their point of divergence? We shall find it, I believe, fairly expressed in the dying words of Plotinus, the great father of Neoplatonism. "I am striving to bring the God which is in us into harmony with the God which is in the universe." Whether or not Plotinus actually so spoke, that was what his disciples not only said that he spoke, but what they would have wished him to speak. That one sentence expresses the whole object of their philosophy.

But to that Pantænus, Origen, Clement, and Augustine would have answered: "And we, on the other hand, assert that the God which is in the universe, is the same as the God which is in you, and is striving to bring you into harmony with Himself." There is the *experimentum crucis*. There is the vast gulf between the Christian and the Heathen schools, which when any man had overleaped, the whole problem of the universe was from that moment inverted. With Plotinus and his school man is seeking for God: with Clement and his, God is seeking for man. With the former, God is passive, and man active: with the latter, God is active, man is passive—passive, that is, in so far as his business is to listen when he is spoken to, to look at the light which is unveiled to him, to submit himself to the inward laws which he feels reproving and checking him at every turn, as Socrates was reproved and checked by his inward Dæmon.

Whether of these two theorems gives the higher conception either of the Divine Being, or of man, I leave it for you to judge. To those old Alexandrian Christians, a being who was not seeking after every single creature, and trying to raise him, could not be a Being of absolute Righteousness, Power, Love; could not be a Being worthy of respect or admiration, even of philosophic speculation. Human righteousness and love flows forth disinterestedly to all around it, however unconscious, however unworthy they may be; human power associated with goodness, seeks for objects which it may raise and benefit by that power. We must confess this, with the Christian schools, or, with the Heathen schools, we must allow another theory, which brought them into awful depths; which may bring any generation which holds it into the same depths.

If Clement had asked the Neoplatonists: "You believe, Plotinus, in an absolutely Good Being. Do you believe that it desires to shed forth its goodness on all?" "Of course," they would have answered, "on those who seek for it, on the philosopher."

"But not, it seems, Plotinus, on the herd, the brutal, ignorant mass, wallowing in those foul crimes above which you have risen?" And at that question there would have been not a little hesitation. These brutes in human form, these souls wallowing in earthly mire, could hardly, in the Neoplatonists' eyes, be objects of the Divine desire.

"Then this Absolute Good, you say, Plotinus, has no relation with them, no care to raise them. In fact, it cannot raise them, because they have nothing in common with it. Is that your notion?" And the Neoplatonists would have, on the whole, allowed that argument. And if Clement had answered, that such was not his notion of Goodness, or of a Good Being, and that therefore the goodness of their Absolute Good, careless of the degradation and misery around it, must be something very different from his notions of human goodness; the Neoplatonists would have answered—indeed they did answer—"After all, why not? Why should the Absolute Goodness be like our human goodness?" This is Plotinus's own belief. It is a question with him, it was still more a question with those who came after him, whether virtues could be predicated of the Divine nature; courage, for instance, of one who had nothing to fear; self-restraint, of one who had nothing to desire. And thus, by setting up a different standard of morality for the divine and for the human, Plotinus gradually arrives at the conclusion, that virtue is not the end, but the means; not the Divine nature itself, as the Christian schools held, but only the purgative process by which man was to ascend into heaven, and which was necessary to arrive at that nature—that nature itself being—what?

And how to answer that last question was the abysmal problem of the whole of Neoplatonic philosophy, in searching for which it wearied itself out, generation after generation, till tired equally of seeking and of speaking, it fairly lay down and died. In proportion as it refused to acknowledge a common divine nature with the degraded mass, it deserted its first healthy instinct, which told it that the spiritual world is identical with the moral world, with right, love, justice; it tried to find new definitions for the spiritual; it conceived it to be identical with the intellectual. That did not satisfy its heart. It had to repeople the spiritual world, which it had emptied of its proper denizens, with ghosts; to reinvent the old dæmonologies and polytheisms—from thence to descend into lower depths, of which we will speak hereafter.

But in the meanwhile we must look at another quarrel which arose between the two twin schools of Alexandria. The Neoplatonists said that there is a divine element in man. The Christian philosophers assented fervently, and raised the old disagreeable question: "Is it in every man? In the publicans and harlots as well as in the philosophers? We say that it is." And there again the Neoplatonist finds it over hard to assent to a doctrine, equally contrary to outward appearance, and galling to Pharisaic pride; and enters into a hundred honest self-puzzles and self-contradictions, which seem to justify him at last in saying, No. It is in the philosopher, who is ready by nature, as Plotinus has it, and as it were furnished with wings, and not needing to sever himself from matter like the rest, but disposed already to ascend to that which is above. And in a degree too, it is in the "lover," who, according to Plotinus, has a certain innate recollection of beauty, and hovers round it, and desires it, wherever he sees it. Him you may raise to the apprehension of the one incorporeal Beauty, by teaching him to separate beauty from the various objects in which it appears scattered and divided. And it is even in the third class, the lowest of whom there is hope, namely, the musical man, capable of being passively affected by beauty, without having any active appetite for it; the sentimentalist, in short, as we should call him nowadays.

But for the herd, Plotinus cannot say that there is anything divine in them. And thus it gradually comes out in all Neoplatonist writings which I have yet examined, that the Divine only exists in a man, in proportion as he is conscious of its existence in him. From which spring two conceptions of the Divine in man. First, is it a part of him, if it is dependent for its existence on his consciousness of it? Or is it, as Philo, Plutarch, Marcus Aurelius would have held, as the Christians held, something independent of him, without him, a Logos or Word speaking to his reason and conscience? With this question Plotinus grapples, earnestly, shrewdly, fairly. If you wish to see how he does it, you should read the fourth and fifth books of the sixth Ennead, especially if you be lucky enough to light on a copy of that rare book, Taylor's faithful though crabbed translation.

Not that the result of his search is altogether satisfactory. He enters into subtle and severe disquisitions concerning soul. Whether it is one or many. How it can be both one and many. He has the strongest perception that, to use the noble saying of the Germans, "Time and Space are no gods." He sees clearly that the soul, and the whole unseen world of truly existing being, is independent of time and space: and yet, after he has wrestled with the two Titans, through page after page, and apparently conquered them, they slip in again unawares into the battle-field, the moment his back is turned. He denies that the one Reason has parts—it must exist as a whole wheresoever it exists: and yet he cannot express the relation of the individual soul to it, but by saying that we are parts of it; or that each thing, down to the lowest, receives as much soul as it is capable of possessing. Ritter has worked out at length, though in a somewhat dry and lifeless way, the hundred contradictions of this kind which you meet in Plotinus; contradictions which I suspect to be inseparable from any philosophy starting from his grounds. Is he not looking for the spiritual in a region where it does not exist; in the region of logical conceptions and abstractions, which are not realities, but only, after all, symbols of our own, whereby we express to ourselves the processes of our own brain? May not his Christian contemporaries have been nearer scientific truth, as well as nearer the common sense and practical belief of mankind, in holding that that which is spiritual is personal, and can only be seen or conceived of as residing in persons; and that that which is personal is moral, and has to do, not with abstractions of the intellect, but with right and wrong, love and hate, and all which, in the common instincts of men, involves a free will, a free judgment, a free responsibility and desert? And that, therefore, if there were a Spirit, a Dæmonic Element, an universal Reason, a Logos, a Divine Element, closely connected with man, that one Reason, that one Divine Element, must be a person also? At least, so strong was the instinct of even the Heathen schools in this direction, that the followers of Plotinus had to fill up the void which yawned between man and the invisible things after which he yearned, by reviving the whole old Pagan Polytheism, and adding to it a Dæmonology borrowed partly from the Chaldees, and partly from the Jewish rabbis, which formed a descending chain of persons, downward from the highest Deities to heroes, and to the guardian angel of each man; the meed of the philosopher being, that by self-culture and self-restraint he could rise above the tutelage of some lower and more earthly dæmon, and become the pupil of a God, and finally a God himself.

These contradictions need not lower the great Father of Neoplatonism in our eyes, as a moral being. All accounts of him seem to prove him to have been what Apollo, in a lengthy oracle, declared him to have been, "good and gentle, and benignant exceedingly, and pleasant in all his conversation." He gave good advice about earthly matters, was a faithful steward of moneys deposited with him, a guardian of widows and orphans, a righteous and loving man. In his practical life, the ascetic and gnostic element comes out strongly enough. The body, with him, was not evil, neither was it good; it was simply nothing—why care about it? He would have no portrait taken of his person: "It was humiliating enough to be obliged to carry a shadow about with him, without having a shadow made of that shadow." He refused animal food, abstained from baths, declined medicine in his last illness, and so died about 200 A.D.

It is in his followers, as one generally sees in such cases, that the weakness of his conceptions comes out. Plotinus was an earnest thinker, slavishly enough reverencing the opinion of Plato, whom he quotes as an infallible oracle, with a "He says," as if there were but one he in the universe: but he tried honestly to develop Plato, or what he conceived to be Plato, on the method which Plato had laid down. His dialectic is far superior, both in quantity and in quality, to that of those who come after him. He is a seeker. His followers are not. The great work which marks the second stage of his school is not an inquiry, but a justification, not only of the Egyptian, but of all possible theurgies and superstitions; perhaps the best attempt of the kind which the world has ever seen; that which marks the third is a mere cloud-castle, an inverted pyramid, not of speculation, but of dogmatic assertion, patched together from all accessible rags and bones of the dead world. Some here will, perhaps, guess from my rough descriptions, that I speak of Iamblichus and Proclus.

Whether or not Iamblichus wrote the famous work usually attributed to him, which describes itself as the letter of Abamnon the Teacher to Porphyry, he became the head of that school of Neoplatonists who fell back on theurgy and magic, and utterly swallowed up the more rational, though more hopeless, school of Porphyry. Not that Porphyry, too, with all his dislike of magic and the vulgar superstitions—a dislike intimately connected with his loudly expressed dislike of the common herd, and therefore of Christianity, as a religion for the common herd—did not believe a fact or two, which looks to us, nowadays, somewhat unphilosophical. From him we learn that one Ammonius, trying to crush Plotinus by magic arts, had his weapons so completely turned against himself, that all his limbs were contracted. From him we learn that Plotinus, having summoned in the temple of Isis his familiar spirit, a god, and not a mere dæmon, appeared. He writes sensibly enough however to one Anebos, an Egyptian priest, stating his doubts as to the popular notions of the Gods, as beings subject to human passions and vices, and of theurgy and magic, as material means of compelling them to appear, or alluring them to favour man. The answer of Abamnon, Anebos, Iamblichus, or whoever the real author may have been, is worthy of perusal by every metaphysical student, as a curious phase of thought, not confined to that time, but rife, under some shape or other, in every age of the world's history, and in this as much as in any. There are many passages full of eloquence, many more full of true and noble thought: but on the whole, it is the sewing of new cloth into an old garment; the attempt to suit the old superstition to the new one, by eclectically picking and choosing, and special pleading, on both sides; but the rent is only made worse. There is no base superstition which Abamnon does not unconsciously justify. And yet he is rapidly losing sight of the real eternal human germs of truth round which those superstitions clustered, and is really further from truth and reason than old Homer or Hesiod, because further from the simple, universal, everyday facts, and relations, and duties of man, which are, after all, among the most mysterious, and also among the most sacred objects which man can contemplate.

It was not wonderful, however, that Neoplatonism took the course it did. Spirit, they felt rightly, was meant to rule matter; it was to be freed from matter only for that very purpose. No one could well deny that. The philosopher, as he rose and became, according to Plotinus, a god, or at least approached toward the gods, must partake of some mysterious and transcendental power. No one could well deny that conclusion, granting the premiss. But of what power? What had he to show as the result of his intimate communion with an unseen Being? The Christian Schools, who held that the spiritual is the moral, answered accordingly. He must show righteousness, and love, and peace in a Holy Spirit. That is the likeness of God. In proportion as a man has them, he is partaker of a Divine nature. He can rise no higher, and he needs no more. Platonists had said—No, that is only virtue; and virtue is the means, not the end. We want proof of having something above that; something more than any man of the herd, any Christian slave, can perform; something above nature; portents and wonders. So they set to work to perform wonders; and succeeded, I suppose, more or less. For now one enters into a whole fairyland of those very phenomena which are puzzling us so nowadays—ecstasy, clairvoyance, insensibility to pain, cures produced by the effect of what we now call mesmerism. They are all there, these modern puzzles, in those old books of the long bygone seekers for wisdom. It makes us love them, while it saddens us to see that their difficulties were the same as ours, and that there is nothing new under the sun. Of course, a great deal of it all was "imagination." But the question then, as now is, what is this wonder-working imagination?—unless the word be used as a mere euphemism for lying, which really, in many cases, is hardly fair. We cannot wonder at the old Neo-platonists for attributing these strange phenomena to spiritual influence, when we see some who ought to know better doing the same thing now; and others, who more wisely believe them to be strictly physical and nervous, so utterly unable to give reasons for them, that they feel it expedient to ignore them for awhile, till they know more about those physical phenomena which can be put under some sort of classification, and attributed to some sort of inductive law.

But again. These ecstasies, cures, and so forth, brought them rapidly back to the old priestcrafts. The Egyptian priests, the Babylonian and Jewish sorcerers, had practised all this as a trade for ages, and reduced it to an art. It was by sleeping in the temples of the deities, after due mesmeric manipulations, that cures were even then effected. Surely the old priests were the people to whom to go for information. The old philosophers of Greece were venerable. How much more those of the East, in comparison with whom the Greeks were children? Besides, if these dæmons and deities were so near them, might it not be possible to behold them? They seemed to have given up caring much for the world and its course—

> Effugerant adytis templisque relictis
> Dî quibus imperium steterat.

The old priests used to make them appear—perhaps they might do it again. And if spirit could act directly and preternaturally on matter, in spite of the laws of matter, perhaps matter might act on spirit. After all, were matter and spirit so absolutely different? Was not spirit some sort of pervading essence, some subtle ethereal fluid, differing from matter principally in being less gross and dense? This was the point to which they went down rapidly enough; the point to which all philosophies, I firmly believe, will descend, which do not keep in sight that the spiritual means the moral. In trying to make it mean exclusively the intellectual, they will degrade it to mean the merely logical and abstract; and when that is found to be a barren and lifeless phantom, a mere projection of the human brain, attributing reality to mere conceptions and names, and confusing the subject with the object, as logicians say truly the Neoplatonists did, then in despair, the school will try to make the spiritual something real, or, at least, something conceivable, by reinvesting it with the properties of matter, and talking of it as if it were some manner of gas, or heat, or electricity, or force, pervading time and space, conditioned by the accidents of brute matter, and a part of that nature which is born to die.

The culmination of all this confusion we see in Proclus. The unfortunate Hypatia, who is the most important personage between him and Iamblichus, has left no writings to our times; we can only judge of her doctrine by that of her instructors and her pupils. Proclus was taught by the men who had heard her lecture; and the golden chain of the Platonic succession descended from her to him. His throne, however, was at Athens, not at Alexandria. After the murder of the maiden philosopher, Neoplatonism prudently retired to Greece. But Proclus is so essentially the child of the Alexandrian school that we cannot pass him over. Indeed, according to M. Cousin, as I am credibly informed, he is *the* Greek philosopher; the flower and crown of all its schools; in whom, says the learned Frenchman, "are combined, and from whom shine forth, in no irregular or uncertain rays, Orpheus, Pythagoras, Plato, Aristotle, Zeno, Plotinus, Porphyry, and Iamblichus;" and who "had so comprehended all religions in his mind, and paid them such equal reverence, that he was, as it were, the priest of the whole universe!"

I have not the honour of knowing much of M. Cousin's works. I never came across them but on one small matter of fact, and on that I found him copying at second hand an anachronism which one would have conceived palpable to any reader of the original authorities. This is all I know of him, saving these his raptures over Proclus, of which I have quoted only a small portion, and of which I can only say, in Mr. Thomas Carlyle's words, "What things men will worship, in their extreme need!" Other moderns, however, have expressed their admiration of Proclus; and, no doubt, many neat sayings may be found in him (for after all he was a Greek), which will be both pleasing and useful to those who consider philosophic method to consist in putting forth strings of brilliant apophthegms, careless about either their consistency or coherence: but of the method of Plato or Aristotle, any more than of that of Kant or Mill, you will find nothing in him. He seems to my simplicity to be at once the most timid and servile of commentators, and the most cloudy of declaimers. He can rave symbolism like Jacob Böhmen, but without an atom of his originality and earnestness. He can develop an inverted pyramid of dæmonology, like Father Newman himself, but without an atom of his art, his knowledge of human cravings. He combines all schools, truly, Chaldee and Egyptian as well as Greek; but only scraps from their mummies, drops from their quintessences, which satisfy the heart and conscience as little as they do the logical faculties. His Greek gods and heroes, even his Alcibiades and Socrates, are "ideas;" that is, symbols of certain notions or qualities: their flesh and bones, their heart and brain, have been distilled away, till nothing is left but a word, a notion, which may patch a hole in his huge heaven-and-earth-embracing system. He, too, is a commentator and a deducer; all has been discovered; and he tries to discover nothing more. Those who followed him seem to have commented on his comments. With him Neoplatonism properly ends. Is its last utterance a culmination or a fall? Have the Titans scaled heaven, or died of old age, "exhibiting," as Gibbon says of them, "a deplorable instance of the senility of the human mind?" Read Proclus, and judge for yourselves: but first contrive to finish everything else you have to do which can possibly be useful to any human being. Life is short, and Art—at least the art of obtaining practical guidance from the last of the Alexandrians—very long.

And yet—if Proclus and his school became gradually unfaithful to the great root-idea of their philosophy, we must not imitate them. We must not believe that the last of the Alexandrians was under no divine teaching, because he had be-systemed himself into confused notions of what that teaching was like. Yes, there was good in poor old Proclus; and it too came from the only source whence all good comes. Were there no good in him I could not laugh at him as I have done; I could only hate him. There are moments when he rises above his theories; moments when he recurs in spirit, if not in the letter, to the faith of Homer, almost to the faith of Philo. Whether these are the passages of his which his modern admirers prize most, I cannot tell. I should fancy not: nevertheless I will read you one of them.

He is about to commence his discourses on the Parmenides, that book in which we generally now consider that Plato has been most untrue to himself, and fallen from his usual inductive method to the ground of a mere *à priori* theoriser—and yet of which Proclus is reported to have said, and, I should conceive, said honestly, that if it, the Timæus, and the Orphic fragments were preserved, he did not care whether every other book on earth were destroyed. But how does he commence?

"I pray to all the gods and goddesses to guide my reason in the speculation which lies before me, and having kindled in me the pure light of truth, to direct my mind upward to the very knowledge of the things which are, and to open the doors of my soul to receive the divine guidance of Plato, and, having directed my knowledge into the very brightness of being, to withdraw me from the various forms of opinion, from the apparent wisdom, from the wandering about things which do not exist, by that purest intellectual exercise about the things which do exist, whereby alone the eye of the soul is nourished and brightened, as Socrates says in the Phædrus; and that the Noetic Gods will give to me the perfect reason, and the Noeric Gods the power which leads up to this, and that the rulers of the Universe above the heaven will impart to me an energy unshaken by material notions and emancipated from them, and those to whom the world is given as their dominion a winged life, and the angelic choirs a true manifestation of divine things, and the good dæmons the fulness of the inspiration which comes from the Gods, and the heroes a grand, and venerable, and lofty fixedness of mind, and the whole divine race together a perfect preparation for sharing in Plato's most mystical and far-seeing speculations, which he declares to us himself in the Parmenides, with the profundity befitting such topics, but which *he* (*i.e.* his master Syrianus) completed by his most pure and luminous apprehensions, who did most truly share the Platonic feast, and was the medium for transmitting the divine truth, the guide in our speculations, and the hierophant of these divine words; who, as I think, came down as a type of philosophy, to do good to the souls that are here, in place of idols, sacrifices, and the whole mystery of purification, a leader of salvation to the men who are now and who shall be hereafter. And may the whole band of those who are above us be propitious; and may the whole force which they supply be at hand, kindling before us that light which, proceeding from them, may guide us to them."

Surely this is an interesting document. The last Pagan Greek prayer, I believe, which we have on record; the death-wail of the old world—not without a touch of melody. One cannot altogether admire the style; it is inflated, pedantic, written, I fear, with a considerable consciousness that he was saying the right thing and in the very finest way: but still it is a prayer. A cry for light—by no means, certainly, like that noble one in Tennyson's "In Memoriam:"

> So runs my dream. But what am I?
> An infant crying in the night;
> An infant crying for the light;
> And with no language but a cry.

Yet he asks for light: perhaps he had settled already for himself—like too many more of us—what sort of light he chose to have: but still the eye is turned upward to the sun, not inward in conceited fancy that self is its own illumination. He asks—surely not in vain. There was light to be had for asking. That prayer certainly was not answered in the letter: it may have been ere now in the spirit. And yet it is a sad prayer enough. Poor old man, and poor old philosophy!

This he and his teachers had gained by despising the simpler and yet far profounder doctrine of the Christian schools, that the Logos, the Divine Teacher in whom both Christians and Heathens believed, was the very archetype of men, and that He had proved that fact by being made flesh, and dwelling bodily among them, that they might behold His glory, full of grace and truth, and see that it was at once the perfection of man and the perfection of God: that that which was most divine was most human, and that which was most human, most divine. That was the outcome of *their* metaphysic, that they had found the Absolute One; because One existed in whom the apparent antagonism between that which is eternally and that which becomes in time, between the ideal and the actual, between the spiritual and the material, in a word, between God and man, was explained and reconciled for ever.

And Proclus's prayer, on the other hand, was the outcome of the Neoplatonists' metaphysic, the end of all *their* search after the One, the Indivisible, the Absolute, this cry to all manner of innumerable phantoms, ghosts of ideas, ghosts of traditions, neither things nor persons, but thoughts, to give the philosopher each something or other, according to the nature of each. Not that he very clearly defines what each is to give him; but still he feels himself in want of all manner of things, and it is as well to have as many friends at court as possible—Noetic Gods, Noeric Gods, rulers, angels, dæmons, heroes—to enable him to do what? To understand Plato's most mystical and far-seeing speculations. The Eternal Nous, the Intellectual Teacher has vanished further and further off; further off still some dim vision of a supreme Goodness. Infinite spaces above that looms through the mist of the abyss a Primæval One. But even that has a predicate, for it is one; it is not pure essence. Must there not be something beyond that again, which is not even one, but is nameless, inconceivable, absolute? What an abyss! How shall the human mind find anything whereon to rest, in the vast nowhere between it and the object of its search? The search after the One issues in a wail to the innumerable; and kind gods, angels, and heroes, not human indeed, but still conceivable enough to satisfy at least the imagination, step in to fill the void, as they have done since, and may do again; and so, as Mr. Carlyle has it, "the bottomless pit got roofed over," as it may be again ere long.

Are we then to say, that Neoplatonism was a failure? That Alexandria, during four centuries of profound and earnest thought, added nothing? Heaven forbid that we should say so of a philosophy which has exercised on European thought, at the crisis of its noblest life and action, an influence as great as did the Aristotelian system during the Middle Ages. We must never forget, that during the two centuries which commence with the fall of Constantinople, and end with our civil wars, not merely almost all great thinkers, but courtiers, statesmen, warriors, poets, were more or less Neoplatonists. The Greek grammarians, who migrated into Italy, brought with them the works of Plotinus, Iamblichus, and Proclus; and their gorgeous reveries were welcomed eagerly by the European mind, just revelling in the free thought of youthful manhood. And yet the Alexandrian impotence for any practical and social purposes was to be manifested, as utterly as it was in Alexandria or in Athens of old. Ficinus and Picus of Mirandola worked no deliverance, either for Italian morals or polity, at a time when such deliverance was needed bitterly enough. Neoplatonism was petted by luxurious and heathen popes, as an elegant play of the cultivated fancy, which could do their real power, their practical system, neither good nor harm. And one cannot help feeling, while reading the magnificent oration on Supra-sensual Love, which Castiglione, in his admirable book "The Courtier," puts into the mouth of the profligate Bembo, how near mysticism may lie not merely to dilettantism or to Pharisaism, but to sensuality itself. But in England, during Elizabeth's reign, the practical weakness of

Neoplatonism was compensated by the noble practical life which men were compelled to live in those great times; by the strong hold which they had of the ideas of family and national life, of law and personal faith. And I cannot but believe it to have been a mighty gain to such men as Sidney, Raleigh, and Spenser, that they had drunk, however slightly, of the wells of Proclus and Plotinus. One cannot read Spenser's "Fairy Queen," above all his Garden of Adonis, and his cantos on Mutability, without feeling that his Neoplatonism must have kept him safe from many a dark eschatological superstition, many a narrow and bitter dogmatism, which was even then tormenting the English mind, and must have helped to give him altogether a freer and more loving conception, if not a consistent or accurate one, of the wondrous harmony of that mysterious analogy between the physical and the spiritual, which alone makes poetry (and I had almost said philosophy also) possible, and have taught him to behold alike in suns and planets, in flowers and insects, in man and in beings higher than man, one glorious order of love and wisdom, linking them all to Him from whom they all proceed, rays from His cloudless sunlight, mirrors of His eternal glory.

But as the Elizabethan age, exhausted by its own fertility, gave place to the Caroline, Neoplatonism ran through much the same changes. It was good for us, after all, that the plain strength of the Puritans, unphilosophical as they were, swept it away. One feels in reading the later Neoplatonists, Henry More, Smith, even Cudworth (valuable as he is), that the old accursed distinction between the philosopher, the scholar, the illuminate, and the plain righteous man, was growing up again very fast. The school from which the "Religio Medici" issued was not likely to make any bad men good, or any foolish men wise.

Besides, as long as men were continuing to quote poor old Proclus as an irrefragable authority, and believing that he, forsooth, represented the sense of Plato, the new-born Baconian philosophy had but little chance in the world. Bacon had been right in his dislike of Platonism years before, though he was unjust to Plato himself. It was Proclus whom he was really reviling; Proclus as Plato's commentator and representative. The lion had for once got into the ass's skin, and was treated accordingly. The true Platonic method, that dialectic which the Alexandrians gradually abandoned, remains yet to be tried, both in England and in Germany; and I am much mistaken, if, when fairly used, it be not found the ally, not the enemy, of the Baconian philosophy; in fact, the inductive method applied to words, as the expressions of Metaphysic Laws, instead of to natural phenomena, as the expressions of Physical ones. If you wish to see the highest instances of this method, read Plato himself, not Proclus. If you wish to see how the same method can be applied to Christian truth, read the dialectic passages in Augustine's "Confessions." Whether or not you shall agree with their conclusions, you will not be likely, if you have a truly scientific habit of mind, to complain that they want either profundity, severity, or simplicity.

So concludes the history of one of the Alexandrian schools of Metaphysic. What was the fate of the other is a subject which I must postpone to my next Lecture.

LECTURE IV.

THE CROSS AND THE CRESCENT.

I TRIED to point out, in my last Lecture, the causes which led to the decay of the Pagan metaphysic of Alexandria. We have now to consider the fate of the Christian school.

You may have remarked that I have said little or nothing about the positive dogmas of Clement, Origen, and their disciples; but have only brought out the especial points of departure between them and the Heathens. My reason for so doing was twofold: first, I could not have examined them without entering on controversial ground; next, I am very desirous to excite some of my hearers, at least, to examine these questions for themselves.

I entreat them not to listen to the hasty sneer to which many of late have given way, that the Alexandrian divines were mere mystics, who corrupted Christianity by an admixture of Oriental and Greek thought. My own belief is that they expanded and corroborated Christianity, in spite of great errors and defects on certain points, far more than they corrupted it; that they presented it to the minds of cultivated and scientific men in the only form in which it would have satisfied their philosophic aspirations, and yet contrived, with wonderful wisdom, to ground their philosophy on the very same truths which they taught to the meanest slaves, and to appeal in the philosophers to the same inward faculty to which they appealed in the slave; namely, to that inward eye, that moral sense and reason, whereby each and every man can, if he will, "judge of himself that which is right." I boldly say that I believe the Alexandrian Christians to have made the best, perhaps the only, attempt yet made by men, to proclaim a true world-philosophy; whereby I mean a philosophy common to all races, ranks, and intellects, embracing the whole phenomena of humanity, and not an arbitrarily small portion of them, and capable of being understood and appreciated by every human being from the highest to the lowest. And when you hear of a system of reserve in teaching, a *disciplina arcani*, of an esoteric and exoteric, an inner and outer school, among these men, you must not be frightened at the words, as if they spoke of priestcraft, or an intellectual aristocracy, who kept the kernel of the nut for themselves, and gave the husks to the mob. It was not so with the Christian schools; it was so with the Heathen ones. The Heathens were content that the mob, the herd, should have the husks. Their avowed intention and wish was to leave the herd, as they called them, in the mere outward observance of the old idolatries, while they themselves, the cultivated philosophers, had the monopoly of those deeper spiritual truths which were contained under the old superstitions, and were too sacred to be profaned by the vulgar eyes. The Christian method was the exact opposite. They boldly called those vulgar eyes to enter into the very holy of holies, and there gaze on the very deepest root-ideas of their philosophy. They owned no ground for their own speculations which was not common to the harlots and the slaves around. And this was what enabled them to do this; this was what brought on them the charge of demagogism, the hatred of philosophers, the persecution of princes—that their ground was a *moral* ground, and not a merely intellectual one; that they started, not from any notions of the understanding, but from the inward conscience, that truly pure Reason in which the intellectual and the moral spheres are united, which they believed to exist, however dimmed or crushed, in every human being, capable of being awakened, purified, and raised up to a noble and heroic life. They concealed nothing *moral* from their disciples: only they forbade them to meddle with intellectual matters, before they had had a regular intellectual training. The witnesses of reason and conscience were sufficient guides for all men, and at them the many might well stop short. The teacher only needed to proceed further, not into a higher region, but into a lower one, namely, into the region of the logical understanding, and there make deductions from, and illustrations of, those higher truths which he held in common with every slave, and held on the same ground as they.

And the consequence of this method of philosophising was patent. They were enabled to produce, in the lives of millions, generation after generation, a more immense moral improvement than the world had ever seen before. Their disciples did actually become righteous and good men, just in proportion as they were true to the lessons they learnt. They did, for centuries, work a distinct and palpable deliverance on the earth; while all the solemn and earnest meditation of the Neoplatonists, however good or true, worked no deliverance whatsoever. Plotinus longed at one time to make a practical attempt. He asked the Emperor Gallienus, his patron, to rebuild for him a city in Campania; to allow him to call it Platonopolis, and put it into the hands of him and his disciples, that they might there realise Plato's ideal republic. Luckily for the reputation of Neoplatonism, the scheme was swamped by the courtiers of Gallienus, and the earth was saved the sad and ludicrous sight of a realised Laputa; probably a very quarrelsome one. That was his highest practical conception: the foundation of a new society: not the regeneration of society as it existed.

That work was left for the Christian schools; and up to a certain point they performed it. They made men good. *This* was the test, which of the schools was in the right: this was the test, which of the two had hold of the eternal roots of metaphysic. Cicero says, that he had learnt more philosophy from the Laws of the Twelve Tables than from all the Greeks. Clement and his school might have said the same of the Hebrew Ten Commandments and Jewish Law, which are so marvellously analogous to the old Roman laws, founded, as they are, on the belief in a Supreme Being, a Jupiter—literally a Heavenly Father—who is the source and the sanction of law; of whose justice man's justice is the pattern; who is the avenger of crimes against marriage, property, life; on whom depends the sanctity of an oath. And so, to compare great things with small, there was a truly practical human element here in the Christian teaching; purely ethical and metaphysical, and yet palpable to the simplest and lowest, which gave to it a regenerating force which the highest efforts of Neoplatonism could never attain.

And yet Alexandrian Christianity, notoriously enough, rotted away, and perished hideously. Most true. But what if the causes of its decay and death were owing to its being untrue to itself?

I do not say that they had no excuses for being untrue to their own faith. We are not here to judge them. That peculiar subtlety of mind, which rendered the Alexandrians the great thinkers of the then world, had with Christians, as well as Heathens, the effect of alluring them away from practice to speculation. The Christian school, as was to be expected from the moral ground of their philosophy, yielded to it far more slowly than the Heathen, but they did yield, and especially after they had conquered and expelled the Heathen school. Moreover, the long battle with the Heathen school had stirred up in them habits of exclusiveness, of denunciation; the spirit which cannot assert a fact, without dogmatising rashly and harshly on the consequences of denying that fact. Their minds assumed a permanent habit of combativeness. Having no more Heathens to fight, they began fighting each other, excommunicating each other; denying to all who differed from them any share of that light, to claim which for all men had been the very ground of their philosophy. Not that they would have refused the Logos to all men in words. They would have cursed a man for denying the existence of the Logos in every man; but they would have equally cursed him for acting on his existence in practice, and treating the heretic as one who had that within him to which a preacher might appeal. Thus they became Dogmatists; that is, men who assert a truth so fiercely, as to forget that a truth is meant to be used, and not merely asserted—if, indeed, the fierce assertion of a truth in frail man is not generally a sign of some secret doubt of it, and in inverse proportion to his practical living faith in it: just as he who is always telling you that he is a man, is not the most likely to behave like a man. And why did this befall them? Because they forgot practically that the light proceeded from a Person. They could argue over notions and dogmas deduced from the notion of His personality: but they were shut up in those notions; they had forgotten that if He was a Person, His eye was on them, His rule and kingdom within them; and that if He was a Person, He had a character, and that that character was a righteous and a loving character: and therefore they were not ashamed, in defending these notions and dogmas about Him, to commit acts abhorrent to His character, to lie, to slander, to intrigue, to hate, even to murder, for the sake of what they madly called His glory: but which was really only their own glory—the glory of their own dogmas; of propositions and conclusions in their own brain, which, true or false, were equally heretical in their mouths, because they used them only as watchwords of division. Orthodox or unorthodox, they lost the knowledge of God, for they lost the knowledge of righteousness, and love, and peace. That Divine Logos, and theology as a whole, receded further and further aloft into abysmal heights, as it became a mere dreary system of dead scientific terms, having no practical bearing on their hearts and lives; and then they, as the Neoplatonists had done before them, filled up the void by those dæmonologies, images, base Fetish worships, which made the Mohammedan invaders regard them, and I believe justly, as polytheists and idolaters, base as the pagan Arabs of the desert.

I cannot but believe them, moreover, to have been untrue to the teaching of Clement and his school, in that coarse and materialist admiration of celibacy which ruined Alexandrian society, as their dogmatic ferocity ruined Alexandrian thought. The Creed which taught them that in the person of the Incarnate Logos, that which was most divine had been proved to be most human, that which was most human had been proved to be most divine, ought surely to have given to them, as it has given to modern Europe, nobler, clearer, simpler views of the true relation of the sexes. However, on this matter they did not see their way. Perhaps, in so debased an age, so profligate a world, as that out of which Christianity had risen, it was impossible to see the true beauty and sanctity of those primary bonds of humanity. And while the relation of the sexes was looked on in a wrong light, all other social relations were necessarily also misconceived. "The very ideas of family and national life," as it has been said, "those two divine roots of the Church, severed from which she is certain to wither away into that most cruel and most godless of spectres, a religious world, had perished in the East, from the evil influence of the universal practice of slave-holding, as well as from the degradation of that Jewish nation which had been for ages the great witness for these ideas; and all classes, like their forefather Adam—like, indeed, the Old Adam—the selfish, cowardly, brute nature in every man and in every age—were shifting the blame of sin from their own consciences to human relationships and duties, and therein, to the God who had appointed them; and saying, as of old, 'The woman whom Thou gavest to be with me, she gave me of the tree, and I did eat.'"

Much as Christianity did, even in Egypt, for woman, by asserting her moral and spiritual equality with the man, there seems to have been no suspicion that she was the true complement of the man, not merely by softening him, but by strengthening him; that true manhood can be no more developed without the influence of the woman, than true womanhood without the influence of the man. There is no trace among the Egyptian celibates of that chivalrous woman-worship which our Gothic forefathers brought with them into the West, which shed a softening and ennobling light round the mediæval convent life, and warded off for centuries the worst effects of monasticism. Among the religious of Egypt, the monk regarded the nun, the nun the monk, with dread and aversion; while both looked on the married population of the opposite sex with a coarse contempt and disgust which is hardly credible, did not the foul records of it stand written to this day, in Rosweyde's extraordinary "Vitæ Patrum Eremiticorum;" no barren school of metaphysic, truly, for those who are philosophic enough to believe that all phenomena whatsoever of the human mind are worthy matter for scientific induction.

And thus grew up in Egypt a monastic world, of such vastness that it was said to equal in number the laity. This produced, no doubt, an enormous increase in the actual amount of moral evil. But it produced three other effects, which were the ruin of Alexandria. First, a continually growing enervation and numerical decrease of the population; next, a carelessness of, and contempt for social and political life; and lastly, a most brutalising effect on the lay population; who, told that they were, and believing themselves to be, beings of a lower order, and living by a lower standard, sank down more and more generation after generation. They were of the world, and the ways of the world they must follow. Political life had no inherent sanctity or nobleness; why act holily and nobly in it? Family life had no inherent sanctity or nobleness; why act holily and nobly in it either, if there were no holy, noble, and divine principle or ground for it? And thus grew up, both in Egypt, Syria, and Byzantium, a chaos of profligacy and chicanery, in rulers and people, in the home and the market, in the theatre and the senate, such as the world has rarely seen before or since; a chaos which reached its culmination in the seventh century, the age of Justinian and Theodora, perhaps the two most hideous sovereigns, worshipped by the most hideous empire of parasites and hypocrites, cowards and wantons, that ever insulted the long-suffering of a righteous God.

But, for Alexandria at least, the cup was now full. In the year 640 the Alexandrians were tearing each other in pieces about some Jacobite and Melchite controversy, to me incomprehensible, to you unimportant, because the fighters on both sides seem to have lost (as all parties do in their old age) the knowledge of what they were fighting for, and to have so bewildered the question with personal intrigues, spites, and quarrels, as to make it nearly as enigmatic as that famous contemporary war between the blue and green factions at Constantinople, which began by backing in the theatre, the charioteers who drove in blue dresses, against those who drove in green; then went on to identify themselves each with one of the prevailing theological factions; gradually developed, the one into an aristocratic, the other into a democratic, religious party; and ended by a civil war in the streets of Constantinople, accompanied by the most horrible excesses, which had nearly, at one time, given up the city to the flames, and driven Justinian from his throne.

In the midst of these Jacobite and Melchite controversies and riots, appeared before the city the armies of certain wild and unlettered Arab tribes. A short and fruitless struggle followed; and, strange to say, a few months swept away from the face of the earth, not only the wealth, the commerce, the castles, and the liberty, but the philosophy and the Christianity of Alexandria; crushed to powder by one fearful blow, all that had been built up by Alexander and the Ptolemies, by Clement and the philosophers, and made void, to all appearance, nine hundred years of human toil. The people, having no real hold on their hereditary Creed, accepted, by tens of thousands, that of the Mussulman invaders. The Christian remnant became tributaries; and Alexandria dwindled, from that time forth, into a petty seaport town.

And now—can we pass over this new metaphysical school of Alexandria? Can we help inquiring in what the strength of Islamism lay? I, at least, cannot. I cannot help feeling that I am bound to examine in what relation the creed of Omar and Amrou stands to the Alexandrian speculations of five hundred years, and how it had power to sweep those speculations utterly from the Eastern mind. It is a difficult problem; to me, as a Christian priest, a very awful problem. What more awful historic problem, than to see the lower creed destroying the higher? to see God, as it were, undoing his own work, and repenting Him that He had made man? Awful indeed: but I can honestly say, that it is one from the investigation of which I have learnt—I cannot yet tell how much: and of this I am sure, that without that old Alexandrian philosophy, I should not have been able to do justice to Islam; without Islam I should not have been able to find in that Alexandrian philosophy, an ever-living and practical element.

I must, however, first entreat you to dismiss from your minds the vulgar notion that Mohammed was in anywise a bad man, or a conscious deceiver, pretending to work miracles, or to do things which he did not do. He sinned in one instance: but, as far as I can see, only in that one—I mean against what he must have known to be right. I allude to his relaxing in his own case those wise restrictions on polygamy which he had proclaimed. And yet, even in this case, the desire for a child may have been the true cause of his weakness. He did not see the whole truth, of course: but he was an infinitely better man than the men around: perhaps, all in all, one of the best men of his day. Many here may have read Mr. Carlyle's vindication of Mohammed in his Lectures on Hero Worship; to those who have not, I shall only say, that I entreat them to do so; and that I assure them, that though I differ in many things utterly from Mr. Carlyle's inferences and deductions in that lecture, yet that I am convinced, from my own acquaintance with the original facts and documents, that the picture there drawn of Mohammed is a true and a just description of a much-calumniated man.

Now, what was the strength of Islam? The common answer is, fanaticism and enthusiasm. To such answers

I can only rejoin: Such terms must be defined before they are used, and we must be told what fanaticism and enthusiasm are. Till then I have no more *à priori* respect for a long word ending in -ism or -asm than I have for one ending in -ation or -ality. But while fanaticism and enthusiasm are being defined—a work more difficult than is commonly fancied—we will go on to consider another answer. We are told that the strength of Islam lay in the hope of their sensuous Paradise and fear of their sensuous Gehenna. If so, this is the first and last time in the world's history that the strength of any large body of people—perhaps of any single man—lay in such a hope. History gives us innumerable proofs that such merely selfish motives are the parents of slavish impotence, of pedantry and conceit, of pious frauds, often of the most devilish cruelty: but, as far as my reading extends, of nothing better. Moreover, the Christian Greeks had much the same hopes on those points as the Mussulmans; and similar causes should produce similar effects: but those hopes gave them no strength. Besides, according to the Mussulmans' own account, this was *not* their great inspiring idea; and it is absurd to consider the wild battle-cries of a few imaginative youths, about black-eyed and green-kerchiefed Houris calling to them from the skies, as representing the average feelings of a generation of sober and self-restraining men, who showed themselves actuated by far higher motives.

Another answer, and one very popular now, is that the Mussulmans were strong, because they believed what they said; and the Greeks weak, because they did not believe what they said. From this notion I shall appeal to another doctrine of the very same men who put it forth, and ask them, Can any man be strong by believing a lie? Have you not told us, nobly enough, that every lie is by its nature rotten, doomed to death, certain to prove its own impotence, and be shattered to atoms the moment you try to use it, to bring it into rude actual contact with fact, and Nature, and the eternal laws? Faith to be strong, must be faith in something which is not one's self; faith in something eternal, something objective, something true, which would exist just as much though we and all the world disbelieved it. The strength of belief comes from that which is believed in; if you separate it from that, it becomes a mere self-opinion, a sensation of positiveness; and what sort of strength that will give, history will tell us in the tragedies of the Jews who opposed Titus, of the rabble who followed Walter the Penniless to the Crusades, of the Munster Anabaptists, and many another sad page of human folly. It may give the fury of idiots; not the deliberate might of valiant men. Let us pass this by, then; believing that faith can only give strength where it is faith in something true and right: and go on to another answer almost as popular as the last.

We are told that the might of Islam lay in a certain innate force and savage virtue of the Arab character. If we have discovered this in the followers of Mohammed, they certainly had not discovered it in themselves. They spoke of themselves, rightly or wrongly, as men who had received a divine light, and that light a moral light, to teach them to love that which was good, and refuse that which was evil; and to that divine light they stedfastly and honestly attributed every right action of their lives. Most noble and affecting, in my eyes, is that answer of Saad's aged envoy to Yezdegird, king of Persia, when he reproached him with the past savagery and poverty of the Arabs. "Whatsoever thou hast said," answered the old man, "regarding the former condition of the Arabs is true. Their food *was* green lizards; they buried their infant daughters alive; nay, some of them feasted on dead carcases, and drank blood; while others slew their kinsfolk, and thought themselves great and valiant, when by so doing they became possessed of more property. They *were* clothed with hair garments, they knew not good from evil, and made no distinction between that which was lawful and unlawful. Such was our state; but God in his mercy has sent us, by a holy prophet, a sacred volume, which teaches us the true faith."

These words, I think, show us the secret of Islam. They are a just comment on that short and rugged chapter of the Koran which is said to have been Mohammed's first attempt either at prophecy or writing; when, after long fasting and meditation among the desert hills, under the glorious eastern stars, he came down and told his good Kadijah that he had found a great thing, and that she must help him to write it down. And what was this which seemed to the unlettered camel-driver so priceless a treasure? Not merely that God was one God—vast as that discovery was—but that he was a God "who showeth to man the thing which he knew not;" a "most merciful God;" a God, in a word, who could be trusted; a God who would teach and strengthen; a God, as he said, who would give him courage to set his face like a flint, and would put an answer in his mouth when his idolatrous countrymen cavilled and sneered at his message to them, to turn from their idols of wood and stone, and become righteous men, as Abraham their forefather was righteous.

"A God who showeth to man the thing which he knew not." That idea gave might to Islam, because it was a real idea, an eternal fact; the result of a true insight into the character of God. And that idea alone, believe me, will give conquering might either to creed, philosophy, or heart of man. Each will be strong, each will endure, in proportion as it believes that God is one who shows to man the thing which he knew not: as it believes, in short, in that Logos of which Saint John wrote, that He was the light who lightens every man who comes into the world.

In a word, the wild Koreish had discovered, more or less clearly, that end and object of all metaphysic whereof I have already spoken so often; that external and imperishable beauty for which Plato sought of old; and had seen that its name was righteousness, and that it dwelt absolutely in an absolutely righteous person; and moreover, that this person was no careless self-contented epicurean deity; but that He was, as they loved to call Him, the most merciful God; that He cared for men; that He desired to make men righteous. Of that they could not doubt. The fact was palpable, historic, present. To them the degraded Koreish of the desert, who as they believed, and I think believed rightly, had fallen from the old Monotheism of their forefathers Abraham and Ismael, into the lowest fetishism, and with that into the lowest brutality and wretchedness—to them, while they were making idols of wood and stone; eating dead carcases; and burying their daughters alive; careless of chastity, of justice, of property; sunk in unnatural crimes, dead in trespasses and sins; hateful and hating one another—a man, one of their own people had come, saying: "I have a message from the one righteous God. His curse is on all this, for it is unlike Himself. He will have you righteous men, after the pattern of your forefather Abraham. Be that, and arise, body, soul, and spirit, out of your savagery and brutishness. Then you shall be able to trample under foot the profligate idolaters, to sweep the Greek tyrants from the land which they have been oppressing for centuries, and to recover the East for its rightful heirs, the children of Abraham." Was this not, in every sense, a message from God? I must deny the philosophy of Clement and Augustine, I must deny my own conscience, my own reason, I must outrage my own moral sense, and confess that I have no immutable standard of right, that I know no eternal source of right, if I deny it to have been one; if I deny what seems to me the palpable historic fact, that those wild Koreish had in them a reason and a conscience, which could awaken to that message, and perceive its boundless beauty, its boundless importance, and that they did accept that message, and lived by it in proportion as they received it fully, such lives as no men in those times, and few in after times, have been able to live. If I feel, as I do feel, that Abubekr, Omar, Abu Obeidah, and Amrou, were better men than I am, I must throw away all that Philo—all that a Higher authority—has taught me: or I must attribute their lofty virtues to the one source of all in man which is not selfishness, and fancy, and fury, and blindness as of the beasts which perish.

Why, then, has Islamism become one of the most patent and complete failures upon earth, if the true test of a system's success be the gradual progress and amelioration of the human beings who are under its influence? First, I believe, from its allowing polygamy? I do not judge Mohammed for having allowed it. He found it one of the ancestral and immemorial customs of his nation. He found it throughout the Hebrew Scriptures. He found it in the case of Abraham, his ideal man; and, as he believed, the divinely-inspired ancestor of his race. It seemed to him that what was right for Abraham, could not be wrong for an Arab. God shall judge him, not I. Moreover, the Christians of the East, divided into either monks or profligates; and with far lower and more brutal notions of the married state than were to be found in Arab poetry and legend, were the very last men on earth to make him feel the eternal and divine beauty of that pure wedded love which Christianity has not only proclaimed, but commanded, and thereby emancipated woman from her old slavery to the stronger sex. And I believe, from his chivalrous faithfulness to his good wife Kadijah, as long as she lived, that Mohammed was a man who could have accepted that great truth in all its fulness, had he but been taught it. He certainly felt the evil of polygamy so strongly as to restrict it in every possible way, except the only right way—namely, the proclamation of the true ideal of marriage. But his ignorance, mistake, sin, if you will, was a deflection from the right law, from the true constitution of man, and therefore it avenged itself. That chivalrous respect for woman, which was so strong in the early Mohammedans, died out. The women themselves—who, in the first few years of Islamism, rose as the men rose, and became their helpmates, counsellors, and fellow-warriors—degenerated rapidly into mere playthings. I need not enter into the painful subject of woman's present position in the East, and the social consequences thereof. But I firmly believe, not merely as a theory, but as a fact which may be proved by abundant evidence, that to polygamy alone is owing nine-tenths of the present decay and old age of every Mussulman nation; and that till it be utterly abolished, all Western civilisation and capital, and all the civil and religious liberty on earth, will not avail one jot toward their revival. You must regenerate the family before you can regenerate the nation, and the relation of husband and wife before the family; because, as long as the root is corrupt, the fruit will be corrupt also.

But there is another cause of the failure of Islamism, more intimately connected with those metaphysical questions which we have been hitherto principally considering.

Among the first Mussulmans, as I have said, there was generally the most intense belief in each man that he was personally under a divine guide and teacher. But their creed contained nothing which could keep up that belief in the minds of succeeding generations. They had destroyed the good with the evil, and they paid the penalty of their undistinguishing wrath. In sweeping away the idolatries and fetish worships of the Syrian Catholics, the Mussulmans had swept away also that doctrine which alone can deliver men from idolatry and fetish worships—if not outward and material ones, yet the still more subtle, and therefore more dangerous idolatries of the intellect. For they had swept away the belief in the Logos; in a divine teacher of every human soul, who was, in some mysterious way, the pattern and antitype of human virtue and wisdom. And more, they had swept away that belief in the incarnation of the Logos, which alone can make man feel that his divine teacher is one who can enter into the human duties, sorrows, doubts, of each human spirit. And, therefore, when Mohammed and his personal friends were dead, the belief in a present divine teacher, on the whole, died with them; and the Mussulmans began to put the Koran in the place of Him of whom the Koran spoke. They began to worship the book—which after all is not a book, but only an irregular collection of Mohammed's meditations, and notes for sermons—with the most slavish and ridiculous idolatry. They fell into a cabbalism, and a superstitious reverence for the mere letters and words of the Koran, to which the cabbalism of the old Rabbis was moderate and rational. They surrounded it, and the history of Mohammed, with all ridiculous myths, and prodigies, and lying wonders, whereof the book itself contained not a word; and which Mohammed, during his existence, had denied and repudiated, saying that he worked no miracles, and that none were needed; because only reason was required to show a man the hand of a good God in all human affairs. Nevertheless, these later Mussulmans found the miracles necessary to confirm their faith: and why? Because they had lost the sense of a present God, a God of order; and therefore hankered, as men in such a mood always will, after prodigious and unnatural proofs of His having been once present with their founder Mohammed.

And in the meanwhile that absolute and omnipotent Being whom Mohammed, arising out of his great darkness, had so nobly preached to the Koreish, receded in the minds of their descendants to an unapproachable and abysmal distance. For they had lost the sense of His present guidance, His personal care. They had lost all which could connect Him with the working of their own souls, with their human duties and struggles, with the belief that His mercy and love were counterparts of human mercy and human love; in plain English, that He was loving and merciful at all. The change came very gradually, thank God; you may read of noble sayings and deeds here and there, for many centuries after Mohammed: but it came; and then their belief in God's omnipotence and absoluteness dwindled into the most dark, and slavish, and benumbing fatalism. His unchangeableness became in their minds not an unchangeable purpose to teach, forgive, and deliver men—as it seemed to Mohammed to have been—but a mere brute necessity, an unchangeable purpose to have His own way, whatsoever that way might be. That dark fatalism, also, has helped toward the decay of the Mohammedan nations. It has made them careless of self-improvement; faithless of the possibility of progress; and has kept, and will keep, the Mohammedan nations, in all intellectual matters, whole ages behind the Christian nations of the West.

How far the story of Omar's commanding the baths of Alexandria to be heated with the books from the great library is true, we shall never know. Some have doubted the story altogether: but so many fresh corroborations of it are said to have been lately discovered, in Arabic writers, that I can hardly doubt that it had some foundation in fact. One cannot but believe that John Philoponus, the last of the Alexandrian grammarians, when he asked his patron Amrou the gift of the library, took care to save some, at least, of its treasures; and howsoever strongly Omar may have felt or said that all books which agreed with the Koran were useless, and all which disagreed with it only fit to be destroyed, the general feeling of the Mohammedan leaders was very different. As they settled in the various countries which they conquered, education seems to have been considered by them an important object. We even find some of them, in the same generation as Mohammed, obeying strictly the Prophet's command to send all captive children to school—a fact which speaks as well for the Mussulmans' good sense, as it speaks ill for the state of education among the degraded descendants of the Greek conquerors of the East. Gradually philosophic Schools arose, first at Bagdad, and then at Cordova; and the Arabs carried on the task of commenting on Aristotle's Logic, and Ptolemy's Megiste Syntaxis—which last acquired from them the name of Almagest, by which it was so long known during the Middle Ages.

But they did little but comment, though there was no Neoplatonic or mystic element in their commentaries. It seems as if Alexandria was preordained, by its very central position, to be the city of commentators, not of originators. It is worthy of remark, that Philoponus, who may be considered as the man who first introduced the simple warriors of the Koreish to the treasures of Greek thought, seems to have been the first rebel against the Neoplatonist eclecticism. He maintained, and truly, that Porphyry, Proclus, and the rest, had entirely misunderstood Aristotle, when they attempted to reconcile him with Plato, or incorporate his philosophy into Platonism. Aristotle was henceforth the text-book of Arab savants. It was natural enough. The Mussulman mind was trained in habits of absolute obedience to the authority of fixed dogmas. All those attempts to follow out metaphysic to its highest object, theology, would be useless if not wrong in the eyes of a Mussulman, who had already his simple and sharply-defined creed on all matters relating to the unseen world. With him metaphysic was a study altogether divorced from man's higher life and aspirations. So also were physics. What need had he of Cosmogonies? what need to trace the relations between man and the universe, or the universe and its Maker? He had his definite material Elysium and Tartarus, as the only ultimate relation between man and the universe; his dogma of an absolute fiat, creating arbitrary and once for all, as the only relation between the universe and its Maker: and further it was not lawful to speculate. The idea which I believe unites both physic and metaphysic with man's highest inspirations and widest speculations—the Alexandria idea of the Logos, of the Deity working in time and space by successive thoughts—he had not heard of; for it was dead, as I have said, in Alexandria itself; and if he had heard of it, he would have spurned it as detracting from the absoluteness of that abysmal one Being, of whom he so nobly yet so partially bore witness. So it was to be; doubtless it was right that it should be so. Man's eye is too narrow to see a whole truth, his brain too weak to carry a whole truth. Better for him, and better for the world, is perhaps the method on which man has been educated in every age, by which to each school, or party, or nation, is given some one great truth, which they are to work out to its highest development, to exemplify in actual life, leaving some happier age—perhaps, alas! only some future state—to reconcile that too favoured dogma with other truths which lie beside it, and without which it is always incomplete, and sometimes altogether barren.

But such schools of science, founded on such a ground as this, on the mere instinct of curiosity, had little chance of originality or vitality. All the great schools of the world, the elder Greek philosophy, the Alexandrian, the present Baconian school of physics, have had a deeper motive for their search, a far higher object which they hope to discover. But indeed, the Mussulmans did not so much wish to discover truth, as to cultivate their own intellects. For that purpose a sharp and subtle systematist, like Aristotle, was the very man whom they required; and from the destruction of Alexandria may date the rise of the Aristotelian philosophy. Translations of his works were made into Arabic, first, it is said, from Persian and Syriac translations; the former of which had been made during the sixth and seventh centuries, by the wreck of tho Neoplatonist party, during their visit to the philosophic Chozroos. A century after, they filled Alexandria. After them Almansoor, Hairoun Alraschid, and their successors, who patronised the Nestorian Christians, obtained from them translations of the philosophic, medical, and astronomical Greek works; while the last of the Omniades, Abdalrahman, had introduced the same literary taste into Spain, where, in the thirteenth century, Averroës and Maimonides rivalled the fame of Avicenna, who had flourished at Bagdad a century before.

But, as I have said already, these Arabs seem to have invonted nothing; they only commented. And yet not only commented; for they preserved for us those works of whose real value they were so little aware. Averroës, in quality of commentator on Aristotle, became his rival in the minds of the mediæval schoolmen; Avicenna, in quality of commentator on Hippocrates and Galen, was for centuries the text-book of all European physicians; while Albatani and Aboul Wefa, as astronomers, commented on Ptolemy, not however without making a few important additions to his knowledge; for Aboul Wefa discovered a third inequality of the moon's motion, in addition to the two mentioned by Ptolemy, which he did, according to Professor Whewell, in a truly philosophic manner—an apparently solitary instance, and one which, in its own day, had no effect; for the fact was forgotten, and rediscovered centuries after by Tycho Brahe. To Albatani, however, we owe two really valuable heir-looms. The one is the use of the sine, or half-chord of the double arc, instead of the chord of the arc itself, which had been employed by the Greek astronomers; the other, of even more practical benefit, was the introduction of the present decimal arithmetic, instead of the troublesome sexagesimal arithmetic of the Greeks. These ten digits, however, seem, says Professor Whewell, by the confession of the Arabians themselves, to be of Indian origin, and thus form no exception to the sterility of the Arabian genius in scientific inventions. Nevertheless we are bound, in all fairness, to set against his condemnation of the Arabs Professor De Morgan's opinion of the Moslem, in his article on Euclid: "Some writers speak slightingly of this progress, the results of which they are too apt to compare with those of our own time. They ought rather to place the Saracens by the side of their own Gothic ancestors; and making some allowance for the more advantageous circumstances under which the first started, they should view the second systematically dispersing the remains of Greek civilisation, while the first were concentrating the geometry of Alexandria, the arithmetic and algebra of India, and the astronomy of both, to form a nucleus for the present state of science."

To this article of Professor De Morgan's on Euclid,* and to Professor Whewell's excellent "History of the Inductive Sciences," from which I, being neither Arabic scholar nor astronomer, have drawn most of my facts about physical science, I must refer those who wish to know more of the early rise of physics, and of their preservation by the Arabs, till a great and unexpected event brought them back again to the quarter of the globe where they had their birth, and where alone they could be regenerated into a new and practical life.

That great event was the Crusades. We have heard little of Alexandria lately. Its intellectual glory had departed westward and eastward, to Cordova and to Bagdad; its commercial greatness had left it for Cairo and Damietta. But Egypt was still the centre of communication between the two great stations of the Moslem power, and indeed, as Mr. Lane has shown in his most valuable translation of the "Arabian Nights," possessed a peculiar life and character of its own.

It was the rash object of the Crusaders to extinguish that life. Palestine was their first point of attack: but the later Crusaders seem to have found, like the rest of the world, that the destinies of Palestine could not be separated from those of Egypt; and to Damietta, accordingly, was directed that last

* Smith's "Classical Dictionary."

disastrous attempt of St. Louis, which all may read so graphically described in the pages of Joinville.

The Crusaders failed utterly of the object at which they aimed. They succeeded in an object of which they never dreamed; for in those Crusades the Moslem and the Christian had met face to face, and found that both were men, that they had a common humanity, a common eternal standard of nobleness and virtue. So the Christian knights went home humbler and wiser men, when they found in the Saracen emirs the same generosity, truth, mercy, chivalrous self-sacrifice, which they had fancied their own peculiar possession, and added to that, a civilisation and a learning which they could only admire and imitate. And thus, from the era of the Crusades, a kindlier feeling sprang up between the Crescent and the Cross, till it was again broken by the fearful invasions of the Turks throughout Eastern Europe. The learning of the Moslem, as well as their commerce, began to pour rapidly into Christendom, both from Spain, Egypt, and Syria; and thus the Crusaders were, indeed, rewarded according to their deeds. They had fancied that they were bound to vindicate the possession of the earth for Him to whom they believed the earth belonged. He showed them—or rather He has shown us, their children—that He can vindicate His own dominion better far than man can do it for Him; and their cruel and unjust aim was utterly foiled. That was not the way to make men know or obey Him. They took the sword, and perished by the sword. But the truly noble element in them—the element which our hearts and reasons recognise and love, in spite of all the loud words about the folly and fanaticism of the Crusades, whensoever we read "The Talisman" or "Ivanhoe"—the element of loyal faith and self-sacrifice—did not go unrequited. They learnt wider, juster views of man and virtue, which I cannot help believing must have had great effect in weakening in their minds their old, exclusive, and bigoted notions, and in paving the way for the great outburst of free thought, and the great assertion of the dignity of humanity, which the fifteenth century beheld. They opened a path for that influx of scientific knowledge which has produced, in after centuries, the most enormous effects on the welfare of Europe, and made life possible for millions who would otherwise have been pent within the narrow bounds of Europe, to devour each other in the struggle for room and bread.

But those Arabic translations of Greek authors were a fatal gift for Egypt, and scarcely less fatal gift for Bagdad. In that Almagest of Ptolemy, in that Organon of Aristotle, which the Crusaders are said to have brought home, lay, rude and embryotic, the germs of that physical science, that geographical knowledge which has opened to the European the commerce and the colonisation of the globe. Within three hundred years after his works reached Europe, Ptolemy had taught the Portuguese to sail round Africa; and from that day the stream of eastern wealth flowed no longer through the Red Sea, or the Persian Gulf, on its way to the new countries of the West; and not only Alexandria, but Damietta and Bagdad, dwindled down to their present insignificance. And yet the whirligig of time brings about its revenges. The stream of commerce is now rapidly turning back to its old channel; and British science bids fair to make Alexandria once more the inn of all the nations.

It is with a feeling of awe that one looks upon the

huge possibilities of her future. Her own physical capacities, as the great mind of Napoleon saw, are what they always have been, inexhaustible; and science has learnt to set at naught the only defect of situation which has ever injured her prosperity, namely, the short land passage from the Nile to the Red Sea. The fate of Palestine is now more than ever bound up with her fate; and a British or French colony might, holding the two countries, develop itself into a nation as vast as sprang from Alexander's handful of Macedonians, and become the meeting point for the nations of the West and those great Anglo-Saxon peoples who seem destined to spring up in the Australian ocean. Wide as the dream may appear, steam has made it a far narrower one than the old actual fact, that for centuries the Phœnician and the Arabian interchanged at Alexandria the produce of Britain for that of Ceylon and Hindostan. And as for intellectual development, though Alexandria wants, as she has always wanted, that insular and exclusive position which seems almost necessary to develop original thought and original national life, yet she may still act as the point of fusion for distinct schools and polities, and the young and buoyant vigour of the new-born nations may at once teach, and learn from, the prudence, the experience, the traditional wisdom of the ancient Europeans.

This vision, however possible, may be a far-off one: but the first step towards it, at least, is being laid before our eyes—and that is, a fresh reconciliation between the Crescent and the Cross. Apart from all political considerations, which would be out of place here, I hail, as a student of philosophy, the school which is now, both in Alexandria and in Constantinople, teaching to Moslem and to Christians the same lesson which the Crusaders learnt in Egypt five hundred years ago. A few years' more perseverance in the valiant and righteous course which Britain has now chosen, will reward itself by opening a vast field for capital and enterprise, for the introduction of civil and religious liberty among the down-trodden peasantry of Egypt; as the Giaour becomes an object of respect, and trust, and gratitude to the Moslem; and as the feeling that Moslem and Giaour own a common humanity, a common eternal standard of justice and mercy, a common sacred obligation to perform our promises, and to succour the oppressed, shall have taken place of the old brute wonder at our careless audacity, and awkward assertion of power, which now expresses itself in the somewhat left-handed Alexandrian compliment—"There is one Satan, and there are many Satans: but there is no Satan like a Frank in a round hat."

It would be both uncourteous and unfair of me to close these my hasty Lectures, without expressing my hearty thanks for the great courtesy and kindness which I have received in this my first visit to your most noble and beautiful city; and often, I am proud to say, from those who differ from me deeply on many important points; and also for the attention with which I have been listened to while trying, clumsily enough, to explain dry and repulsive subjects, and to express opinions which may be new, and perhaps startling, to many of my hearers. If my imperfect hints shall have stirred up but one hearer to investigate this obscure and yet most important subject, and to examine for himself the original documents, I shall feel that my words in this place have not been spoken in vain; for even if such a seeker should arrive at conclusions different from my own (and I pretend to no infallibility), he will at least have learnt new facts, the parents of new thought, perhaps of new action; he will have come face to face with new human beings, in whom he will have been compelled to take a human interest; and will surely rise from his researches, let them lead him where they will, at least somewhat of a wider-minded and a wider-hearted man.

THE ANCIEN RÉGIME.

THE ANCIEN RÉGIME.

PREFACE.

The rules of the Royal Institution forbid (and wisely) religious or political controversy. It was therefore impossible for me in these Lectures, to say much which had to be said, in drawing a just and complete picture of the Ancien Régime in France. The passages inserted between brackets, which bear on religious matters, were accordingly not spoken at the Royal Institution.

But more. It was impossible for me in these Lectures, to bring forward as fully as I could have wished, the contrast between the continental nations and England, whether now, or during the eighteenth century. But that contrast cannot be too carefully studied at the present moment. In proportion as it is seen and understood, will the fear of revolution (if such exists) die out among the wealthier classes; and the wish for it (if such exists) among the poorer; and a large extension of the suffrage will be looked on as—what it actually is—a safe and harmless concession to the wishes—and, as I hold, to the just rights—of a large portion of the British nation.

There exists in Britain now, as far as I can see, no one of those evils which brought about the French Revolution. There is no widespread misery, and therefore no widespread discontent, among the classes who live by hand-labour. The legislation of the last generation has been steadily in favour of the poor, as against the rich; and it is even more true now than it was in 1789, that—as Arthur Young told the French mob which stopped his carriage—the rich pay many taxes (over and above the poor-rates, a direct tax on the capitalist in favour of the labourer) more than are paid by the poor. "In England" (says M. de Tocqueville of even the eighteenth century) "the poor man enjoyed the privilege of exemption from taxation; in France, the rich." Equality before the law is as well-nigh complete as it can be, where some are rich and others poor; and the only privileged class, it sometimes seems to me, is the pauper, who has neither the responsibility of self-government, nor the toil of self-support.

A minority of malcontents, some justly, some unjustly, angry with the present state of things, will always exist in this world. But a majority of malcontents we shall never have, as long as the workmen are allowed to keep untouched and unthreatened their rights of free speech, free public meeting, free combination for all purposes which do not provoke a breach of the peace. There may be (and probably are) to be found in London and the large towns, some of those revolutionary propagandists who have terrified and tormented continental statesmen since the year 1815. But they are far fewer in number than in 1848; far fewer still (I believe) than in 1831; and their habits, notions, temper, whole mental organisation, is so utterly alien to that of the average Englishman, that it is only the sense of wrong which can make him take counsel with them, or make common cause with them. Meanwhile, every man who is admitted to a vote, is one more person withdrawn from the temptation to disloyalty, and enlisted in maintaining the powers that be—when they are in the wrong, as well as when they are in the right. For every Englishman is by his nature conservative; slow to form an opinion; cautious in putting it into effect; patient under evils which seem irremediable; persevering in abolishing such as seem remediable; and then only too ready to acquiesce in the earliest practical result; to "rest and be thankful." His faults, as well as his virtues, make him anti-revolutionary. He is generally too dull to take in a great idea; and if he does take it in, often too selfish to apply it to any interest save his own. But now and then, when the sense of actual injury forces upon him a great idea, like that of Free-trade or of Parliamentary Reform, he is indomitable, however slow and patient, in translating his thought into fact: and they will not be wise statesmen who resist his dogged determination. If at this moment he demands an extension of the suffrage eagerly and even violently, the wise statesman will give at once, gracefully and generously, what the Englishman will certainly obtain one day, if he has set his mind upon it. If, on the other hand, he asks for it calmly, then the wise statesman (instead of mistaking English reticence for apathy) will listen to his wishes all the more readily; seeing in the moderation of the demand, the best possible guarantee for moderation in the use of the thing demanded.

And, be it always remembered, that in introducing these men into the "balance of the Constitution," we introduce no unknown quantity. Statesmen ought to know them, if they know themselves; to judge what the working man would do by what they do themselves. He who imputes virtues to his own class imputes them also to the labouring class. He who imputes vices to the labouring class, imputes them to his own class. For both are not only of the same flesh and blood, but, what is infinitely more important, of the same spirit; of the same race; in innumerable cases, of the same ancestors. For centuries past the most able of these men have been working upwards into the middle class, and through it, often, to the highest dignities, and the highest family connections; and the whole nation knows how they have comported themselves therein. And, by a reverse process (of which the physiognomist and genealogist can give abundant proof), the weaker members of that class which was dominant during the Middle Age have been sinking downward, often to the rank of mere day-labourers, and carrying downward with them—sometimes in a very tragical and pathetic fashion—somewhat of the dignity and the refinement which they had learnt from their ancestors.

Thus has the English nation (and as far as I can see, the Scotch likewise) become more homogeneous than any nation of the Continent, if we except France since the extermination of the Frankish nobility. And for that very reason, as it seems to me, it is more fitted than any other European nation for the exercise of equal political rights; and not to be debarred of them by arguments drawn from countries which have been governed—as England has not been—by a caste.

The civilisation, not of mere book-learning, but of the heart; all that was once meant by "manners"—good breeding, high feeling, respect for self and respect for others—are just as common (as far as I have seen) among the hand-workers of England and Scotland, as among any other class; the only difference is, that these qualities develop more early in the richer classes, owing to that severe discipline of our public schools, which makes mere lads often fit to govern, because they have learnt to obey: while they develop later—generally not till middle age—in the classes who have not gone through in their youth that Spartan training, and who indeed (from a mistaken conception of liberty) would not endure it for a day. This and other social drawbacks which are but too patent, retard the manhood of the working classes. That it should be so, is a wrong. For if a citizen have one right above all others to demand anything of his country, it is that he should be educated; that whatever capabilities he may have in him, however small, should have their fair and full chance of development. But the cause of the wrong is not the existence of a caste, or a privileged class, or of anything save the plain fact, that some men will be always able to pay more for their children's education than others; and that those children will, inevitably, win in the struggle of life.

Meanwhile, in this fact is to be found the most weighty, if not the only argument against manhood suffrage, which would admit many—but too many, alas!—who are still mere boys in mind. To a reasonable household suffrage it cannot apply. The man who (being almost certainly married, and having children) can afford to rent a £5 tenement in a town, or in the country either, has seen quite enough of life, and learnt quite enough of it, to form a very fair judgment of the man who offers to represent him in Parliament; because he has learnt, not merely something of his own interest, or that of his class, but—what is infinitely more important—the difference between the pretender and the honest man.

The causes of this state of society, which is peculiar to Britain, must be sought far back in the ages. It would seem that the distinction between "earl and churl" (the noble and the non-noble freeman) was crushed out in this island by the two Norman conquests—that of the Anglo-Saxon nobility by Sweyn and Canute; and that of the Anglo-Danish nobility by William and his Frenchmen. Those two terrible calamities, following each other in the short space of fifty years, seem to have welded together, by a community of suffering, all ranks and races, at least south of the Tweed; and when the English rose after the storm, they rose as one homogeneous people, never to be governed again by an originally alien race. The English nobility were, from the time of Magna Charta, rather an official nobility, than, as in most continental countries, a separate caste; and whatever caste tendencies had developed themselves before the Wars of the Roses (as such are certain to do during centuries of continued wealth and power), were crushed out by the great revolutionary events of the next hundred years. Especially did the discovery of the New World, the maritime struggle with Spain, the outburst of commerce and colonisation during the reigns of Elizabeth and James, help toward this good result. It was in vain for the Lord Oxford of the day, sneering at Raleigh's sudden elevation, to complain that as on the virginals, so in the State, "Jacks went up, and heads went down." The proudest noblemen were not ashamed to have their ventures on the high seas, and to send their younger sons trading, or buccaneering, under the conduct of low-born men like Drake, who "would like to see the gentleman that would not set his hand to a rope, and hale and draw with the mariners." Thus sprang up that respect for, even fondness for, severe bodily labour, which the educated class of no nation save our own has ever felt; and which has stood them in such good stead, whether at home or abroad. Thus, too, sprang up the system of society by which (as the ballad sets forth) the squire's son might be a "'prentice good," and marry

> "The bailiff's daughter dear
> That dwelt at Islington,"

without tarnishing, as he would have done on the Continent, the scutcheon of his ancestors. That which has saved England from a central despotism, such as crushed, during the eighteenth century, every nation on the Continent, is the very same peculiarity which makes the advent of the masses to a share in political power safe and harmless; namely, the absence of caste, or rather (for there is sure to be a moral fact underlying and causing every political fact) the absence of that wicked pride which perpetuates caste; forbidding those to intermarry whom nature and fact pronounce to be fit mates before God and man.

These views are not mine only. They have been already set forth so much more forcibly by M. de Tocqueville, that I should have thought it unnecessary to talk about them, were not the rhetorical phrases, "Caste," "Privileged Classes," "Aristocratic Exclusiveness," and such-like, bandied about again just now, as if they represented facts. If there remain in this kingdom any facts which correspond to those words, let them be abolished as speedily as possible: but that such do remain was not the opinion of the master of modern political philosophy, M. de Tocqueville.

He expresses his surprise "that the fact which distinguishes England from all other modern nations, and which alone can throw light on her peculiarities, . . . has not attracted more attention, . . . and that habit has rendered it, as it were, imperceptible to the English themselves—that England was the only country in which the system of caste had been not only modified, but effectually destroyed. The nobility and the middle classes followed the same business, embraced the same professions, and, what is far more significant, intermarried with each other. The daughter of the greatest nobleman" (and this, if true of the eighteenth century, has become far more true of the nineteenth) "could already, without disgrace, marry a man of yesterday." . . .

"It has often been remarked that the English nobility has been more prudent, more able, and less exclusive than any other. It would have been much nearer the truth to say, that in England, for a very long time past, no nobility, properly so called, have existed, if we take the word in the ancient and limited sense it has everywhere else retained." . . .

"For several centuries the word 'gentleman'" (he might have added, "burgess") "has altogether changed its meaning in England; and the word 'roturier' has ceased to exist. In each succeeding century it is applied to persons placed somewhat lower in the social scale" (as the "bagman" of Pickwick has become, and has deserved to become, the "commercial gentleman" of our day). "At length it travelled with the English to America, where it is used to designate every citizen indiscriminately. Its history is that of democracy itself." . . .

"If the middle classes of England, instead of making war upon the aristocracy, have remained so intimately connected with it, it is not especially because the aristocracy is open to all, but rather, because its outline was indistinct, and its limit unknown: not so much because any man might be admitted into it, as because it was impossible to say with certainty when he took rank there: so that all who approached it might look on themselves as belonging to it; might take part in its rule, and derive either lustre or profit from its influence."

Just so; and therefore the middle classes of Britain, of whatever their special political party, are conservative in the best sense of that word.

For there are not three, but only two, classes in England; namely, rich and poor: those who live by capital (from the wealthiest landlord to the smallest village shopkeeper); and those who live by hand-labour. Whether the division between those two classes is increasing or not, is a very serious question. Continued legislation in favour of the hand-labourer, and a beneficence towards him, when in need, such as no other nation on earth has ever shown, have done much to abolish the moral division. But the social division has surely been increased during the last half century, by the inevitable tendency, both in commerce and agriculture, to employ one large capital, where several small ones would have been employed a century ago. The large manufactory, the large shop, the large estate, the large farm, swallows up the small ones.

The yeoman, the thrifty squatter who could work at two or three trades as well as till his patch of moor, the hand-loom weaver, the skilled village craftsman, have all but disappeared. The handworker, finding it more and more difficult to invest his savings, has been more and more tempted to squander them. To rise to the dignity of a capitalist, however small, was growing impossible to him, till the rise of that co-operative movement, which will do more than any social or political impulse in our day for the safety of English society, and the loyalty of the English working classes. And meanwhile—ere that movement shall have spread throughout the length and breadth of the land, and have been applied, as it surely will be some day, not only to distribution, not only to manufacture, but to agriculture likewise—till then, the best judges of the working men's worth must be their employers; and especially the employers of the northern manufacturing population. What their judgment is, is sufficiently notorious. Those who depend most on the working men, who have the best opportunities of knowing them, trust them most thoroughly. As long as great manufacturers stand forward as the political sponsors of their own workmen, it behoves those who cannot have had their experience, to consider their opinion as conclusive. As for that "influence of the higher classes" which is said to be endangered just now; it will exist, just as much as it deserves to exist. Any man who is superior to the many, whether in talents, education, refinement, wealth, or anything else, will always be able to influence a number of men —and if he thinks it worth his while, of votes—by just and lawful means. And as for unjust and unlawful means, let those who prefer them keep up heart. The world will go on much as it did before; and be always quite bad enough to allow bribery and corruption, jobbery and nepotism, quackery and arrogance, their full influence over our home and foreign policy. An extension of the suffrage, however wide, will not bring about the millennium. It will merely make a large number of Englishmen contented and loyal, instead of discontented and disloyal. It may make, too, the educated and wealthy classes wiser by awakening a wholesome fear—perhaps, it may be, by awakening a chivalrous emulation. It may put the younger men of the present aristocracy upon their mettle, and stir them up to prove that they are not in the same effete condition as was the French noblesse in 1789. It may lead them to take the warnings which have been addressed to them, for the last thirty years, by their truest friends—often by kinsmen of their own. It may lead them to ask themselves why, in a world which is governed by a just God, such great power as is palpably theirs at present is entrusted to them, save that they may do more work, and not less, than other men, under the penalties pronounced against those to whom much is given, and of whom much is required. It may lead them to discover that they are in a world where it is not safe to sit under the tree, and let the ripe fruit drop into your mouth; where the "competition of species" works with ruthless energy among all ranks of being, from kings upon their thrones to the weeds upon the waste; where "he that is not hammer, is sure to be anvil;" and he who will not work, neither shall he eat. It may lead them to devote that energy (in which they surpass so far the continental aristocracies) to something better than outdoor amusements or indoor dilettantisms. There are those among them who, like one section of the old French noblesse, content themselves with mere complaints of "the revolutionary tendencies of the age." Let them beware in time; for when the many are on the march, the few who stand still are certain to be walked over. There are those among them who, like another section of the French noblesse, are ready, more generously than wisely, to throw away their own social and political advantages, and play (for it will never be really more than playing) at democracy. Let them, too, beware. The penknife and the axe should respect each other; for they were wrought from the same steel: but the penknife will not be wise in trying to fell trees. Let them accept their own position, not in conceit and arrogance, but in fear and trembling; and see if they cannot play the man therein, and save their own class; and with it, much which it has needed many centuries to accumulate and to organise, and without which no nation has yet existed for a single century. They are no more like the old French noblesse, than are the commercial class like the old French bourgeoisie, or the labouring like the old French peasantry. Let them prove that fact by their deeds during the next generation; or sink into the condition of mere rich men, exciting, by their luxury and laziness, nothing but envy and contempt.

Meanwhile, behind all classes and social forces—I had almost said, above them all—stands a fourth estate, which will, ultimately, decide the form which English society is to take: a Press as different from the literary class of the Ancien Régime as is everything else English; and different in this—that it is free.

The French Revolution, like every revolution (it

seems to me) which has convulsed the nations of Europe for the last eighty years, was caused immediately—whatever may have been its more remote causes—by the suppression of thought; or, at least, by a sense of wrong among those who thought. A country where every man, be he fool or wise, is free to speak that which is in him, can never suffer a revolution. The folly blows itself off like steam, in harmless noise; the wisdom becomes part of the general intellectual stock of the nation, and prepares men for gradual, and therefore for harmless, change.

As long as the press is free, a nation is guaranteed against sudden and capricious folly, either from above or from below. As long as the press is free, a nation is guaranteed against the worse evil of persistent and obstinate folly, cloaking itself under the venerable shapes of tradition and authority. For under a free press, a nation must ultimately be guided not by a caste, not by a class, not by mere wealth, not by the passions of a mob: but by mind; by the net result of all the common-sense of its members; and in the present default of genius, which is un-common sense, common-sense seems to be the only, if not the best, safeguard for poor humanity.

1867.

LECTURE I.

Delivered at the Royal Institution, London, 1867.

CASTE.

These Lectures are meant to be comments on the state of France before the French Revolution. To English society, past or present, I do not refer. For reasons which I have set forth at length in an introductory discourse, there never was any Ancien Régime in England.

Therefore, when the Stuarts tried to establish in England a system which might have led to a political condition like that of the Continent, all classes combined and exterminated them; while the course of English society went on as before.

On the contrary, England was the mother of every movement which undermined, and at last destroyed, the Ancien Régime.

From England went forth those political theories which, transmitted from America to France, became the principles of the French Revolution. From England went forth the philosophy of Locke, with all its immense results. It is noteworthy, that when Voltaire tries to persuade people, in a certain famous passage, that philosophers do not care to trouble the world—of the ten names to whom he does honour, seven names are English. "It is," he says, "neither Montaigne, nor Locke, nor Boyle, nor Spinoza, nor Hobbes, nor Lord Shaftesbury, nor Mr. Collins, nor Mr. Toland, nor Fludd, nor Baker, who have carried the torch of discord into their countries." It is worth notice, that not only are the majority of these names English, but that they belong not to the latter but to the former half of the eighteenth century; and indeed, to the latter half of the seventeenth.

So it was with that Inductive Physical Science, which helped more than all to break up the superstitions of the Ancien Régime, and to set man face to face with the facts of the universe. From England, towards the end of the seventeenth century, it was promulgated by such men as Newton, Boyle, Sydenham, Ray, and the first founders of our Royal Society.

In England, too, arose the great religious movements of the seventeenth and eighteenth centuries—and especially that of a body which I can never mention without most deep respect—the Society of Friends. At a time when the greater part of the Continent was sunk in spiritual sleep, these men were reasserting doctrines concerning man, and his relation to his Creator, which, whether or not all believe them (as I believe them) to be founded on eternal fact, all must confess to have been of incalculable benefit to the cause of humanity and civilisation.

From England, finally, about the middle of the eighteenth century, went forth—promulgated by English noblemen—that freemasonry which seems to have been the true parent of all the secret societies of Europe. Of this curious question, more hereafter. But enough has been said to show that England, instead of falling, at any period, into the stagnation of the Ancien Régime, was, from the middle of the seventeenth century, in a state of intellectual growth and ferment which communicated itself finally to the continental nations. This is the special honour of England; universally confessed at the time. It was to England that the slowly-awakening nations looked, as the source of all which was noble, true, and free, in the dawning future.

It will be seen, from what I have said, that I consider the Ancien Régime to begin in the seventeenth century. I should date its commencement—as far as that of anything so vague, unsystematic, indeed anarchic, can be defined—from the end of the Thirty Years' War, and the peace of Westphalia in 1648.

For by that time the mighty spiritual struggles and fierce religious animosities of the preceding century had worn themselves out. And, as always happens, to a period of earnest excitement had succeeded one of weariness, disgust, half-unbelief in the many questions for which so much blood had been shed. No man had come out of the battle with altogether clean hands; some not without changing sides more than once. The war had ended as one, not of nations, not even of zealots, but of mercenaries. The body of Europe had been pulled in pieces between them all; and the poor soul thereof—as was to be expected—had fled out through the gaping wounds. Life, mere existence, was the most pressing need. If men could —in the old prophet's words—find the life of their hand, they were content. High and low only asked to be let live. The poor asked it—slaughtered on a hundred battle-fields, burnt out of house and home: vast tracts of the centre of Europe were lying desert;

the population was diminished for several generations. The trading classes, ruined by the long war, only asked to be let live, and make a little money. The nobility, too, only asked to be let live. They had lost, in the long struggle, not only often lands and power, but their ablest and bravest men; and a weaker and meaner generation was left behind, to do the governing of the world. Let them live, and keep what they had. If signs of vigour still appeared in France, in the wars of Louis XIV. they were feverish, factitious, temporary—soon, as the event proved, to droop into the general exhaustion. If wars were still to be waged they were to be wars of succession, wars of diplomacy; not wars of principle, waged for the mightiest invisible interests of man. The exhaustion was general; and to it we must attribute alike the changes and the conservatism of the Ancien Régime. To it is owing that growth of a centralising despotism, and of arbitrary regal power, which M. de Tocqueville has set forth in a book which I shall have occasion often to quote. To it is owing, too, that longing, which seems to us childish, after ancient forms, etiquettes, dignities, court costumes, formalities diplomatic, legal, ecclesiastical. Men clung to them as to keepsakes of the past—revered relics of more intelligible and better-ordered times. If the spirit had been beaten out of them in a century of battle, that was all the more reason for keeping up the letter. They had had a meaning once, a life once; perhaps there was a little life left in them still; perhaps the dry bones would clothe themselves with flesh once more, and stand upon their feet. At least it was useful that the common people should so believe. There was good hope that the simple masses, seeing the old dignities and formalities still parading the streets, should suppose that they still contained men, and were not mere wooden figures, dressed artistically in official costume. And, on the whole, that hope was not deceived. More than a century of bitter experience was needed ere the masses discovered that their ancient rulers were like the suits of armour in the Tower of London—empty iron astride of wooden steeds, and armed with lances which every ploughboy could wrest out of their hands, and use in his own behalf.

The mistake of the masses was pardonable. For those suits of armour had once held living men; strong, brave, wise; men of an admirable temper; doing their work according to their light, not altogether well—what man does that on earth?—but well enough to make themselves necessary to, and loyally followed by, the masses whom they ruled. No one can read fairly the "Gesta Dei per Francos in Oriente," or the deeds of the French Nobility in their wars with England, or those tales—however legendary—of the mediæval knights, which form so noble an element in German literature, without seeing, that however black were these men's occasional crimes, they were a truly noble race, the old Nobility of the Continent; a race which ruled simply because, without them, there would have been naught but anarchy and barbarism. To their chivalrous ideal they were too often, perhaps for the most part, untrue: but, partial and defective as it is, it is an ideal such as never entered into the mind of Celt or Gaul, Hun or Sclav; one which seems continuous with the spread of the Teutonic conquerors. They ruled because they did practically raise the ideal of humanity in the countries which they conquered, a whole stage higher. They ceased to rule when they were, through their own sins, caught up and surpassed in the race of progress by the classes below them.

But, even when at its best, their system of government had in it—like all human invention—original sin; an unnatural and unrighteous element, which was certain, sooner or later, to produce decay and ruin. The old Nobility of Europe was not a mere aristocracy. It was a caste: a race not intermarrying with the races below it. It was not a mere aristocracy. For that, for the supremacy of the best men, all societies strive, or profess to strive. And such a true aristocracy may exist independent of caste, or the hereditary principle at all. We may conceive an Utopia, governed by an aristocracy which should be really democratic; which should use, under developed forms, that method which made the mediæval priesthood the one great democratic institution of old Christendom; bringing to the surface and utilising the talents and virtues of all classes, even to the lowest. We may conceive an aristocracy choosing out, and gladly receiving into its own ranks as equals, every youth, every maiden, who was distinguished by intellect, virtue, valour, beauty, without respect to rank or birth; and rejecting in turn, from its own ranks, each of its own children who fell below some lofty standard, and showed by weakliness, dulness, or baseness, incapacity for the post of guiding and elevating their fellow-citizens. Thus would arise a true aristocracy; a governing body of the really most worthy—the most highly organised in body and in mind—perpetually recruited from below: from which, or from any other ideal, we are yet a few thousand years distant.

But the old Ancien Régime would have shuddered, did shudder, at such a notion. The supreme class was to keep itself pure, and avoid all taint of darker blood, shutting its eyes to the fact that some of its most famous heroes had been born of such left-handed marriages as that of Robert of Normandy with the tanner's daughter of Falaise. "Some are so curious in this behalf," says quaint old Burton, writing about 1650, "as these old Romans, our modern Venetians, Dutch, and French, that if two parties dearly love, the one noble, the other ignoble, they may not, by their laws, match, though equal otherwise in years, fortunes, education, and all good affection. In Germany, except they can prove their gentility by three descents, they scorn to match with them. A nobleman must marry a noblewoman; a baron, a baron's daughter; a knight, a knight's. As slaters sort their slates, do they degrees and families."

And doubtless this theory—like all which have held their ground for many centuries—at first represented a fact. These castes were, at first, actually superior to the peoples over whom they ruled. I cannot, as long as my eyes are open, yield to the modern theory of the equality—indeed of the non-existence—of races. Holding, as I do, the primæval unity of the human race, I see in that race the same inclination to sport into fresh varieties, the same competition of species between those varieties, which Mr. Darwin has pointed out among plants and mere animals. A distinguished man arises; from him a distinguished family; from it a distinguished tribe, stronger, cunninger than those around. It asserts its supremacy over its neighbours at first exactly as a plant or animal would do, by destroying, and, where possible, eating them; next, having grown more prudent, by enslaving them; next, having gained a little morality in addition to its prudence, by civilising them, raising them more or less toward its own standard. And thus, in every land, civilisation and national life has arisen out of the patriarchal state; and the Eastern scheik, with his wives, free and slave, and his hundreds of fighting men born in his house, is the type of all primæval rulers. He is the best man of his horde—in every sense of the word best; and whether he have a right to rule them or not, they consider that he has, and are the better men for his guidance.

Whether this ought to have been the history of primæval civilisation, is a question not to be determined here. That it is the history thereof, is surely patent to anyone who will imagine to himself what must have been. In the first place, the strongest and cunningest savage must have had the chance of producing children more strong and cunning than the average; he would have—the strongest savage has still—the power of obtaining a wife, or wives, superior in beauty and in household skill, which involves superiority of intellect; and therefore his children would—some of them at least—be superior to the average, both from the father's and the mother's capacities. They again would marry select wives; and their children again would do the same; till, in a very few generations, a family would have established itself, considerably superior to the rest of the tribe in body and mind, and become assuredly its ruling race.

Again, if one of that race invented a new weapon, a new mode of tillage, or aught else which gave him power, that would add to the superiority of his whole family. For the invention would be jealously kept among them as a mystery, a hereditary secret. To this simple cause, surely, is to be referred the system of hereditary caste occupations, whether in Egypt or Hindoostan. To this, too, the fact that alike in Greek and in Teutonic legend the chief so often appears, not merely as the best warrior and best minstrel, but as the best smith, armourer, and handicraftsman of his tribe. If, however, the inventor happened to be a low-born genius, its advantages would still accrue to the ruling race. For nothing could be more natural or more easy—as more than one legend intimates—than that the king should extort the new secret from his subject, and then put him to death to prevent any further publicity.

Two great inventive geniuses we may see dimly through the abysses of the past, both of whom must have become in their time great chiefs, founders of mighty aristocracies—it may be, worshipped after their death as gods.

The first, who seems to have existed after the age in which the black race colonised Australia, must have been surely a man worthy to hold rank with our Brindleys, Watts, and Stephensons. For he invented (and mind, one man must have invented the thing first, and by the very nature of it, invented it all at once) an instrument so singular, unexpected, unlike anything to be seen in nature, that I wonder it has not been called, like the plough, the olive, or the vine, a gift of the immortal gods: and yet an instrument so simple, so easy, and so perfect, that it spread over all races in Europe and America, and no substitute could be found for it till the latter part of the fifteenth century. Yes, a great genius was he, and the consequent founder of a great aristocracy and conquering race, who first invented for himself and his children after him a—bow and arrow.

The next—whether before or after the first in time, it suits me to speak of him in second place—was the man who was the potential ancestor of the whole Ritterschaft, Chivalry, and knightly caste of Europe; the man who first, finding a foal upon the steppe, deserted by its dam, brought it home, and reared it; and then bethought him of the happy notion of making it draw—presumably by its tail—a fashion which endured long in Ireland, and had to be forbidden by law, I think as late as the sixteenth century. A great aristocrat must that man have become. A greater still he who first substituted the bit for the halter. A greater still he who first thought of wheels. A greater still he who conceived the yoke and pole for bearing up his chariot; for that same yoke, and pole, and chariot, became the peculiar instrument of conquerors like him who mightily oppressed the children of Israel, for he had nine hundred chariots of iron. Egyptians, Syrians, Assyrians, Greeks, Romans—none of them improved on the form of the conquering biga, till it was given up by a race who preferred a pair of shafts to their carts, and who had learnt to ride instead of drive. A great aristocrat, again, must he have been among those latter races who first conceived the notion of getting on his horse's back, accommodating his motions to the beast's, and becoming a centaur, half-man, half-horse. That invention must have tended, in the first instance, as surely toward democracy as did the invention of firearms. A tribe of riders must have been always, more or less, equal and free. Equal because a man on a horse would feel himself a man indeed; because the art of riding called out an independence, a self-help, a skill, a consciousness of power, a personal pride and vanity, which would defy slavery. Free, because a tribe of riders might be defeated, exterminated, but never enchained. They could never become *glebæ adscripti*, bound to the soil, as long as they could take horse and saddle, and away. History gives us more than one glimpse of such tribes—the scourge and terror of the non-riding races with whom they came in contact. Some, doubtless, remember how in the wars between Alfred and the Danes, "the army" (the Scandinavian invaders) again and again horse themselves, steal away by night from the Saxon infantry, and ride over the land (whether in England or in France), "doing unspeakable evil." To that special instinct of horsemanship, which still distinguishes their descendants, we may attribute mainly the Scandinavian settlement of the north and east of England. Some, too, may recollect the sketch of the primæval Hun, as he first appeared to the astonished and disgusted old Roman soldier Ammianus Marcellinus; the visages "more like cakes than faces;" the "figures like those which are hewn out with an axe on the poles at bridge-ends;" the rat-skin coats, which they wore till they rotted off their limbs; their steaks of meat cooked between the saddle and the thigh; the little horses on which "they eat and drink, buy and sell, and sleep lying forward along his narrow neck, and indulging in every variety of dream." And over and above, and more important politically, the common councils "held on horseback, under the authority of no king, but content with the irregular government of nobles, under whose leading they force their way through all obstacles." A race—like those Cossacks who are probably their lineal descendants—to be feared, to be hired, to be petted, but not to be conquered.

Instances nearer home of free equestrian races we have in our own English borderers, among whom (as Mr. Froude says) the farmers and their farm-servants had but to snatch their arms and spring into their saddles and they became at once the Northern Horse, famed as the finest light cavalry in the world. And equal to them—superior even, if we recollect that they preserved their country's freedom for centuries against the superior force of England—were those troops of Scots who, century after century, swept across the border on their little garrons, their bag of oatmeal hanging by the saddle, with the iron griddle whereon to bake it; careless of weather and of danger; men too swift to be exterminated, too independent to be enslaved.

But if horsemanship had, in these cases, a levelling tendency it would have the very opposite when a riding tribe conquered a non-riding one. The conquerors would, as much as possible, keep the art and mystery of horsemanship hereditary among themselves, and become a Ritterschaft or chivalrous caste. And they would be able to do so: because the conquered race would not care or dare to learn the new and dangerous art. There are persons, even in England, who can never learn to ride. There are whole populations in Europe, even now, when races have become almost indistinguishably mixed, who seem unable to learn. And this must have been still more the case when the races were more strongly separated in blood and habits. So the

Teutonic chief, with his gesitha, comites, or select band of knights, who had received from him, as Tacitus has it, the war-horse and the lance, established himself as the natural ruler—and oppressor—of the non-riding populations; first over the aborigines of Germany proper, tribes who seem to have been enslaved, and their names lost, before the time of Tacitus; and then over the non-riding Romans and Gauls to the South and West, and the Wendish and Sclavonic tribes to the East. Very few in numbers, but mighty in their unequalled capacity of body and mind, and in their terrible horsemanship, the Teutonic Ritterschaft literally rode roughshod over the old world; never checked, but when they came in contact with the free-riding hordes of the Eastern steppes; and so established an equestrian caste, of which the *ἱππεῖς* of Athens and the Equites of Rome had been only hints ending in failure and absorption.

Of that equestrian caste the symbol was the horse. The favourite, and therefore the chosen sacrifice of Odin, their ancestor and God, the horse's flesh was eaten at the sacrificial meal; the horse's head, hung on the ash in Odin's wood, gave forth oracular responses. As Christianity came in, and the eating of horse-flesh was forbidden as impiety by the Church, while his oracles dwindled down to such as that which Falada's dead head gives to the goose-girl in the German tale, the magic power of the horse figured only in ballads and legends: but his real power remained.

The art of riding became an hereditary and exclusive science—at last a pedantry, hampered by absurd etiquettes, and worse than useless traditions; but the power and right to ride remained on the whole the mark of the dominant caste. Terribly did they often abuse that special power. The faculty of making a horse carry him no more makes a man a good man, than the faculties of making money, making speeches, making books, or making a noise about public abuses. And of all ruffians, the worst, if history is to be trusted, is the ruffian on a horse; to whose brutality of mind is superadded the brute power of his beast. A ruffian on a horse—what is there that he will not ride over, and ride on, careless and proud of his own shame? When the ancient chivalry of France descended to that level, or rather delegated their functions to mercenaries of that level—when the knightly hosts who fought before Jerusalem allowed themselves to be superseded by the dragoons and dragonnades of Louis XIV.—then the end of the French chivalry was at hand, and came. But centuries before that shameful fall there had come in with Christianity the new thought, that domination meant responsibility; that responsibility demanded virtue. The words which denoted rank, came to denote likewise high moral excellencies. The nobilis, or man who was known, and therefore subject to public opinion, was bound to behave nobly. The gentleman—gentile-man—who respected his own gens, or family and pedigree, was bound to be gentle. The courtier, who had picked up at court some touch of Roman civilisation from Roman ecclesiastics, was bound to be courteous. He who held an "honour" or "edel" of land was bound to be honourable; and he who held a "weorthig," or worthy, thereof, was bound himself to be worthy. In like wise, he who had the right to ride a horse, was expected to be chivalrous in all matters befitting the hereditary ruler, who owed a sacred debt to a long line of forefathers, as well as to the state in which he dwelt; all dignity, courtesy, purity, self-restraint, devotion—such as they were understood in those rough days—centred themselves round the idea of the rider as the attributes of the man whose supposed duty, as well as his supposed right, was to govern his fellow-men, by example, as well as by law and force;—attributes which gathered themselves up into that one word—Chivalry: an idea, which, perfect or imperfect, God forbid that mankind should ever forget, till it has become the possession—as it is the God-given right—of the poorest slave that ever trudged on foot; and every collier-lad shall have become—as some of those Barnsley men proved but the other day they had become already:

> A very gentle perfect knight.

Very unfaithful was chivalry to its ideal—as all men are to all ideals. But bear in mind, that if the horse was the symbol of the ruling caste, it was not at first its only strength. Unless that caste had had at first spiritual, as well as physical force on its side, it would have been soon destroyed—nay, it would have destroyed itself—by internecine civil war. And we must believe that those Franks, Goths, Lombards, and Burgunds, who in the early Middle Age leaped on the backs (to use Mr. Carlyle's expression) of the Roman nations, were actually, in all senses of the word, better men than those whom they conquered. We must believe it from reason; for if not, how could they, numerically few, have held for a year, much more for centuries, against millions, their dangerous elevation? We must believe it, unless we take Tacitus's "Germania," which I absolutely refuse to do, for a romance.

We must believe that they were better than the Romanised nations whom they conquered, because the writers of those nations, Augustine, Salvian, and Sidonius Apollinaris, for example, say that they were such, and give proof thereof. Not good men according to our higher standard—far from it; though Sidonius's picture of Theodoric, the East Goth, in his palace of Narbonne, is the picture of an eminently good and wise ruler. But not good, I say, as a rule—the Franks, alas! often very bad men: but still better, wiser, abler, than those whom they ruled. We must believe, too, that they were better, in every sense of the word, than those tribes on their eastern frontier, whom they conquered in after centuries, unless we discredit (which we have no reason to do) the accounts which the Roman and Greek writers give of the horrible savagery of those tribes.

So it was in later centuries. One cannot read fairly the history of the Middle Ages without seeing that the robber knight of Germany or of France, who figures so much in modern novels, must have been the exception, and not the rule: that an aristocracy which lived by the saddle would have as little chance of perpetuating itself, as a priesthood composed of hypocrites and profligates; that the mediæval Nobility has been as much slandered as the mediæval Church; and the exceptions taken—as more salient and exciting—for the average: that side by side with ruffians like Gaston de Foix hundreds of honest gentlemen were trying to do their duty to the best of their light, and were raising, and not depressing, the masses below them—one very important item in that duty being, the doing the whole fighting of the country at their own expense, instead of leaving it to a standing army of mercenaries, at the beck and call of a despot; and that, as M. de Tocqueville says: "In feudal times, the Nobility were regarded pretty much as the government is regarded in our own; the burdens they imposed were endured in consequence of the security they afforded. The nobles had many irksome privileges; they possessed many onerous rights: but they maintained public order, they administered justice, they caused the law to be executed, they came to the relief of the weak, they conducted the business of the community. In proportion as they ceased to do these things, the burden of their privileges appeared more oppressive, and their existence became an anomaly in proportion as they ceased to do these things." And the Ancien Régime may be defined as the period in which they ceased to do these things—in which they began to play the idlers, and expected to take their old wages without doing their old work.

But in any case, government by a ruling caste, whether of the patriarchal or of the feudal kind, is no ideal or permanent state of society. So far from it, it is but the first or second step out of primæval savagery. For the more a ruling race becomes conscious of its own duty, and not merely of its own power—the more it learns to regard its peculiar gifts as entrusted to it for the good of men—so much the more earnestly will it labour to raise the masses below to its own level, by imparting to them its own light; and so will it continually tend to abolish itself, by producing a general equality, moral and intellectual; and fulfil that law of self-sacrifice which is the beginning and the end of all virtue.

A race of noblest men and women, trying to make

all below them as noble as themselves—that is at least a fair ideal, tending toward, though it has not reached, the highest ideal of all.

But suppose that the very opposite tendency—inherent in the heart of every child of man—should conquer. Suppose the ruling caste no longer the physical, intellectual, and moral superiors of the mass, but their equals. Suppose them—shameful, but not without example—actually sunk to be their inferiors. And that such a fall did come—nay, that it must have come—is matter of history. And its cause, like all social causes, was not a political nor a physical, but a moral cause. The profligacy of the French and Italian aristocracies, in the sixteenth century, avenged itself on them by a curse (derived from the newly-discovered America) from which they never recovered. The Spanish aristocracy suffered, I doubt not very severely. The English and German, owing to the superior homeliness and purity of ruling their lives, hardly at all. But the continental caste, instead of recruiting their tainted blood by healthy blood from below, did all, under pretence of keeping it pure, to keep it tainted by continual intermarriage; and paid, in increasing weakness of body and mind, the penalty of their exclusive pride. It is impossible for anyone who reads the French memoirs of the sixteenth and seventeenth centuries, not to perceive, if he be wise, that the aristocracy therein depicted was ripe for ruin—yea, already ruined—under any form of government whatsoever, independent of all political changes. Indeed, many of the political changes were not the causes but the effects of the demoralisation of the noblesse. Historians will tell you how, as early as the beginning of the seventeenth century, Henry IV. complained that the nobles were quitting their country districts; how succeeding kings and statesmen, notably Richelieu and Louis XIV., tempted the noblesse up to Paris, that they might become mere courtiers, instead of powerful country gentlemen; how those who remained behind were only the poor *hobereaux*, little hobby-hawks among the gentry, who considered it degradation to help in governing the parish, as their forefathers had governed it, and lived shabbily in their chateaux, grinding the last farthing out of their tenants, that they might spend it in town during the winter. No wonder that with such an aristocracy, who had renounced that very duty of governing the country, for which alone they and their forefathers had existed, there arose government by intendants and sub-delegates, and all the other evils of administrative centralisation, which M. de Tocqueville anatomises and deplores. But what was the cause of the curse? Their moral degradation. What drew them up to Paris save vanity and profligacy? What kept them from intermarrying with the middle class save pride? What made them give up the office of governors save idleness? And if vanity, profligacy, pride, and idleness be not injustices and moral vices, what are?

The race of heroic knights and nobles who fought under the walls of Jerusalem—who wrestled, and not in vain, for centuries with the equally heroic English, in defence of their native soil—who had set to all Europe the example of all knightly virtues, had rotted down to this; their only virtue left, as Mr. Carlyle says, being—a perfect readiness to fight duels.

Every Intendant, chosen by the Comptroller-General out of the lower-born members of the Council of State; a needy young plebeian with his fortune to make, and a stranger to the province, was, in spite of his greed, ambition, chicane, arbitrary tyranny, a better man—abler, more energetic, and often, to judge from the pages of De Tocqueville, with far more sympathy and mercy for the wretched peasantry—than was the count or marquis in the chateau above, who looked down on him as a roturier; and let him nevertheless become first his deputy, and then his master.

Understand me—I am not speaking against the hereditary principle of the Ancien Régime, but against its caste principle — two widely different elements, continually confounded nowadays.

The hereditary principle is good, because it is founded on fact and nature. If men's minds come into the world blank sheets of paper—which I much doubt—every other part and faculty of them comes in stamped with hereditary tendencies and peculiarities. There are such things as transmitted capabilities for good and for evil; and as surely as the offspring of a good horse or dog is likely to be good, so is the offspring of a good man, and still more of a good woman. If the parents have any special ability, their children will probably inherit it, at least in part; and over and above, will have it developed in them by an education worthy of their parents and themselves. If man were—what he is not—a healthy and normal species, a permanent hereditary caste might go on intermarrying, and so perpetuate itself. But the same moral reason which would make such a caste dangerous—indeed, fatal to the liberty and development of mankind, makes it happily impossible. Crimes and follies are certain, after a few generations, to weaken the powers of any human caste; and unless it supplements its own weakness by mingling again with the common stock of humanity, it must sink under that weakness, as the ancient noblesse sank by its own vice. Of course there were exceptions. The French Revolution brought those exceptions out into strong light; and like every day of judgment, divided between the good and the evil. But it lies not in exceptions to save a caste, or an institution; and a few Richelieus, Liancourts, Rochefoucaulds, Noailles, Lafayettes were but the storks among the cranes involved in the wholesale doom due not to each individual, but to a system and a class.

Profligacy, pride, idleness—these are the vices which we have to lay to the charge of the Teutonic Nobility of the Ancien Régime in France especially; and (though in a less degree perhaps) over the whole continent of Europe. But below them, and perhaps the cause of them all, lay another and deeper vice—godlessness—atheism.

I do not mean merely want of religion, doctrinal unbelief. I mean want of belief in duty, in responsibility. Want of belief that there was a living God governing the universe, who had set them their work, and would judge them according to their work. And therefore, want of belief, yea, utter unconsciousness, that they were set in their places to make the masses below them better men; to impart to them their own civilisation, to raise them to their own level. They would have shrunk from that which I just now defined as the true duty of an aristocracy, just because it would have seemed to them madness to abolish themselves. But the process of abolition went on, nevertheless, only now from without instead of from within. So it must always be, in such a case. If a ruling class will not try to raise the masses to their own level, the masses will try to drag them down to theirs. That sense of justice which allowed privileges, when they were as strictly official privileges as the salary of a judge, or the immunity of a member of the House of Commons; when they were earned, as in the Middle Age, by severe education, earnest labour, and life and death responsibility in peace and war, will demand the abolition of those privileges, when no work is done in return for them, with a voice which must be heard, for it is the voice of truth and justice.

But with that righteous voice will mingle another, most wicked, and yet, alas! most flattering to poor humanity—the voice of envy, simple and undisguised; of envy, which moralists hold to be one of the basest of human passions; which can never be justified, however hateful or unworthy be the envied man. And when a whole people, or even a majority thereof, shall be possessed by that, what is there that they will not do?

Some are surprised and puzzled when they find, in the French Revolution of 1793, the noblest and the foulest characters labouring in concert, and side by side—often, too, paradoxical as it may seem, united in the same personage. The explanation is simple. Justice inspired the one; the other was the child of simple envy. But this passion of envy, if it becomes permanent and popular, may avenge itself, like all other sins. A nation may say to itself, "Provided we have no superiors to fall our pride, we are content. Liberty is a slight matter, provided we have equality. Let us be slaves, provided we are all slaves alike." It may destroy every standard of humanity above its own mean average; it may forget that the old ruling class, in spite of all its defects and crimes, did at least pretend to represent something higher than man's necessary wants, plus the greed of amassing money; never meeting (at least in the country districts) any one wiser or more refined than an official or a priest drawn from the peasant class, it may lose the belief that any standard higher than that is needed; and, all but forgetting the very existence of civilisation, sink contented into a dead level of intellectual mediocrity and moral barbarism, crying, "Let us eat and drink, for to-morrow we die."

A nation in such a temper will surely be taken at its word. Where the carcase is, there the eagles will be gathered together; and there will not be wanting to such nations—as there were not wanting in old Greece and Rome—despots who will give them all they want, and more, and say to them: "Yes, you shall eat and drink; and yet you shall not die. For I, while I take care of your mortal bodies, will see that care is taken of your immortal souls."

For there are those who have discovered, with the kings of the Holy Alliance, that infidelity and scepticism are political mistakes, not so much because they promote vice, as because they promote (or are supposed to promote) free thought; who see that religion (no matter of what quality) is a most valuable assistant to the duties of a minister of police. They will quote in their own behalf Montesquieu's opinion that religion is a column necessary to sustain the social edifice; they will quote, too, that sound and true saying of De Tocqueville's: * "If the first American who might be met, either in his own country, or abroad, were to be stopped and asked whether he considered

* Mr. H. Reeve's translation of De Tocqueville's "France before the Revolution of 1789." p. 280.

religion useful to the stability of the laws and the good order of society, he would answer, without hesitation, that no civilised society, but more especially none in a state of freedom, can exist without religion. Respect for religion is, in his eyes, the greatest guarantee of the stability of the State, and of the safety of the community. Those who are ignorant of the science of government, know that fact at least."

M. de Tocqueville, when he wrote these words, was lamenting that in France, "freedom was forsaken;" "a thing for which it is said that no one any longer cares in France." He did not, it seems to me, perceive that, as in America the best guarantee of freedom is the reverence for a religion or religions, which are free themselves, and which teach men to be free; so in other countries the best guarantee of slavery is, reverence for religions which are not free, and which teach men to be slaves.

But what M. de Tocqueville did not see, there are others who will see; who will say: "If religion be the pillar of political and social order, there is an order which is best supported by a religion which is adverse to free thought, free speech, free conscience, free communion between man and God. The more enervating the superstition, the more exacting and tyrannous its priesthood, the more it will do our work, if we help it to do its own. If it permit us to enslave the body, we will permit it to enslave the soul."

And so may be inaugurated a period of that organised anarchy of which the poet says:

> It is not life, but death, when nothing stirs.

LECTURE II.

CENTRALISATION.

The degradation of the European nobility caused, of course, the increase of the kingly power, and opened the way to central despotisms. The bourgeoisie, the commercial middle class, whatever were its virtues, its value, its real courage, were never able to stand alone against the kings. Their capital, being invested in trade, was necessarily subject to such sudden dangers from war, political change, bad seasons, and so forth, that its holders, however individually brave, were timid as a class. They could never hold out on strike against the governments, and had to submit to the powers that were, whatever they were, under penalty of ruin.

But on the Continent, and especially in France and Germany, unable to strengthen itself by intermarriage with the noblesse, they retained that timidity which is the fruit of the insecurity of trade; and had to submit to a more and more centralised despotism, and grow up as they could, in the face of exasperating hindrances to wealth, to education, to the possession, in many parts of France, of large landed estates; leaving the noblesse to decay in isolated uselessness and weakness, and in many cases debt and poverty.

The system—or rather anarchy—according to which France was governed during this transitional period, may be read in that work of M. de Tocqueville's which I have already quoted, and which is accessible to all classes, through Mr. H. Reeve's excellent translation. Every student of history is, of course, well acquainted with that book. But as there is reason to fear, from language which is becoming once more too common, both in speech and writing, that the general public either do not know it, or have not understood it, I shall take the liberty of quoting from it somewhat largely. I am justified in so doing by the fact that M. de Tocqueville's book is founded on researches into the French Archives, which have been made (as far as I am aware) only by him; and contains innumerable significant facts, which are to be found (as far as I am aware) in no other accessible work.

The French people—says M. de Tocqueville—made, in 1789, the greatest effort which was ever made by any nation to cut, so to speak, their destiny in halves, and to separate by an abyss that which they had heretofore been, from that which they sought to become hereafter. But he had long thought that they had succeeded in this singular attempt much less than was supposed abroad; and less than they had at first supposed themselves. He was convinced that they had unconsciously retained, from the former state of society, most of the sentiments, the habits, and even the opinions, by means of which they had effected the destruction of that state of things; and that, without intending it, they had used its remains to rebuild the edifice of modern society. This is his thesis, and this he proves, it seems to me, incontestably by documentary evidence. Not only does he find habits which we suppose—or supposed till lately—to have died with the eighteenth century, still living and working, at least in France, in the nineteenth, but the new opinions which we look on usually as the special children of the nineteenth century, he shows to have been born in the eighteenth. France, he considers, is still at heart what the Ancien Régime made her.

He shows that the hatred of the ruling caste, the intense determination to gain and keep equality, even at the expense of liberty, had been long growing up, under those influences of which I spoke in my first lecture.

He shows, moreover, that the acquiescence in a centralised administration; the expectation that the government should do everything for the people, and nothing for themselves; the consequent loss of local liberties, local peculiarities; the helplessness of the towns and the parishes: and all which issued in making Paris France, and subjecting the whole of a vast country to the arbitrary dictates of a knot of despots in the capital, was not the fruit of the Revolution, but of the Ancien Régime which preceded it; and that Robespierre and his "Comité de Salut Public," and commissioners sent forth to the four winds of heaven in bonnet rouge and carmagnole complete, to build up and pull down, according to their wicked will, were only handling, somewhat more roughly, the same wires which had been handled for several generations by the Comptroller-General and Council of State, with their provincial intendants.

"Do you know," said Law to the Marquis d'Argenson, "that this kingdom of France is governed by thirty intendants? You have neither parliament, nor estates, nor governors. It is upon thirty masters of request, despatched into the provinces, that their evil or their good, their fertility or their sterility, entirely depend."

To do everything for the people, and let them do nothing for themselves—this was the Ancien Régime. To be more wise and more loving than Almighty God, who certainly does not do everything for the sons of men, but forces them to labour for themselves by bitter need, and after a most Spartan mode of education; who allows them to burn their hands as often as they are foolish enough to put them into the fire; and to be filled with the fruits of their own folly, even though the folly be one of necessary ignorance; treating them with that seeming neglect which is after all the most provident care, because by it alone can men be trained to experience, self-help, science, true humanity; and so become not tolerably harmless dolls, but men and women worthy of the name; with

> The reason firm, the temperate will,
> Endurance, foresight, strength, and skill;
> The perfect spirit, nobly planned
> To cheer, to counsel, and command.

Such seems to be the education and government appointed for man by the voluntatem Dei in rebus revelatum, and the education, therefore, which the man of science will accept and carry out. But the men of the Ancien Régime—in as far as it was a régime at all—tried to be wiser than the Almighty. Why not? They were not the first, nor will be the last, by many who have made the same attempt. So this Council of State settled arbitrarily, not only taxes, and militia, and roads, but anything and everything. Its members meddled, with their whole hearts and minds. They tried to teach agriculture by schools and pamphlets and prizes; they sent out plans for every public work. A town could not establish an octroi, levy a rate, mortgage, sell, sue, farm, or administer their property, without an order in council. The Government ordered public rejoicings, saw to the firing of salutes, and illuminating of houses —in one case mentioned by M. de Tocqueville, they fined a member of the burgher guard for absenting himself from a Te Deum. All self-government was gone. A country parish was, says Turgot, nothing but "an assemblage of cabins, and of inhabitants as passive as the cabins they dwelt in. Without an order of council, the parish could not mend the steeple after a storm, or repair the parsonage gable. If they grumbled at the intendant, he threw some of the chief persons into prison, and made the parish pay the expenses of the horse patrol, which formed the arbitrary police of France. Everywhere was meddling. There were reports on statistics—circumstantial, inaccurate, and useless—as statistics are too often wont to be. Sometimes, when the people were starving, the Government sent down charitable donations to certain parishes, on condition that the inhabitants should raise a sum on their part. When the sum offered was sufficient, the Comptroller-General wrote on the margin, when he returned the report to the intendant, "Good—express satisfaction." If it was more than sufficient, he wrote, "Good—express satisfaction and sensibility." There is nothing new under the sun. In 1761, the Government, jealous enough of newspapers, determined to start one for itself, and for that purpose took under its tutelage the *Gazette de France.* So the public newsmongers were of course to be the provincial intendants, and their sub-newsmongers, of course, the sub-delegates.

But alas! the poor sub-delegates seem to have found either very little news, or very little which it was politic to publish. One reports that a smuggler of salt has been hung, and has displayed great courage; another that a woman in his district has had three girls at a birth; another that a dreadful storm has happened, but—has done no mischief; a fourth—living in some specially favoured Utopia—declares that in spite of all his efforts he has found nothing worth recording, but that he himself will subscribe to so useful a journal, and will exhort all respectable persons to follow his example: in spite of which loyal endeavours, the journal seems to have proved a failure, to the great disgust of the king and his minister, who had of course expected to secure fine weather by nailing, like the schoolboy before a holiday, the hand of the weather-glass.

Well had it been, if the intermeddling of this bureaucracy had stopped there. But, by a process of evocation (as it was called), more and more causes, criminal as well as civil, were withdrawn from the regular tribunals, to those of the intendants and the Council. Before the intendant all the lower order of people were generally sent for trial. Bread-riots were a common cause of such trials, and M. de Tocqueville asserts that he has found sentences, delivered by the intendant, and a local council chosen by himself, by which men were condemned to the galleys, and even to death. Under such a system, under which an intendant must have felt it his interest to pretend at all risks, that all was going right, and to regard any disturbance as a dangerous exposure of himself and his chiefs—one can understand easily enough that scene which Mr. Carlyle has dramatised from Lacretelle, concerning the canaille, the masses, as we used to call them a generation since:

"A dumb generation—their voice only an inarticulate cry. Spokesman, in the king's council, in the world's forum, they have none that finds credence. At rare intervals (as now, in 1775) they will fling down their hoes, and hammers; and, to the astonishment of mankind, flock hither and thither, dangerous, aimless, get the length even of Versailles. Turgot is altering the corn trade, abrogating the absurdest corn laws; there is dearth, real, or were it even factitious, an indubitable scarcity of bread. And so, on the 2nd day of May, 1775, these waste multitudes do here, at Versailles chateau, in widespread wretchedness, in sallow faces, squalor, winged raggedness, present as in legible hieroglyphic writing their petition of grievances. The chateau-gates must be shut; but the king will appear on the balcony and speak to them. They have seen the king's face; their petition of grievances has been, if not read, looked at. In answer, two of them are hanged, on a new gallows forty feet high, and the rest driven back to their dens for a time."

Of course. What more exasperating and inexpiable insult to the ruling powers was possible than this? To persist in being needy and wretched, when a whole bureaucracy is toiling day and night to make them prosperous and happy? An insult only to be avenged in blood. Remark meanwhile, that this centralised bureaucracy was a failure; that after all the trouble taken to govern these masses, they were not governed, in the sense of being made better, and not worse. The truth is, that no centralised bureaucracy, or so-called "paternal government," yet invented on earth, has been anything but a failure, or is it like to be anything else: because it is founded on an error; because it regards and treats men as that which they are not, as things; and not as that which they are, as persons. If the bureaucracy were a mere Briareus giant, with a hundred hands, helping the weak throughout the length and breadth of the empire, the system might be at least tolerable. But what if the Government were not a Briareus with a hundred hands, but a Hydra with a hundred heads and mouths, each far more intent on helping itself than on helping the people? What if sub-delegates and other officials, holding office at the will of the intendant, had to live, and even provide against a rainy day? What if intendants, holding office at the will of the Comptroller-General, had to do more than live, and found it prudent to realise as large a fortune as possible, not only against disgrace, but against success, and the dignity fit for a new member of the Noblesse de la Robe? Would not the system, then, soon become intolerable? Would there not be evil times for the masses, till they became something more than masses?

It is an ugly name, that of "The Masses," for the great majority of human beings in a nation. He who uses it speaks of them not as human beings, but as things; and as things not bound together in one living body, but lying in a fortuitous heap. A swarm of ants is not a mass. It has a polity and a unity. Not the ants, but the fir-needles and sticks, of which the ants have piled their nest, are a mass.

The term, I believe, was invented during the

Ancien Régime. Whether it was or not, it expresses very accurately the life of the many in those days. No one would speak, if he wished to speak exactly, of the masses of the United States; for there every man is, or is presumed to be, a personage; with his own independence, his own activities, his own rights and duties. No one, I believe, would have talked of the masses in the old feudal times; for then each individual was someone's man, bound to his master by ties of mutual service, just or unjust, honourable or base, but still giving him a personality of duties and rights, and dividing him from his class.

Dividing, I say. The poor of the Middle Age had little sense of a common humanity. Those who owned allegiance to the lord in the next valley were not their brothers; and at their own lord's bidding, they buckled on sword and slew the next lord's men, with joyful heart and good conscience. Only now and then misery compressed them into masses; and they ran together, as sheep run together to face a dog. Some wholesale wrong made them aware that they were brothers, at least in the power of starving; and they joined in the cry which was heard, I believe, in Mecklenburg as late as 1790: "Den Edelman wille wi dodschlagen." Then, in Wat Tyler's insurrections, in Munster Anabaptisms, in Jacqueries, they proved themselves to be masses, if nothing better, striking for awhile, by the mere weight of numbers, blows terrible, though aimless—soon to be dispersed and slain in their turn by a disciplined and compact aristocracy. Yet not always dispersed, if they could find a leader; as the Polish nobles discovered to their cost in the middle of the seventeenth century. Then Bogdan the Cossack, a wild warrior, not without his sins, but having deserved well of James Sobieski and the Poles, found that the neighbouring noble's steward had taken a fancy to his windmill and his farm upon the Dnieper. He was thrown into prison on a frivolous charge, and escaped to the Tatars, leaving his wife dishonoured, his house burnt, his infant lost in the flames, his eldest son scourged for protesting against the wrong. And he returned, at the head of an army of Tatars, Socinians, Greeks, or what not, to set free the serfs, and exterminate Jesuits, Jews, and nobles, throughout Podolia, Volhynia, Red Russia; to desecrate the altars of God, and slay his servants; to destroy the nobles by lingering tortures; to strip noble ladies and maidens, and hunt them to death with the whips of his Cossacks; and after defeating the nobles in battle after battle, to inaugurate an era of misery and anarchy from which Poland never recovered.

Thus did the masses of Southern Poland discover, for one generation at least, that they were not many things, but one thing; a class, capable of brotherhood and unity, though, alas! only of such as belongs to a pack of wolves. But such outbursts as this were rare exceptions. In general, feudalism kept the people divided, and therefore helpless. And as feudalism died out, and with it the personal self-respect and loyalty which were engendered by the old relations of master and servant, the division still remained; and the people, in France especially, became merely masses, a swarm of incoherent and disorganised things intent on the necessaries of daily bread, like mites crawling over each other in a cheese.

Out of this mass were struggling upwards perpetually, all who had a little ambition, a little scholarship, or a little money, endeavouring to become members of the middle class by obtaining a Government appointment. "A man," says M. de Tocqueville, "endowed with some education and small means, thought it not decorous to die without having been a Government officer." "Every man, according to his condition," says a contemporary writer, "wants to be something by command of the king."

It was not merely the "natural vanity" of which M. de Tocqueville accuses his countrymen, which stirred up in them this eagerness after place; for we see the same eagerness in other nations of the Continent, who cannot be accused (as wholes) of that weakness. The fact is, a Government place, or a Government decoration, cross, ribbon, or what not, is, in a country where self-government is unknown or dead, the only method, save literary fame, which is left to men in order to assert themselves either to themselves or their fellow-men.

A British or American shopkeeper or farmer asks nothing of his Government. He can, if he chooses, be elected to some local office (generally unsalaried) by the votes of his fellow-citizens. But that is his right, and adds nothing to his respectability. The test of that latter, in a country where all honest callings are equally honourable, is the amount of money he can make; and a very sound practical test that is, in a country where intellect and capital are free. Beyond that, he is what he is, and wishes to be no more, save what he can make himself. He has his rights, guaranteed by law and public opinion; and as long as he stands within them, and (as he well phrases it) behaves like a gentleman, he considers himself as good as any man; and so he is. But under the bureaucratic régime of the Continent, if a man had not "something by command of the king," he was nothing; and something he naturally wished to be, even by means of a Government which he disliked and despised. So in France, where innumerable petty posts were regular articles of sale, anyone, it seems, who had saved a little money, found it most profitable to invest it in a beadledom of some kind—to the great detriment of the country, for he thus withdrew his capital from trade; but to his own clear gain, for he thereby purchased some immunity from public burdens, and, as it were, compounded once and for all for his taxes. The petty German princes, it seems, followed the example of France, and sold their little beadledoms likewise; but even where offices were not sold, they must be obtained by any and every means, by everyone who desired not to be as other men were, and to become Notables, as they were called in France; so he migrated from the country into the nearest town, and became a member of some small body—guild, town council, or what not, bodies which were infinite in number. In one small town M. de Tocqueville discovers thirty-six such bodies, "separated from each other by diminutive privileges, the least honourable of which was still a mark of honour." Quarrelling perpetually with each other for precedence, despising and oppressing the very *menu peuple* from whom they had for the most part sprung, these innumerable small bodies, instead of uniting their class, only served to split it up more and more; and when the Revolution broke them up, once and for all, with all other privileges whatsoever, no bond of union was left; and each man stood alone, proud of his individuality" —his complete social isolation; till he discovered that, in ridding himself of superiors, he had rid himself also of fellows; fulfilling, every man in his own person, the old fable of the bundle of sticks; and had to submit, under the Consulate and the Empire, to a tyranny to which the Ancien Régime was freedom itself.

For, in France at least, the Ancien Régime was no tyranny. The middle and upper classes had individual liberty—it may be, only too much; the liberty of disobeying a Government which they did not respect. "However submissive the French may have been before the Revolution to the will of the king, one sort of obedience was altogether unknown to them. They knew not what it was to bow before an illegitimate and contested power—a power but little honoured, frequently despised, but willingly endured because it may be serviceable, or because it may hurt. To that degrading form of servitude they were ever strangers. The king inspired them with feelings . . . . which have become incomprehensible to this generation. . . . . They loved him with the affection due to a father; they revered him with the respect due to God. In submitting to the most arbitrary of his commands, they yielded less to compulsion than to loyalty; and thus they frequently preserved great freedom of mind, even in the most complete dependence. This liberty, irregular, intermittent," says M. de Tocqueville, "helped to form those vigorous characters, those proud and daring spirits, which were to make the French Revolution at once the object of the admiration and the terror of succeeding generations."

This liberty—too much akin to anarchy, in which indeed it issued for awhile—seems to have asserted itself in continual petty resistance to officials whom they did not respect, and who, in their turn, were more than a little afraid of the very men out of whose ranks they had sprung.

The French Government—one may say, every Government on the Continent in those days—had the special weakness of all bureaucracies; namely, that want of moral force which compels them to fall back at last on physical force, and transforms the ruler into a bully, and the soldier into a policeman and a gaoler. A Government of parvenus, uncertain of its own position, will be continually trying to assert itself to itself, by vexatious intermeddling and intruding pretensions; and then, when it meets with the resistance of free and rational spirits, will either recoil in awkward cowardice, or fly into a passion, and appeal to the halter and the sword. Such a Government can never take itself for granted, because it knows that it is not taken for granted by the people. It never can possess the quiet assurance, the courteous dignity, without swagger, yet without hesitation, which belongs to hereditary legislators; by which term is to be understood, not merely kings, not merely noblemen, but every citizen of a free nation, however democratic, who has received from his forefathers the right, the duty, and the example of self-government.

Such was the political and social state of the Ancien Régime, not only in France, but if we are to trust (as we must trust) M. de Tocqueville, in almost every nation in Europe, except Britain.

And as for its moral state. We must look for that —if we have need, which happily all have not—in its lighter literature.

I shall not trouble you with criticisms on French memoirs—of which those of Madame de Sévigné are on the whole, the most painful (as witness her comments on the Marquise de Brinvilliers's execution), because written by a woman better and more human than ordinary. Nor with "Menagiana," or other 'ana's—as vain and artificial as they are often foul; nor with novels and poems, long since deservedly forgotten. On the first perusal of this lighter literature, you will be charmed with the ease, grace, lightness with which everything is said. On the second, you will be somewhat cured of your admiration, as you perceive how little there is to say. The head proves to be nothing but a cunning mask, with no brains inside. Especially is this true of a book, which I must beg those who have read it already, to recollect. To read it I recommend no human being. We may consider it, as it was considered in its time, the typical novel of the Ancien Régime. A picture of Spanish society, written by a Frenchman, it was held to be—and doubtless with reason—a picture of the whole European world. Its French editor (of 1836) calls it a *grande épopée*; "one of the most prodigious efforts of intelligence, exhausting all forms of humanity"—in fact, a second Shakespeare, according to the lights of the year 1715. I mean, of course, "Gil Blas." So picturesque is the book, that it has furnished inexhaustible *motifs* to the draughtsman. So excellent is its workmanship, that the enthusiastic editor of 1836 tells us—and doubtless he knows best —that it is the classic model of the French tongue; and that, as Le Sage "had embraced all that belonged to man in his composition, he dared to prescribe to himself to embrace the whole French language in his work." It has been the parent of a whole school of literature—the Bible of tens of thousands, with admiring commentators in plenty; on whose souls may God have mercy!

And no wonder. The book has a solid value, and will always have, not merely from its perfect art (according to its own measure and intention), but from its perfect truthfulness. It is the Ancien Régime itself. It set forth to the men thereof, themselves, without veil or cowardly reticence of any kind; and inasmuch as every man loves himself, the Ancien Régime loved "Gil Blas," and said, "The problem of humanity is solved at last." But, ye long-suffering powers of heaven, what a solution! It is beside the matter to call the book ungodly, immoral, base. Le Sage would have answered: "Of course it is; for so is the world of which it is a picture." No; the most notable thing about the book is its intense stupidity; its dreariness, barrenness, shallowness, ignorance of the human heart, want of any human interest. If it be an epos, the actors in it are not men and women, but ferrets—with here and there, of course, a stray rabbit, on whose brains they may feed. It is the inhuman mirror of an inhuman age, in which the healthy human heart can find no more interest than in a pathological museum.

That last, indeed, "Gil Blas" is; a collection of diseased specimens. No man or woman in the book, lay or clerical, gentle or simple, as far as I can remember, do their duty in any wise, even if they recollect that they have any duty to do. Greed, chicane, hypocrisy, uselessness are the ruling laws of human society. A new book of Ecclesiastes, crying, "Vanity of vanity, all is vanity;" the "conclusion of the whole matter" being left out, and the new Ecclesiastes rendered thereby diabolic, instead of like that old one, divine. For, instead of "Fear God and keep his commandments, for that is the whole duty of man," Le Sage sends forth the new conclusion, "Take care of thyself, and feed on thy neighbours, for that is the whole duty of man." And very faithfully was his advice (easy enough to obey at all times) obeyed for nearly a century after "Gil Blas" appeared.

About the same time there appeared, by a remarkable coincidence, another work, like it the child of the Ancien Régime, and yet as opposite to it as light to darkness. If Le Sage drew men as they were, Fénelon tried at least to draw them as they might have been, and still might be, were they governed by sages and by saints, according to the laws of God. "Télémaque" is an ideal—imperfect, doubtless, as all ideals must be in a world in which God's ways and thoughts are for ever higher than man's; but an ideal nevertheless. If its construction is less complete than that of "Gil Blas," it is because its aim is infinitely higher; because the form has to be subordinated, here and there, to the matter. If its political economy be imperfect, often chimerical, it is because the mind of one man must needs have been too weak to bring into shape and order the chaos, social and economic, which he saw around him. M. de Lamartine, in his brilliant little life of Fénelon, does not hesitate to trace to the influence of "Télémaque," the Utopias which produced the revolutions of 1793 and 1848. "The saintly poet was," he says, "without knowing it, the first Radical and the first communist of his century." But it is something to have preached to princes doctrines till then unknown, or at least forgotten for many a generation—free trade, peace, international arbitration, and the "carrière ouverte aux talents" for all ranks. It is something to have warned his generation of the dangerous overgrowth of the metropolis; to have prophesied, as an old Hebrew might have done, that the despotism which he saw around him would end in a violent revolution. It is something to have combined the highest Christian morality with a hearty appreciation of old Greek life; of its reverence for bodily health and prowess; its joyous and simple country society; its sacrificial feasts, dances, games; its respect for the gods; its belief that they helped, guided, inspired the sons of men. It is something to have himself believed in God; in a living God, who, both in this life and in all lives to come, rewarded the good and punished the evil by inevitable laws. It is something to have warned a young prince, in an age of doctrinal bigotry and practical atheism, that a living God still existed, and that his laws were still in force; to have shown him Tartarus crowded with the souls of wicked monarchs, while a few of kingly race rested in Elysium, and among them old pagans—Inachus, Cecrops, Erichthon, Triptolemus, and Sesostris—rewarded for ever for having done their duty, each according to his light, to the flocks which the gods had committed to their care. It is something to have spoken to a prince, in such an age, without servility, and without etiquette, of the frailties and the dangers which beset arbitrary rulers; to have told him that royalty, "when assumed to content oneself, is a monstrous tyranny; when assumed to fulfil its duties, and to conduct an innumerable people as a father conducts his children, a crushing slavery, which demands an heroic courage and patience."

Let us honour the courtier who dared speak such truths; and still more the saintly celibate who had sufficient catholicity of mind to envelop them in old Grecian dress, and, without playing false for a moment to his own Christianity, seek in the writings of heathen sages a wider and a healthier view of humanity than was afforded by an ascetic creed.

No wonder that the appearance of "Télémaque," published in Holland without the permission of Fénelon, delighted throughout Europe that public which is always delighted with new truths, as long as it is not required to practise them. To read "Télémaque" was the right and the enjoyment of everyone. To obey it, the duty only of princes. No wonder that, on the other hand, this "Vengeance de peuples, leçon des rois," as M. de Lamartine calls it, was taken for the bitterest satire by Louis XIV., and completed the disgrace of one who had dared to teach the future king of France that he must show himself, in all things, the opposite of his grandfather. No wonder if Madame de Maintenon and the court looked on its portraits of wicked ministers and courtiers as caricatures of themselves; portraits too, which, "composed thus in the palace of Versailles, under the auspices of that confidence which the king had placed in the preceptor of his heir, seemed a domestic treason." No wonder, also, if the foolish and envious world outside was of the same opinion; and after enjoying for awhile this exposure of the great ones of the earth, left "Télémaque" as an Utopia with which private folks had no concern; and betook themselves to the easier and more practical model of "Gil Blas."

But there are solid defects in "Télémaque"—indicating corresponding defects in the author's mind—which would have, in any case, prevented its doing the good work which Fénelon desired; defects which are natural, as it seems to me, to his position as a Roman Catholic priest, however saintly and pure, however humane and liberal. The king, with him, is to be always the father of his people; which is tantamount to saying that the people are to be always children, and in a condition of tutelage; voluntary, if possible: if not, of tutelage still. Of self-government, and education of human beings into free manhood by the exercise of self-government, free will, free thought—of this Fénelon had surely not a glimpse. A generation or two passed by, and then the peoples of Europe began to suspect that they were no longer children, but come to manhood; and determined (after the example of Britain and America) to assume the rights and duties of manhood, at whatever risk of excesses or mistakes: and then "Télémaque" was relegated—half unjustly—as the slavish and childish dream of a past age, into the schoolroom, where it still remains.

But there is a defect in "Télémaque" which is perhaps deeper still. No woman in it exercises influence over man, except for evil. Minerva, the guiding and inspiring spirit, assumes of course, as Mentor, a male form; but her speech and thought is essentially masculine, and not feminine. Antiope is a mere lay-figure, introduced at the end of the book because Telemachus must needs be allowed to have hope of marrying someone or other. Venus plays but the same part as she does in the Tannenhäuser legends of the Middle Age. Her hatred against Telemachus is an integral element of the plot. She, with the other women or nymphs of the romance, in spite of all Fénelon's mercy and courtesy towards human frailties, really rise no higher than the witches of the Malleus Maleficanum. Woman—as the old monk held who derived femina from fe, faith, and minus, less, because women have less faith than men—is, in "Télémaque," whenever she thinks or acts, the temptress, the enchantress; the victim (according to a very ancient calumny) of passions more violent, often more lawless, than man's.

Such a conception of women must make "Télémaque," to the end of time, useless as a wholesome book of education. It must have crippled its influence, especially in France, in its own time. For there, for good and for evil, woman was asserting more and more her power, and her right to power, over the mind and heart of man. Rising from the long degradation of the Middle Ages, which had really respected her only when unsexed and celibate, the French woman had assumed, often lawlessly, always triumphantly, her just freedom; her true place as the equal, the coadjutor, the counsellor of man. Of all problems connected with the education of a young prince, that of the influence of woman was, in the France of the Ancien Régime, the most important. And it was just that which Fénelon did not, perhaps dared not, try to touch; and which he most certainly could not have solved. Meanwhile, not only Madame de Maintenon, but women whose names it were a shame to couple with hers, must have smiled at, while they hated, the saint who attempted to dispense not only with them, but with the ideal queen who should have been the helpmeet of the ideal king.

To those who believe that the world is governed by a living God, it may seem strange, at first sight, that this moral anarchy was allowed to endure; that the avenging, and yet most purifying storm of the French Revolution, inevitable from Louis XIV.'s latter years, was not allowed to burst two generations sooner than it did. Is not the answer—that the question always is not of destroying the world, but of amending it? And that amendment must always come from within, and not from without? That men must be taught to become men, and mend their world themselves? To educate men into self-government—that is the purpose of the government of God; and some of the men of the eighteenth century did not learn that lesson. As the century rolled on, the human mind arose out of the slough in which Le Sage found it, into manifold and beautiful activity, increasing hatred of shams and lies, increasing hunger after truth and usefulness. With mistakes and confusions innumerable they worked: but still they worked; planting good seed; and when the fire of the French Revolution swept over the land, it burned up the rotten and the withered, only to let the fresh herbage spring up from underneath.

But that purifying fire was needed. If we inquire why the many attempts to reform the Ancien Régime, which the eighteenth century witnessed, were failures one and all; why Pombal failed in Portugal, Aranda in Spain, Joseph II. in Austria, Ferdinand and Caroline in Naples—for these last, be it always remembered, began as humane and enlightened sovereigns, patronising liberal opinions, and labouring to ameliorate the condition of the poor, till they were driven by the murder of Marie Antoinette into a paroxysm of rage and terror—why, above all, Louis XVI., who attempted deeper and wiser reforms than any other sovereign, failed more disastrously than any—is not the answer this, that all these reforms would but have cleansed the outside of the cup and the platter, while they left the inside full of extortion and excess? It was not merely institutions which required to be reformed, but men and women. The spirit of "Gil Blas" had to be cast out. The deadness, selfishness, isolation of men's souls; their unbelief in great duties, great common causes, great self-sacrifices—in a word, their unbelief in God, and themselves, and mankind—all that had to be reformed; and till that was done all outward reform would but have left them, at best, in brute ease and peace, to that soulless degradation, which (as in the Byzantine empire of old, and seemingly in the Chinese empire of to-day) hides the reality of barbarism under a varnish of civilisation. Men had to be awakened; to be taught to think for themselves, act for themselves, to dare and suffer side by side for their country and for their children; in a word, to arise and become men once more.

And, what is more, men had to punish—to avenge. Those are fearful words. But there is, in this God-guided universe, a law of retribution, which will find men out, whether men choose to find it out or not; a law of retribution; of vengeance inflicted justly, though not necessarily by just men. The public executioner was seldom a very estimable personage, at least under the old Régime; and those who have been the scourges of God have been, in general, mere scourges, and nothing better; smiting blindly, rashly, confusedly; confounding too often the innocent with the guilty, till they have seemed only to punish crime by crime, and replace old sins by new. But, however insoluble, however saddening that puzzle be, I must believe—as long as I believe in any God at all—that such men as Robespierre were His instruments, even in their crimes.

In the case of the French Revolution, indeed, the wickedness of certain of its leaders was part of the retribution itself. For the noblesse existed surely to make men better. It did, by certain classes, the very opposite. Therefore it was destroyed by wicked men, whom it itself had made wicked. For over and above all political, economic, social wrongs, there were wrongs personal, human, dramatic; which stirred not merely the springs of covetousness or envy, or even of a just demand for the freedom of labour and enterprise: but the very deepest springs of rage, contempt, and hate; wrongs which caused, as I believe, the horrors of the Revolution.

It is notorious how many of the men most deeply implicated in those horrors were of the artist class—by which I signify not merely painters and sculptors—as the word artist has now got, somewhat strangely, to signify, at least in England—but what the French meant by *artistes*—producers of luxuries and amusements, play-actors, musicians, and suchlike, down to that "distracted peruke-maker with two fiery torches," who, at the storm of the Bastile, "was for burning the saltpetres of the Arsenal, had not a woman run screaming; had not a patriot, with some tincture of natural philosophy, instantly struck the wind out of him, with butt of musket on pit of stomach, overturned the barrels, and stayed the devouring element." The distracted peruke-maker may have had his wrongs—perhaps such a one as that of poor Triboulet the fool, in "Le Roi s'amuse"—and his own sound reasons for blowing down the Bastile, and the system which kept it up.

For these very ministers of luxury—then miscalled art—from the periwig-maker to the play-actor—who like them had seen the frivolity, the baseness, the profligacy, of the rulers to whose vices they pandered, whom they despised while they adored! Figaro himself may have looked up to his master the Marquis as a superior being as long as the law enabled the Marquis to send him to the Bastile by a lettre de cachet; yet Figaro may have known and seen enough to excuse him, when lettres de cachet were abolished, for handing the Marquis over to a Comité de Salut Public. Disappointed play-actors, like Collet d'Herbois; disappointed poets, like Fabre d'Olivet, were, they say, especially ferocious. Why not? Ingenious, sensitive spirits, used as lap-dogs and singing-birds by men and women whom they felt to be their own flesh and blood, they had, it may be, a juster appreciation of the actual worth of their patrons than had our own Pitt and Burke. They had played the valet: and no man was a hero to them. They had seen the nobleman expose himself before his own helots: they would try if the helot was not as good as the nobleman. The nobleman had played the mountebank: why should not the mountebank, for once, play the nobleman? The nobleman's God had been his five senses, with (to use Mr. Carlyle's phrase) the sixth sense of vanity: why should not the mountebank worship the same God, like Carriére at Nantes, and see what grace and gifts he too might obtain at that altar?

But why so cruel? Because, with many of these men, I more than suspect, there were wrongs to be avenged deeper than any wrongs done to the sixth sense of vanity. Wrongs common to them, and to a great portion of the respectable middle class, and much of the lower class: but wrongs to which they and their families, being most in contact with the noblesse, would be especially exposed; namely, wrongs to women.

Everyone who knows the literature of that time, must know what I mean: what had gone on for more than a century, it may be more than two, in France, in Italy, and—I am sorry to have to say it—Germany likewise. All historians know what I mean, and how enormous was the evil. I only wonder that they have so much overlooked that item in the causes of the Revolution. It seems to me to have been more patent and potent in the sight of men, as it surely was in the sight of Almighty God, than all the political and economic wrongs put together. They might have issued in a change of dynasty or of laws. That, issued in the blood of the offenders. Not a girl was enticed into Louis XV.'s Petit Trianon, or other den of aristocratic iniquity, but left behind her, parents nursing shame and sullen indignation, even while they fingered the ill-gotten price of their daughter's honour; and left behind also, perhaps, some unhappy boy of her own class, in whom disappointment and jealousy were transformed—and who will blame him?—into righteous indignation, and a very sword of God; all the more indignant, and all the more righteous, if education helped him to see, that the maiden's acquiescence, her pride in her own shame, was the ugliest feature in the whole crime, and the most potent reason for putting an end, however fearful, to a state of things in which such a fate was thought an honour and a gain, and not a disgrace and a ruin; in which the most gifted daughters of the lower classes had learnt to think it more noble to become—that which they became—than the wives of honest men.

If you will read fairly the literature of the Ancien Régime, whether in France or elsewhere, you will see that my facts are true. If you have human hearts in you, you will see in them, it seems to me, an explanation of many a guillotinade and fusillade, as yet explained only on the ground of madness—an hypothesis which (as we do not yet in the least understand what madness is) is no explanation at all.

An age of decay, incoherence, and makeshift, varnish and gilding upon worm-eaten furniture, and mouldering wainscot, was that same Ancien Régime. And for that very reason a picturesque age; like one of its own landscapes. A picturesque bit of uncultivated mountain, swarming with the prince's game; a picturesque old robber schloss above, now in ruins; and below, perhaps, the picturesque new schloss, with its French fountains and gardens, French nymphs of marble, and of flesh and blood likewise, which the prince has partially paid for, by selling a few hundred young men to the English to fight the Yankees. The river, too, is picturesque, for the old bridge has not been repaired since it was blown up in the Seven Years' War; and there is but a single lazy barge floating down the stream, owing to the tolls and tariffs of his Serene Highness; the village is picturesque, for the flower of the young men are at the wars, and the place is tumbling down; and the two old peasants in the foreground, with the single goat and the hamper of vine-twigs, are very picturesque likewise, for they are all in rags.

How sad to see the picturesque element eliminated, and the quiet artistic beauty of the scene destroyed;—to have steamers puffing up and down the river, and a railroad hurrying along its banks the wealth of the

Old World, in exchange for the wealth of the New—or hurrying, it may be, whole regiments of free and educated citizen-soldiers, who fight, they know for what. How sad to see the alte schloss desecrated by tourists, and the neue schloss converted into a cold-water cure. How sad to see the village, church and all, built up again brand-new, and whitewashed to the very steeple-top;—a new school at the town-end—a new crucifix by the wayside. How sad to see the old folk well clothed in the fabrics of England or Belgium, doing an easy trade in milk and fruit, because the land they till has become their own, and not the prince's; while their sons are thriving farmers on the prairies of the far West. Very unpicturesque, no doubt, is wealth and progress, peace and safety, cleanliness and comfort. But they possess advantages unknown to the Ancien Régime, which was, if nothing else, picturesque. Men could paint amusing and often pretty pictures of its people and its places.

Consider that word, "picturesque." It, and the notion of art which it expresses, are the children of the Ancien Régime—of the era of decay. The healthy, vigorous, earnest, progressive Middle Age never dreamed of admiring, much less of painting, for their own sake, rags and ruins; the fashion sprang up at the end of the seventeenth century; it lingered on during the first quarter of our century, kept alive by the reaction from 1815–25. It is all but dead now, before the return of vigorous and progressive thought. An admirer of the Middle Ages now does not build a sham ruin in his grounds; he restores a church, blazing with colour, like a mediæval illumination. He has learnt to look on that which went by the name of picturesque in his great-grandfather's time, as an old

Greek or a Middle Age monk would have done—as something squalid, ugly, a sign of neglect, disease, death; and therefore to be hated and abolished, if it cannot be restored. At Carcassone, now, M. Viollet-le-Duc, under the auspices of the Emperor of the French, is spending his vast learning, and much money, simply in abolishing the picturesque; in restoring stone for stone, each member of that wonderful museum of Middle Age architecture: Roman, Visigothic, Moslem, Romaine, Early English, later French, all is being reproduced exactly as it must have existed centuries since. No doubt that is not the highest function of art: but it is a preparation for the highest, a step toward some future creative school. As the early Italian artists, by careful imitation, absorbed into their minds the beauty and meaning of old Greek and Roman art; so must the artists of our days by the art of the Middle Age and the Renaissance. They must learn to copy, before they can learn to surpass; and, meanwhile, they must learn—indeed they have learnt—that decay is ugliness, and the imitation of decay, a making money out of the public shame.

The picturesque sprang up, as far as I can discover, suddenly, during the time of exhaustion and recklessness which followed the great struggles of the sixteenth century. Salvator Rosa and Callot, two of the earliest professors of picturesque art, have never been since surpassed. For indeed, they drew from life. The rags and the ruins, material, and alas! spiritual, were all around them; the lands and the creeds alike lay waste. There was ruffianism and misery among the masses of Europe; unbelief and artificiality among the upper classes; churches and monasteries defiled, cities sacked, farmsteads plundered and ruinate, and all the wretchedness which Callot has immortalised—for a warning to evil rulers—in his Misères de la Guerre. The world was all gone wrong: but as for setting it right again—who could do that? And so men fell into a sentimental regret for the past, and its beauties, all exaggerated by the foreshortening of time; while they wanted strength or faith to reproduce it. At last they became so accustomed to the rags and ruins, that they looked on them as the normal condition of humanity, as the normal field for painters.

Only now and then, and especially toward the latter half of the eighteenth century, when thought began to revive, and men dreamed of putting the world to rights once more, there rose before them glimpses of an Arcadian ideal. Country life—the primæval calling of men—how graceful and pure it might be! How graceful—if not pure—it once had been! The boors of Teniers and the beggars of Murillo might be true to present fact; but there was a fairer ideal, which once had been fact, in the Eclogues of Theocritus, and the Loves of Daphnis and Chloe. And so men took to dreaming of shepherds and shepherdesses, and painting them on canvas, and modelling them in china, according to their cockney notions of what they had been once, and always ought to be. We smile now at Sèvres and Dresden shepherdesses; but the wise man will surely see in them a certain pathos. They indicated a craving after something better than boorishness; and the many men and women may have become the gentler and purer by looking even at them, and have said sadly to themselves: "Such might have been the peasantry of half Europe, had it not been for devastations of the Palatinate, wars of succession, and the wicked wills of emperors and kings."

LECTURE III.

THE EXPLOSIVE FORCES.

In a former lecture in this Institution, I said that the human race owed more to the eighteenth century than to any century since the Christian era. It may seem a bold assertion to those who value duly the century which followed the revival of Greek literature, and consider that the eighteenth century was but the child, or rather grandchild, thereof. But I must persist in my opinion, even though it seem to be inconsistent with my description of the very same era as one of decay and death. For side by side with the death, there was manifold fresh birth; side by side with the decay there was active growth;—side by side with them, fostered by them, though generally in strong opposition to them, whether conscious or unconscious. We must beware, however, of trying to find between that decay and that growth a bond of cause and effect where there is really none. The general decay may have determined the course of many men's thoughts; but it no more set them thinking than (as I have heard said) the decay of the

Ancien Régime produced the new Régime—a loose metaphor, which, like all metaphors, will not hold water, and must not be taken for a philosophic truth. That would be to confess man—what I shall never confess him to be—the creature of circumstances; it would be to fall into the same fallacy of spontaneous generation as did the ancients, when they believed that bees were bred from the carcass of a dead ox. In the first place, the bees were no bees, but flies—unless when some true swarm of honey bees may have taken up their abode within the empty ribs, as Samson's bees did in that of the lion. But bees or flies, each sprang from an egg, independent of the carcass, having a vitality of its own: it was fostered by the carcass it fed on during development; but bred from it it was not, any more than Marat was bred from the decay of the Ancien Régime. There are flies which, by feeding on putridity, become poisonous themselves, as did Marat: but even they owe their vitality and organisation to something higher than that on which they feed; and each of them, however, defaced and debased, was at first a "thought of God." All true manhood consists in the defiance of circumstances; and if any man be the creature of circumstances, it is because he has become so, like the drunkard; because he has ceased to be a man, and sunk downward toward the brute.

Accordingly we shall find, throughout the 18th century, a stirring of thought, an originality, a resistance to circumstances, an indignant defiance of circumstances, which would have been impossible, had circumstances been the true lords and shapers of mankind. Had that latter been the case, the downward progress of the Ancien Régime would have been irremediable. Each generation, conformed more and more to the element in which it lived, would have sunk deeper in dull acquiescence to evil, in ignorance of all cravings save those of the senses; and if at any time intolerable wrong or want had driven it to revolt, it would have issued, not in the proclamation of new and vast ideas, but in an anarchic struggle for revenge and bread.

There are races, alas! which seem, for the present at least, mastered by circumstances. Some, like the Chinese, have sunk back into that state; some, like the negro in Africa, seem not yet to have emerged from it; but in Europe, during the eighteenth century, were working not merely new forces and vitalities (abstractions which mislead rather than explain), but living persons in plenty, men and women, with independent and original hearts and brains, instinct, in spite of all circumstances, with power which we shall most wisely ascribe directly to Him who is the Lord and Giver of Life.

Such persons seemed—I only say seemed—most numerous in England and in Germany. But there were enough of them in France to change the destiny of that great nation for awhile—perhaps for ever.

M. de Tocqueville has a whole chapter, and a very remarkable one, which appears at first sight to militate against my belief—a chapter "showing that France was the country in which men had become most alike."

"The men," he says, "of that time, especially those belonging to the upper and middle ranks of society, who alone were at all conspicuous, were all exactly alike."

And it must be allowed, that if this were true of

the upper and middle classes, it must have been still more true of the mass of the lowest population, who, being most animal, are always most moulded—or rather crushed—by their own circumstances, by public opinion, and by the wants of five senses, common to all alike.

But when M. de Tocqueville attributes this curious fact to the circumstances of their political state—to that "government of one man which in the end has the inevitable effect of rendering all men alike, and all mutually indifferent to their common fate"—we must differ, even from him: for facts prove the impotence of that, or of any other circumstance, in altering the hearts and souls of men, in producing in them anything but a mere superficial and temporary resemblance.

For all the while there was, among these very French, here and there a variety of character and purpose, sufficient to burst through that very despotism, and to develop the nation into manifold, new, and quite original shapes. Thus it was proved that the uniformity had been only in their outside crust and shell. What tore the nation to pieces during the Reign of Terror, but the boundless variety and originality of the characters which found themselves suddenly in free rivalry? What else gave to the undisciplined levies, the bankrupt governments, the parvenu heroes of the Republic, a manifold force, a self-dependent audacity, which made them the conquerors, and the teachers (for good and evil) of the civilised world? If there was one doctrine which the French Revolution specially proclaimed—which it caricatured till it brought it into temporary disrepute—it was this: that no man is like another; that in each is a God-given "individuality," an independent soul, which no government or man has a right to crush, or can crush in the long run: but which ought to have, and must have, a "carrière ouverte aux talents," freely to do the best for itself in the battle of life. The French Revolution, more than any event since twelve poor men set forth to convert the world some eighteen hundred years ago, proves that man ought not to be, and need not be, the creature of circumstances, the puppet of institutions; but, if he will, their conqueror and their lord.

Of these original spirits who helped to bring life out of death, and the modern world out of the decay of the mediæval world, the French *philosophes* and encyclopædists are, of course, the most notorious. They confessed, for the most part, that their original inspiration had come from England. They were, or considered themselves, the disciples of Locke; whose philosophy, it seems to me, their own acts disproved.

And first, a few words on these same *philosophes*. One may be thoroughly aware of their deficiencies, of their sins, moral as well as intellectual; and yet one may demand that everyone should judge them fairly —which can only be done by putting himself in their place; and any fair judgment of them will, I think, lead to the conclusion that they were not mere destroyers, inflamed with hate of everything which mankind had as yet held sacred. Whatever sacred things they despised, one sacred thing they reverenced, which men had forgotten more and more since the seventeenth century—common justice and common humanity. It was this, I believe, which gave them their moral force. It was this which drew towards them the hearts, not merely of educated bourgeois and nobles (on the *menu peuple* they had no influence, and did not care to have any), but of every continental sovereign who felt in himself higher aspirations than those of a mere selfish tyrant—Frederick the Great, Christina of Sweden, Joseph of Austria, and even that fallen Juno, Catharine of Russia, with all her sins. To take the most extreme instance—Voltaire. We may question his being a philosopher at all. We may deny that he had even a tincture of formal philosophy. We may doubt much whether he had any of that human and humorous common sense, which is often a good substitute for the philosophy of the schools. We may feel against him a just and honest indignation when we remember that he dared to travestie into a foul satire the tale of his country's purest and noblest heroine; but we must recollect, at the same time, that he did a public service to the morality of his own country, and of all Europe, by his indignation—quite as just and honest as any which we may feel—at the legal murder of Calas. We must recollect that, if he exposes baseness and foulness with too cynical a license of speech (in which, indeed, he sinned no more than had the average of French writers since the days of Montaigne), he at least never advocates them, as did Le Sage. We must recollect that, scattered throughout his writings, are words in favour of that which is just, merciful, magnanimous, and even, at times, in favour of that which is pure; which proves that in Voltaire, as in most men, there was a double self—the one sickened to cynicism by the iniquity and folly which he saw around him—the other, hungering after a nobler life, and possibly exciting that hunger in one and another, here and there, who admired him for other reasons than the educated mob, which cried after him "Vive la Pucelle."

Rousseau, too. Easy it is to feel disgust, contempt, for the "Confessions" and the "Nouvelle Heloise"—for much, too much, in the man's own life and character. One would think the worse of the young Englishman who did not so feel, and express his feelings roundly and roughly. But all young Englishmen should recollect, that to Rousseau's "Emile" they owe their deliverance from the useless pedantries, the degrading brutalities, of the mediæval system of school education; that "Emile" awakened throughout civilised Europe a conception of education just, humane, rational, truly scientific, because founded upon facts; that if it had not been written by one writhing under the bitter consequences of mis-education, and feeling their sting and their brand day by day on his own spirit, Miss Edgeworth might never have reformed our nurseries, or Dr. Arnold our public schools.

And so with the rest of the *philosophes*. That there were charlatans among them, vain men, pretentious men, profligate men, selfish, self-seeking, and hypocritical men, who doubts? Among what class of men were there not such in those evil days? In what class of men are there not such now, in spite of all social and moral improvement? But nothing but the conviction, among the average, that they were in the right—that they were fighting a battle for which it was worth while to dare, and if need be to suffer, could have enabled them to defy what was then public opinion, backed by overwhelming physical force.

Their intellectual defects are patent. No one can deny that their inductions were hasty and partial: but then they were inductions as opposed to the dull pedantry of the schools, which rested on tradition only half believed, or pretended to be believed. No one can deny that their theories were too general and abstract; but then they were theories as opposed to the no-theory of the Ancien Régime, which was, "Let us eat and drink, for to-morrow we die."

Theories—principles—by them if men do not live, by them men are, at least, stirred into life, at the sight of something more noble than themselves. Only by great ideas, right or wrong, could such a world as that which Le Sage painted, be roused out of its slough of foul self-satisfaction, and equally foul self-discontent.

For mankind is ruled and guided, in the long run, not by practical considerations, not by self-interest, not by compromises; but by theories and principles, and those of the most abstruse, delicate, supernatural, and literally unspeakable kind; which, whether they be according to reason or not, are so little according to logic—that is, to speakable reason—that they cannot be put into speech. Men act, whether singly or in masses, by impulses and instincts for which they give reasons quite incompetent, often quite irrelevant; but which they have caught from each other, as they catch fever or small-pox; as unconsciously, and yet as practically and potently; just as the nineteenth century has caught from the philosophers of the eighteenth most practical rules of conduct, without even (in most cases) having read a word of their works.

And what has this century caught from these philosophers? One rule it has learnt, and that a most practical one—to appeal in all cases, as much as possible, to "Reason and the Laws of Nature." That, at least, the philosophers tried to do. Often they failed. Their conceptions of reason and of the laws of nature being often incorrect, they appealed to unreason and to laws which were not those of nature. "The fixed idea of them all was," says M. de Tocqueville, "to substitute simple and elementary rules, deduced from reason and natural law, for the complicated traditional customs which governed the society of their time." They were often rash, hasty, in the application of their method. They ignored whole classes of facts, which, though spiritual and not physical, are just as much facts, and facts for science, as those which concern a stone or a fungus. They mistook for merely complicated traditional customs, many most sacred institutions which were just as much founded on reason and natural law, as any theories of their own. But who shall say that their method was not correct? That it was not the only method? They appealed to reason. Would you have had them appeal to unreason? They appealed to natural law. Would you have had them appeal to unnatural law?—law according to which God did not make this world? Alas! that had been done too often already. Solomon saw it done in his time, and called it folly, to which he prophesied no good end. Rabelais saw it done in his time; and wrote his chapters on the "Children of Physis and the Children of Antiphysis." But, born in an evil generation, which was already, even in 1500, ripening for the revolution of 1789, he was sensual and, I fear, cowardly enough to hide his light, not under a bushel, but under a dunghill; till men took him for a jester of jests; and his great wisdom was lost to the worse and more foolish generations which followed him, and thought they understood him.

But as for appealing to natural law for that which is good for men, and to reason for the power of discerning that same good—if man cannot find truth by that method, by what method shall he find it?

And thus it happened that, though these philosophers and encyclopædists were not men of science, they were at least the heralds and the coadjutors of science.

We may call them, and justly, dreamers, theorists, fanatics. But we must recollect that one thing they meant to do, and did. They recalled men to facts; they bid them ask of everything they saw—What are the facts of the case? Till we know the facts, argument is worse than useless.

Now the habit of asking for the facts of the case must deliver men more or less from that evil spirit which the old Romans called "Fama;" from her whom Virgil described in the Æneid as the ugliest, the falsest, and the cruellest of monsters.

From "Fama;" from rumours, hearsays, exaggerations, scandals, superstitions, public opinions—whether from the ancient public opinion that the sun went round the earth, or the equally public opinion, that those who dared to differ from public opinion were hateful to the deity, and therefore worthy of death—from all those blasts of Fame's lying trumpet they helped to deliver men; and they therefore helped to insure something like peace and personal security for those quiet, modest, and generally virtuous men, who, as students of physical science, devoted their lives, during the eighteenth century, to asking of nature—What are the facts of the case?

It was no coincidence, but a connection of cause and effect, that during the century of *philosophes* sound physical science throve, as she had never thriven before; that in zoology and botany, chemistry and medicine, geology and astronomy, man after man, both of the middle and the noble classes, laid down on more and more sound, because more and more extended foundations, that physical science which will endure as an everlasting heritage to mankind; endure, even though a second Byzantine period should reduce it to a timid and traditional pedantry, or a second irruption of barbarians sweep it away for awhile, to revive again (as classic philosophy revived in the fifteenth century) among new and more energetic races; when the kingdom of God shall have been taken away from us, and given to a nation bringing forth the fruits thereof.

An eternal heritage, I say, for the human race; which once gained, can never be lost; which stands, and will stand; marches, and will march, proving its growth, its health, its progressive force, its certainty of final victory, by those very changes, disputes, mistakes, which the ignorant and the bigoted hold up to scorn, as proofs of its uncertainty and its rottenness; because they never have dared or cared to ask boldly—What are the facts of the case?—and have never discovered either the acuteness, the patience, the calm justice, necessary for ascertaining the facts, or their awful and divine certainty when once ascertained.

[But these philosophers (it will be said) hated all religion.

Before that question can be fairly discussed, it is surely right to consider what form of religion that was which they found working round them in France, and on the greater part of the Continent. The quality thereof may have surely had something to do (as they themselves asserted) with that "sort of rage" with which (to use M. de Tocqueville's words) "the Christian religion was attacked in France."

M. de Tocqueville is of opinion (and his opinion is likely to be just) that "the Church was not more open to attack in France than elsewhere; that the corruptions and abuses which had been allowed to creep into it were less, on the contrary, there than in most Catholic countries. The Church of France was infinitely more tolerant than it ever had been previously, and than it still was among other nations. Consequently, the peculiar causes of this phenomenon" (the hatred which it aroused) "must be looked for less in the condition of religion than in that of society."

"We no longer," he says, shortly after, "ask in what the Church of that day erred as a religious institution, but how far it stood opposed to the political revolution which was at hand." And he goes on to show how the principles of her ecclesiastical government, and her political position, were such that the *philosophes* must needs have been her enemies. But he mentions another fact which seems to me to belong neither to the category of religion nor to that of politics; a fact which, if he had done us the honour to enlarge upon it, might have led him and his readers to a more true understanding of the disrepute into which Christianity had fallen in France.

"The ecclesiastical authority had been specially employed in keeping watch over the progress of thought; and the censorship of books was a daily annoyance to the *philosophes*. By defending the common liberties of the human mind against the Church, they were combating in their own cause: and they began by breaking the shackles which pressed most closely on themselves."

Just so. And they are not to be blamed if they pressed first and most earnestly reforms which they knew by painful experience to be necessary. All reformers are wont thus to begin at home. It is to their honour if, not content with shaking off their own fetters, they begin to see that others are fettered likewise; and, reasoning from the particular to the universal, to learn that their own cause is the cause of mankind.

There is, therefore, no reason to doubt that these men were honest, when they said that they were combating, not in their own cause merely, but in that of humanity; and that the Church was combating in her own cause, and that of her power and privilege. The Church replied that she, too, was combating for humanity; for its moral and eternal well-being. But that is just what the *philosophes* denied. They said (and it is but fair to take a statement which appears on the face of all their writings; which is the one key-note on which they ring perpetual changes), that the cause of the Church in France was not that of humanity, but of inhumanity; not that of nature, but of unnature; not even that of grace, but of disgrace. Truely or falsely, they complained that the French clergy had not only identified themselves with the repression of free thought, and of physical science, especially that of the Newtonian astronomy, but that they had proved themselves utterly unfit, for centuries past, to exercise any censorship whatsoever over the thoughts of men: that they had identified themselves with the cause of darkness, not of light; with persecution and torture, with the dragonnades of Louis XIV., with the murder of Calas and of Urban Grandier; with celibacy, hysteria, demonology, witchcraft, and the shameful public scandals, like those of Gauffredi, Grandier, and Père Giraud, which had arisen out of mental disease; with forms of worship which seemed to them (rightly or wrongly) idolatry, and miracles which seemed to them (rightly or wrongly) impostures; that the clergy interfered perpetually with the sanctity of family life, as well as with the welfare of the state; that their evil counsels, and specially those of the Jesuits, had been patent and potent causes of much of the misrule and misery of Louis XIV.'s and XV.'s reigns; and that with all these heavy counts against them, their morality was not such as to make other men more moral; and was not—at least among the hierarchy—improving, or likely to improve. To a Mazarin, a De Retz, a Richelieu (questionable men enough) had succeeded a Dubois, a Rohan, a Lomenie de Brienne, a Maury, a Talleyrand; and at the revolution of 1789 thoughtful Frenchmen asked, once and for all, what was to be done with a Church of which these were the hierophants?

Whether these complaints affected the French Church as a "religious" institution, must depend entirely on the meaning which is attached to the word "religion": that they affected her on scientific, rational, and moral grounds, independent of any merely political one, is as patent as that the attack based on them was one-sided, virulent, and often somewhat hypocritical, considering the private morals of many of the assailants. We know—or ought to know—that within that religion which seemed to the *philosophes* (so distorted and defaced had it become) a nightmare dream, crushing the life out of mankind, there lie elements divine, eternal; necessary for man in this life and the life to come. But we are bound to ask—Had they a fair chance of knowing what we know? Have we proof that their hatred was against all religion, or only against that which they saw around them? Have we proof that they would have equally hated, had they been in permanent contact with them, creeds more free from certain faults which seemed to them, in the case of the French Church, ineradicable and inexpiable? Till then we must have charity—which is justice—even for the *philosophes* of the eighteenth century.

This view of the case had been surely overlooked by M. de Tocqueville, when he tried to explain by the fear of revolutions, the fact that both in America and in England, "while the boldest political doctrines of the eighteenth-century philosophers have been adopted, their anti-religious doctrines have made no way."

He confesses that, "Among the English, French irreligious philosophy had been preached, even before the greater part of the French philosophers were born. It was Bolingbroke who set up Voltaire. Throughout the eighteenth century infidelity had celebrated champions in England. Able writers and profound thinkers espoused that cause, but they were never able to render it triumphant as in France." Of these facts there can be no doubt: but the cause which he gives for the failure of infidelity will surely sound new and strange to those who know the English literature and history of that century. It was, he says, "inasmuch as all those who had anything to fear from revolutions, eagerly came to the rescue of the established faith." Surely there was no talk of revolutions; no wish, expressed or concealed, to overthrow either government or society, in the aristocratic clique to whom English infidelity was confined. Such was, at least, the opinion of Voltaire, who boasted that "All the works of the modern philosophers together would never make as much noise in the world as was made in former days by the disputes of the Cordeliers about the shape of their sleeves and hoods." If (as M. de Tocqueville says) Bolingbroke set up Voltaire, neither master nor pupil had any more leaning than Hobbes had toward a democracy which was not dreaded in those days because it had never been heard of. And if (as M. de Tocqueville heartily allows) the English apologists of Christianity triumphed, at least for the time being, the cause of their triumph must be sought in the plain fact that such men as Berkeley, Butler, and Paley, each according to his light, fought the battle fairly, on the common ground of reason and philosophy, instead of on that of tradition and authority; and that the forms of Christianity current in England—whether Quaker, Puritan, or Anglican—offended, less than that current in France, the common-sense and the human instincts of the many, or of the sceptics themselves.]

But the eighteenth century saw another movement, all the more powerful, perhaps, because it was continually changing its shape, even its purpose; and gaining fresh life and fresh adherents with every change. Propagated at first by men of the school of Locke, it became at last a protest against the materialism of that school, on behalf of all that is, or calls itself, supernatural and mysterious. Abjuring, and honestly, all politics, it found itself sucked into the political whirlpool in spite of itself, as all human interests which have any life in them must be at last. It became an active promoter of the Revolution; then it helped to destroy the Revolution, when that had, under Napoleon, become a levelling despotism; then it helped, as actively, to keep revolutionary principles alive, after the reaction of 1815 :—a Protean institution, whose power we in England are as apt to undervalue as the governments of the Continent were apt, during the eighteenth century, to exaggerate it. I mean, of course, Freemasonry, and the secret societies which, honestly and honourably disowned by Freemasonry, yet have either copied it, or actually sprung out of it. In England, Freemasonry never was, it seems, more than a liberal and respectable benefit-club; for secret societies are needless for any further purposes, amid free institutions and a free press. But on the Continent during the eighteenth century, Freemasonry excited profound suspicion and fear on the part of statesmen who knew perfectly well their friends from their foes; and whose precautions were, from their point of view, justified by the results.

I shall not enter into the deep question of the origin of Freemasonry. One uninitiate, as I am, has no right to give an opinion on the great questions of the mediæval lodge of Kilwinning and its Scotch degrees; on the seven Templars, who, after poor Jacques Molay was burnt at Paris, took refuge on the Isle of Mull, in Scotland, found there another Templar and brother Mason, ominously named Harris; took to the trowel in earnest, and revived the Order;—on the Masons who built Magdeburg Cathedral in 876; on the English Masons assembled in Pagan times by "St. Albone, that worthy knight;" on the revival of English Masonry by Edwin, son of Athelstan; on Magnus Grecus, who had been at the building of Solomon's Temple, and taught Masonry to Charles Martel; on the pillars Jachin and Boaz; on the masonry of Hiram of Tyre, and indeed of Adam himself, of whose first fig-leaf the masonic apron may be a type—on all these matters I dare no more decide than on the making of the Trojan Horse, the birth of Romulus and Remus, or the incarnation of Vishnoo.

All I dare say is, that Freemasonry emerges in its present form into history and fact, seemingly about the beginning of George I.'s reign, among Englishmen and noblemen, notably in four lodges in the city of London: (1) at The Goose and Gridiron alehouse in St. Paul's Churchyard; (2) at The Crown alehouse near Drury Lane; (3) at The Apple Tree tavern near Covent Garden; (4) at The Rummer and Grapes tavern, in Charnel Row, Westminster. That its principles were brotherly love and good fellowship, which included in those days port, sherry, claret, and punch; that it was founded on the ground of mere humanity, in every sense of the word; being (as was to be expected from the temper of the times) both aristocratic and liberal, admitting to its ranks virtuous gentlemen "obliged," says an old charge, "only to that religion wherein all men agree, leaving their particular opinions to themselves: that is, to be good men and true, or men of honour and honesty, by whatever denominations or persuasions they may be distinguished; whereby Masonry becomes the centre of union and means of conciliating true friendship among persons that otherwise must have remained at a distance."

Little did the honest gentlemen who established or re-established their society on these grounds, and fenced it with quaint ceremonies, old or new, conceive the importance of their own act; we, looking at it from a distance, may see all that such a society involved, which was quite new to the world just then; and see, that it was the very child of the Ancien Régime—of a time when men were growing weary of the violent factions, political and spiritual, which had torn Europe in pieces for more than a century, and longed to say: "After all, we are all alike in one thing—for we are at least men."

Its spread through England and Scotland, and the seceding bodies which arose from it, as well as the supposed Jacobite tendency of certain Scotch lodges, do not concern us here. The point interesting to us just now is, that Freemasonry was imported to the Continent exclusively by English and Scotch gentlemen and noblemen. Lord Derwentwater is said by some to have founded the "Loge Anglaise" in Paris in 1725; the Duke of Richmond one in his own castle of Aubigny shortly after. It was through Hanoverian influence that the movement seems to have spread into Germany. In 1733, for instance, the English Grand Master, Lord Strathmore, permitted eleven German gentlemen and good brethren to form a lodge in Hamburg. Into this English Society was Frederick the Great, when Crown Prince, initiated, in spite of strict old Frederick William's objections, who had heard of it as an English invention of irreligious tendency. Francis I. of Austria was made a Freemason at the Hague, Lord Chesterfield being in the chair, and then became a Master in London under the name of "Brother Lothringen," to the discontent of Maria Theresa, whose woman's wit saw farther than her husband. Englishmen and Scotchmen introduced the new society into Russia and into Geneva. Sweden and Poland seem to have received it from France; while, in the South, it seems to have been exclusively an

English plant. Sackville, Duke of Middlesex, is said to have founded the first lodge at Florence in 1733, Lord Coleraine at Gibraltar and Madrid, one Gordon in Portugal; and everywhere, at the commencement of the movement, we find either London or Scotland the mother-lodges, introducing on the Continent those liberal and humane ideas of which England was then considered, to her glory, as the only home left on earth.

But, alas! the seed sown grew up into strange shapes, according to the soil in which it rooted. False doctrine, heresy, and schism, according to Herr Findel, the learned and rational historian whom I have chiefly followed, defiled the new Church from its infancy. "In France," so he bemoans himself, "first of all there shot up that baneful seed of lies and frauds, of vanity and presumption, of hatred and discord, the mischievous high degrees; the misstatement that our order was allied to the Templars, and existed at the time of the Crusades; the removal of old charges, the bringing in surreptitiously of a multitude of symbols and forms which awoke the love of secrecy; knighthood; and, in fact, all which tended to poison Freemasonry." Herr Findel seems to attribute these evils principally to the "high degrees." It would have been more simple to have attributed them to the morals of the French noblesse in the days of Louis Quinze. What could a corrupt tree bring forth, but corrupt fruit? If some of the early lodges, like those of "La Félicité" and "L'Ancre," to which women were admitted, resembled not a little the Bacchic mysteries of old Rome, and like them called for the interference of the police, still no great reform was to be expected, when those Sovereign Masonic Princes, the "Emperors of the East and West," quarrelled—knights of the East against knights of the West—till they were absorbed or crushed by the Lodge "Grand Orient," with Philippe Egalité, Duc de Chartres, as their grand master, and as his representative, the hero of the diamond necklace, and disciple of Count Cagliostro—Louis, Prince de Rohan.

But if Freemasonry, among the frivolous and sensual French noblesse, became utterly frivolous and sensual itself, it took a deeper, though a questionably fantastic form, among the more serious and earnest German nobility. Forgetful as they too often were of their duty to their peoples—tyrannical, extravagant, debauched by French opinions, French fashions, French luxuries, till they had begun to despise their native speech, their native literature, almost their native land, and to hide their native homeliness under a clumsy varnish of French outside civilisation, which the years 1807–13 rubbed off them again with a brush of iron—they were yet Germans at heart; and that German instinct for the unseen—call it enthusiasm, mysticism, what you will, you cannot make it anything but a human fact, and a most powerful, and (as I hold) most blessed fact—that instinct for the unseen, I say, which gives peculiar value to German philosophy, poetry, art, religion, and above all to German family life, and which is just the complement needed to prevent our English common-sense, matter-of-fact Lockism from degenerating into materialism—that was only lying hidden, but not dead, in the German spirit.

With the Germans, therefore, Freemasonry assumed a nobler and more earnest shape. Dropping, very soon, that Lockite and *Philosophe* tone which had perhaps recommended it to Frederick the Great in his youth, it became mediævalist and mystic. It craved after a resuscitation of old chivalrous spirit, and the virtues of the knightly ideal, and the old German *biederkeit und tapferkeit,* which were all defiled and overlaid by French fopperies. And not in vain; as no struggle after a noble aim, however confused or fantastic, is ever in vain. Freemasonry was the direct parent of the Tugenbund, and of those secret societies which freed Germany from Napoleon. Whatever follies young members of them may have committed; whatever Jahn and his Turnerei; whatever the iron youths, with their iron decorations and iron boot-heels; whatever, in a word, may have been said or done amiss, in that childishness which (as their own wisest writers often lament) so often defaces the noble childlikeness of the German spirit, let it be always remembered that under the impulse first given by Freemasonry, as much as that given by such heroes as Stein and Scharnhorst, Germany shook off the chains which had fallen on her in her sleep; and stood once more at Leipsic, were it but for a moment, a free people alike in body and in soul.

Remembering this, and the solid benefits which Germany owed to Masonic influences, one shrinks from saying much of the extravagances in which its Masonry indulged before the French Revolution. Yet they are so characteristic of the age, so significant to the student of human nature, that they must be hinted at, though not detailed.

It is clear that Masonry was at first a movement confined to the aristocracy, or at least to the most educated classes; and clear, too, that it fell in with a temper of mind unsatisfied with the dry dogmatism into which the popular creeds had then been frozen—

unsatisfied with their own Frenchified foppery and pseudo-philosophy—unsatisfied with want of all duty, purpose, noble thought, or noble work. With such a temper of mind it fell in: but that very temper was open (as it always is) to those dreams of a royal road to wisdom and to virtue, which have haunted, in all ages, the luxurious and the idle.

Those who will, may read enough, and too much, of the wonderful secrets in nature and science and theosophy, which men expected to find and did not find in the higher degrees of Masonry, till old Voss—the translator of Homer—had to confess, that after "trying for eleven years to attain a perfect knowledge of the inmost penetralia, where the secret is said to be, and of its invisible guardians," all he knew was that "the documents which he had to make known to the initiated were nothing more than a well got-up farce."

But the mania was general. The high-born and the virtuous expected to discover some panacea for their own consciences in what Voss calls, "A multitude of symbols, which are ever increasing the farther you penetrate, and are made to have a moral application through some arbitrary twisting of their meaning, as if I were to attempt expounding the chaos on my writing-desk."

A rich harvest-field was an aristocracy in such a humour, for quacks of every kind; richer even than that of France, in that the Germans were at once more honest and more earnest, and therefore to be robbed more easily. The carcass was there: and the birds of prey were gathered together.

Of Rosa, with his lodge of the Three Hammers, and his Potsdam gold-making;—of Johnson, alias Leuchte, who passed himself off as a Grand Prior sent from Scotland to resuscitate the order of Knights Templars; who informed his disciples that the Grand Master Von Hund commanded 26,000 men; that round the convent (what convent, does not appear) a high wall was erected, which was guarded day and night; that the English navy was in the hands of the Order; that they had MSS. written by Hugo de Paganis (a mythic hero who often figures in these fables); that their treasure was in only three places in the world, in Ballenstadt, in the icy mountains of Savoy, and in China; that whosoever drew on himself the displeasure of the Order, perished both body and soul; who degraded his rival Rosa to the sound of military music, and after having had, like every dog, his day, died in prison in the Wartburg;—of the Rosicrucians, who were accused of wanting to support and advance the Catholic religion—one would think the accusation was very unnecessary, seeing that their actual dealings were with the philosopher's stone, and the exorcism of spirits: and that the first apostle of the new golden Rosicrucian order, one Schröpfer, getting into debt, and fearing exposure, finished his life in an altogether un-catholic manner at Leipsic in 1774, by shooting himself;—of Keller and his Urim and Thummim;—of Wöllner (who caught the Crown Prince Frederick William) with his three names of Chrysophiron, Heliconus, and Ophiron, and his fourth name of Ormesus Magnus, under which all the brethren were to offer up for him solemn prayers and intercessions;—of Baron Heinrich von Ekker and Eckenhofen, gentleman of the bed-chamber and counsellor of the Duke of Coburg Saalfeld, and his Jewish colleague Hirschmann, with their Asiatic brethren and order named Ben Bicca, Cabalistic and Talmudic;

of the Illuminati, and poor Adam Weisshaupt, Professor of Canon and National Law at Ingoldstadt in Bavaria, who set up what he considered an Anti-Jesuitical order on a Jesuit model, with some vague hope, according to his own showing, of "perfecting the reasoning powers interesting to mankind, spreading the knowledge of sentiments both humane and social, checking wicked inclinations, standing up for oppressed and suffering virtue against all wrong, promoting the advancement of men of merit, and in every way facilitating the acquirement of knowledge and science;"—of this honest silly man, and his attempts to carry out all his fine projects by calling himself Spartacus, Bavaria Achaia, Austria Egypt, Vienna Rome, and so forth;—of Knigge, who picked his honest brains, quarrelled with him, and then made money and fame out of his plans, for as long as they lasted;—of Bode, the knight of the lilies of the valley, who, having caught Duke Ernest of Saxe Gotha, was himself caught by Knigge, and his eight, nine, or more ascending orders of unwisdom;—and finally of the Jesuits who, really with considerable excuses for their severity, fell upon these poor foolish Illuminati in 1784 throughout Bavaria, and had them exiled or imprisoned;—of all this you may read in the pages of Dr. Findel, and in many another book. For, forgotten as they are now, they made noise enough in their time.

And so it befell, that this eighteenth century, which is usually held to be the most "materialistic" of epochs, was, in fact, a most "spiritualistic" one; in which ghosts, demons, quacks, philosophers' stones, enchanters' wands, mysteries and mummeries, were as fashionable—as they will probably be again some day.

You have all heard of Cagliostro—"pupil of the sage Althotas, foster-child of the Scheriff of Mecca, probable son of the last king of Trebizond; named also Acharat, and 'Unfortunate child of Nature;' by profession healer of diseases, abolisher of wrinkles, friend of the poor and impotent; grand-master of the Egyptian Mason-lodge of High Science, spirit-summoner, gold-cook, Grand-Cophta, prophet, priest, Thaumaturgic moralist, and swindler"—born Giuseppe Balsamo of Palermo;—of him, and of his lovely Countess Seraphina—née Lorenza Feliciani? You have read what Goethe—and still more important, what Mr. Carlyle has written on him, as on one of the most significant personages of the age? Remember, then, that Cagliostro was no isolated phenomenon; that his success—nay, his having even conceived the possibility of success in the brain that lay within that "brass-faced, bull-necked, thick-lipped" head—was made possible by public opinion. Had Cagliostro lived in our time, public opinion would have pointed out to him other roads to honour—on which he would doubtless have fared as well. For when the silly dace try to be caught and hope to be caught, he is a foolish pike who cannot gorge them. But the method most easy for a pike-nature like Cagliostro's, was in the eighteenth century, as it may be in the latter half of the nineteenth, to trade, in a materialist age, on the unsatisfied spiritual cravings of mankind. For what do all these phantasms betoken, but a generation ashamed of its own materialism, sensuality, insincerity, ignorance, and striving to escape therefrom by any and every mad superstition which seemed likely to give an answer to the awful questions—What are we, and where? and to lay to rest those instincts of the unseen and infinite around it, which tormented it like ghosts by day and night: a sight ludicrous or pathetic, according as it is looked on by a cynical or a human spirit.

It is easy to call such a phenomenon absurd, improbable. It is rather rational, probable, say certain to happen. Rational, I say; for the reason of man tells him, and has always told him, that he is a supernatural being, if by nature is meant that which is cognisable by his five senses: that his coming into this world, his relation to it, his exit from it—which are the three most important facts about him—are supernatural, not to be explained by any deductions from the impressions of his senses. And I make bold to say, that the recent discoveries of physical science—notably those of embryology—go only to justify that old and general belief of man. If man be told that the microscope and scalpel show no difference, in the first stage of visible existence, between him and the lower mammals, then he has a right to answer—as he will answer—So much the worse for the microscope and scalpel: so much the better for my old belief, that there is beneath my birth, life, death, a substratum of supernatural causes, imponderable, invisible, unknowable by any physical science whatsoever. If you cannot render me a reason how I came hither, and what I am, I must go to those who will render me one. And if that craving be not satisfied by a rational theory of life, it will demand satisfaction from some magical theory; as did the mind of the eighteenth century when, revolting from materialism, it fled to magic, to explain the ever-astounding miracle of life.

The old Régime. Will our age, in its turn, ever

be spoken of as an old Régime? Will it ever be spoken of as a Régime at all; as an organised, orderly system of society and polity; and not merely as a chaos, an anarchy, a transitory struggle, of which the money-lender has been the real guide and lord?

But at least it will be spoken of as an age of progress, of rapid developments, of astonishing discoveries.

Are you so sure of that? There was an age of progress once. But what is our age—what is all which has befallen since 1815—save after-swells of that great storm, which are weakening and lulling into heavy calm? Are we on the eve of stagnation? Of a long check to the human intellect? Of a new Byzantine era, in which little men will discuss, and ape, the deeds which great men did in their forefathers' days?

What progress—it is a question which some will receive with almost angry surprise—what progress has the human mind made since 1815?

If the thought be startling, do me the great honour of taking it home, and verifying for yourselves its truth or its falsehood. I do not say that it is altogether true. No proposition concerning human things, stated so broadly, can be. But see for yourselves, whether it is not at least more true than false; whether the ideas, the discoveries, of which we boast most in the nineteenth century, are not really due to the end of the eighteenth. Whether other men did not labour, and we have only entered into their labours. Whether our positivist spirit, our content with the collecting of facts, our dread of vast theories, is not a symptom—wholesome, prudent, modest, but still a symptom—of our consciousness that we are not as our grandfathers were; that we can no longer conceive great ideas, which illumine, for good or evil, the whole mind and heart of man, and drive him on to dare and suffer desperately.

Railroads? Electric telegraphs? All honour to them in their place: but they are not progress; they are only the fruits of past progress. No outward and material thing is progress; no machinery causes progress; it merely spreads and makes popular the results of progress. Progress is inward, of the soul. And, therefore, improved constitutions, and improved book instruction—now miscalled education—are not progress: they are at best only fruits and signs thereof. For they are outward, material; and progress, I say, is inward. The self-help and self-determination of the independent soul—that is the root of progress; and the more human beings who have that, the more progress there is in the world. Give me a man who, though he can neither read nor write, yet dares think for himself, and do the thing he believes: that man will help forward the human race more than any thousand men who have read, or written either, a thousand books apiece, but have not dared to think for themselves. And better for his race, and better, I believe, in the sight of God, the confusions and mistakes of that one sincere brave man, than the second-hand and cowardly correctness of all the thousand.

As for the "triumphs of science," let us honour, with astonishment and awe, the genius of those who invented them; but let us remember that the things themselves are as a gun or a sword, with which we can kill our enemy, but with which also our enemy can kill us. Like all outward and material things, they are equally fit for good and for evil. In England here —they have been as yet, as far as I can see, nothing but blessings: but I have my very serious doubts whether they are likely to be blessings to the whole human race, for many an age to come. I can conceive them—may God avert the omen!—the instruments of a more crushing executive centralisation, of a more utter oppression of the bodies and souls of men, than the world has yet seen. I can conceive—may God avert the omen!—centuries hence, some future world-ruler sitting at the junction of all railroads, at the centre of all telegraph-wires—a world-spider in the omphalos of his world-wide web; and smiting from thence everything that dared to lift its head, or utter a cry of pain, with a swiftness and surety to which the craft of a Justinian or a Philip II. were but clumsy and impotent.

All, all outward things, be sure of it, are good or evil, exactly as far as they are in the hands of good men or of bad.

Moreover, paradoxical as it may seem, railroads and telegraphs, instead of inaugurating an era of progress, may possibly only retard it. "Rester sur un grand succès," which was Rossini's advice to a young singer who had achieved a triumph, is a maxim which the world often follows, not only from prudence, but from necessity. They have done so much that it seems neither prudent nor possible to do more. They will rest and be thankful.

Thus, gunpowder and printing made rapid changes enough; but those changes had no further development. The new art of war, the new art of literature, remained stationary, or rather receded and degenerated, till the end of the eighteenth century.

And so it may be with our means of locomotion and intercommunion, and what depends on them. The vast and unprecedented amount of capital, of social interest, of actual human intellect invested—I may say locked up—in these railroads, and telegraphs, and other triumphs of industry and science, will not enter into competition against themselves. They will not set themselves free to seek new discoveries in directions which are often actually opposed to their own, always foreign to it. If the money of thousands are locked up in these great works, the brains of hundreds of thousands, and of the very shrewdest too, are equally locked up therein likewise; and are to be subtracted from the gross material of social development, and added (without personal fault of their owners, who may be very good men) to the dead weight of vested selfishness, ignorance, and dislike of change.

Yes. A Byzantine and stationary age is possible yet. Perhaps we are now entering upon it; an age in which mankind shall be satisfied with the "triumphs of science," and shall look merely to the greatest comfort (call it not happiness) of the greatest number; and like the debased Jews of old, "having found the life of their hand, be therewith content," no matter in what mud-hole of slavery and superstition.

But one hope there is, and more than a hope—one certainty, that however satisfied enlightened public opinion may become with the results of science, and the progress of the human race, there will be always a more enlightened private opinion or opinions, which will not be satisfied therewith at all; a few men of genius, a few children of light, it may be a few persecuted, and a few martyrs for new truths, who will wish the world not to rest and be thankful, but to be discontented with itself, ashamed of itself, striving and toiling upward, without present hope of gain, till it has reached that unknown goal which Bacon saw afar off, and like all other heroes, died in faith, not having received the promises, but seeking still a polity which has foundations, whose builder and maker is God.

These will be the men of science, whether physical or spiritual. Not merely the men who utilise and apply that which is known (useful as they plainly are), but the men who themselves discover that which was unknown, and are generally deemed useless, if not hurtful, to their race. They will keep the sacred lamp burning unobserved in quiet studies, while all the world is gazing only at the gaslights flaring in the street. They will pass that lamp on from hand to hand, modestly, almost stealthily, till the day comes round again, when the obscure student shall be discovered once more to be, as he has always been, the strongest man on earth. For they follow a mistress whose footsteps may often slip, yet never fall; for she walks forward on the eternal facts of Nature, which are the acted will of God. A giantess she is; young indeed, but humble as yet: cautious and modest beyond her years. She is accused of trying to scale Olympus, by some who fancy that they have already scaled it themselves, and will, of course, brook no rival in their fancied monopoly of wisdom.

The accusation, I believe, is unjust. And yet science may scale Olympus after all. Without intending it, almost without knowing it, she may find herself hereafter upon a summit of which she never dreamed; surveying the universe of God in the light of Him who made it and her, and remakes them both for ever and ever. On that summit she may stand hereafter, if only she goes on, as she goes now, in humility and in patience; doing the duty which lies nearest her; lured along the upward road, not by ambition, vanity, or greed, but by reverent curiosity for every new pebble, and flower, and child, and savage, around her feet.

THE FIRST DISCOVERY OF AMERICA.

THE FIRST DISCOVERY OF AMERICA.

Let me begin this lecture* with a scene in the North Atlantic 863 years since.

"Bjarne Grimolfson was blown with his ship into the Irish Ocean; and there came worms and the ship began to sink under them. They had a boat which they had payed with seals' blubber, for that the sea-worms will not hurt. But when they got into the boat they saw that it would not hold them all. Then said Bjarne, 'As the boat will only hold the half of us, my advice is that we should draw lots who shall go in her; for that will not be unworthy of our manhood.' This advice seemed so good that none gainsaid it; and they drew lots. And the lot fell to Bjarne that he should go in the boat with half his crew. But as he got into the boat, there spake an Icelander who was in the ship and had followed Bjarne from Iceland, 'Art thou going to leave me here, Bjarne?' Quoth Bjarne, 'So it must be.' Then said the man, 'Another thing didst thou promise my father, when I sailed with thee from Iceland, than to desert me thus. For thou saidst that we both should share the same lot.' Bjarne said, 'And that we will not do. Get thou down into the boat, and I will get up into the ship, now I see

* This lecture was delivered in America in 1874.

that thou art so greedy after life.' So Bjarne went up into the ship, and the man went down into the boat; and the boat went on its voyage till they came to Dublin in Ireland. Most men say that Bjarne and his comrades perished among the worms; for they were never heard of after."

This story may serve as a text for my whole lecture. Not only does it smack of the sea-breeze and the salt water, like all the finest old Norse sagas, but it gives a glimpse at least of the nobleness which underlay the grim and often cruel nature of the Norseman. It belongs, too, to the culminating epoch, to the beginning of that era when the Scandinavian peoples had their great times; when the old fierceness of the worshippers of Thor and Odin was tempered, without being effeminated, by the Faith of the "White Christ," till the very men who had been the destroyers of Western Europe became its civilisers.

It should have, moreover, a special interest to Americans. For—as American antiquaries are well aware—Bjarne was on his voyage home from the coast of New England; possibly from that very Mount Hope Bay which seems to have borne the same name in the time of those old Norsemen, as afterwards in the days of King Philip, the last sachem of the Wampanong Indians. He was going back to Greenland, perhaps for reinforcements, finding, he and his fellow-captain, Thorfinn, the Esquimaux who then dwelt in that land too strong for them. For the Norsemen were then on the very edge of discovery, which might have changed the history not only of this continent but of Europe likewise. They had found and colonised Iceland and Greenland. They had found Labrador, and called it Helluland, from its ice-polished rocks. They had found Nova Scotia seemingly, and called it Markland, from its woods. They had found New England, and called it Vinland the Good. A fair land they found it, well wooded, with good pasturage; so that they had already imported cows, and a bull whose lowings terrified the Esquimaux. They had found self-sown corn too, probably maize. The streams were full of salmon. But they had called the land Vinland, by reason of its grapes. Quaint enough, and bearing in its very quaintness the stamp of truth, is the story of the first finding of the wild fox-grapes. How Leif the Fortunate, almost as soon as he first landed, missed a little wizened old German servant of his father's, Tyrker by name, and was much vexed thereat, for he had been brought up on the old man's knee, and hurrying off to find him met Tyrker coming back twisting his eyes about—a trick of his—smacking his lips and talking German to himself in high excitement. And when they get him to talk Norse again, he says: "I have not been far, but I have news for you. I have found vines and grapes!" "Is that true, foster-father?" says Leif. "True it is," says the old German, "for I was brought up where there was never any lack of them."

The saga—as given by Rafn—had a detailed description of this quaint personage's appearance; and it would not be amiss if American wine-growers should employ an American sculptor—and there are great American sculptors—to render that description into marble, and set up little Tyrker in some public place, as the Silenus of the New World.

Thus the first cargoes homeward from Vinland to Greenland had been of timber and of raisins, and of vine-stocks, which were not like to thrive.

And more. Beyond Vinland the Good there was said to be another land, Whiteman's Land—or Ireland the Mickle, as some called it. For these Norse traders from Limerick had found Ari Marson, and Ketla of Ruykjanes, supposed to have been long since drowned at sea, and said that the people had made him and Ketla chiefs, and baptized Ari. What is all this ? and what is this, too, which the Esquimaux children taken in Markland told the Northmen, of a land beyond them where the folk wore white clothes, and carried flags on poles ? Are these all dreams ? or was some part of that great civilisation, the relics whereof your antiquarians find in so many parts of the United States, still in existence some 900 years ago ; and were these old Norse cousins of ours upon the very edge of it ? Be that as it may, how nearly did these fierce Vikings, some of whom seemed to have sailed far south along the shore, become aware that just beyond them lay a land of fruits and spices, gold and gems ? The adverse current of the Gulf Stream, it may be, would have long prevented their getting past the Bahamas into the Gulf of Mexico ; but, sooner or later, some storm must have carried a Greenland viking to San Domingo or to Cuba ; and then, as has been well said, some Scandinavian dynasty might have sat upon the throne of Mexico.

These stories are well known to antiquarians. They may be found, almost all of them, in Professor Rafn's "Antiquitates Americanæ." The action in them stands out often so clear and dramatic, that the internal evidence of historic truth is irresistible. Thorvald, who, when he saw what seems to be, they say, the bluff head of Alderton at the south-east end of Boston Bay, said, "Here should I like to dwell," and, shot by an Esquimaux arrow, bade bury him on that place, with a cross at his head and a cross at his feet, and call the place Cross Ness for evermore; Gudrida, the magnificent widow, who wins hearts and sees strange deeds from Iceland to Greenland, and Greenland to Vinland and back, and at last, worn out and sad, goes off on a pilgrimage to Rome; Helgi and Finnbogi, the Norwegians, who, like our Arctic voyagers in after times, devise all sorts of sports and games to keep the men in humour during the long winter at Hope; and last, but not least, the terrible Freydisa, who, when the Norse are seized with a sudden panic at the Esquimaux and flee from them, as they had three weeks before fled from Thorfinn's bellowing bull, turns, when so weak that she cannot escape, single-handed on the savages, and catching up a slain man's sword, puts them all to flight with her fierce visage and fierce cries —Freydisa the Terrible, who, in another voyage, persuades her husband to fall on Helgi and Finnbogi, when asleep, and murder them and all their men; and then, when he will not murder the five women too, takes up an axe and slays them all herself, and getting back to Greenland, when the dark and unexplained tale comes out, lives unpunished, but abhorred henceforth. All these folks, I say, are no phantoms, but realities; at least, if I can judge of internal evidence.

But beyond them, and hovering on the verge of Mythus and Fairyland, there is a ballad called "Finn the Fair," and how

> An upland Earl had twa braw sons,
> My story to begin;
> The tane was hight Haldane the strong,
> The tither was winsome Finn.

and so forth; which was still sung, with other "rimur," or ballads, in the Faroes, at the end of the last century. Professor Rafn has inserted it, because it talks of Vinland as a well-known place, and because the brothers are sent by the princess to slay American kings; but that Rime has another value. It is of a beauty so perfect, and yet so like the old Scotch ballads in its heroic conception of love, and in all its forms and its qualities, that it is one proof more, to any student of early European poetry, that we and these old Norsemen are men of the same blood.

If anything more important than is told by Professor Rafn and Mr. Black* be now known to the antiquarians of Massachusetts, let me entreat them to pardon my ignorance. But let me record my opinion that, though somewhat too much may have been made in past years of certain rock-inscriptions, and so forth, on this side of the Atlantic, there can be no reasonable doubt that our own race landed and tried to settle on the shore of New England six hundred years before their kinsmen, and, in many cases, their actual descendants, the august Pilgrim Fathers of the seventeenth century. And so, as I said, a Scandinavian dynasty might have been seated now upon the throne of Mexico. And how was that strange chance lost? First, of course, by the length and danger of the coasting voyage. It was one thing to have, like Columbus and Vespucci, Cortes and Pizarro, the Azores as a halfway port; another to have Greenland, or even Iceland. It was one thing to run south-west upon Columbus's track, across the Mar de Damas, the Ladies' Sea, which hardly knows a storm, with the blazing blue above, the blazing

* Black, translator of Mallett's "Northern Antiquities," Supplementary Chapter I., and Rafn's "Antiquitates Americanæ."

blue below, in an ever-warming climate, where every breath is life and joy; another to struggle against the fogs and icebergs, the rocks and currents of the dreary North Atlantic. No wonder, then, that the knowledge of Markland, and Vinland, and Whiteman's Land died away in a few generations, and became but fireside sagas for the winter nights.

But there were other causes, more honourable to the dogged energy of the Norse. They were in those very years conquering and settling nearer home as no other people—unless, perhaps, the old Ionian Greeks—conquered and settled.

Greenland, we have seen, they held—the western side at least—and held it long and well enough to afford, it is said, 2,600 pounds of walrus' teeth as yearly tithe to the Pope, besides Peter's pence, and to build many a convent, and church, and cathedral, with farms and homesteads round; for one saga speaks of Greenland as producing wheat of the finest quality. All is ruined now, perhaps by gradual change of climate.

But they had richer fields of enterprise than Greenland, Iceland, and the Faroes. Their boldest outlaws at that very time—whether from Norway, Sweden, Denmark, or Britain—were forming the imperial life-guard of the Byzantine Emperor, as the once famous Varangers of Constantinople; and that splendid epoch of their race was just dawning, of which my lamented friend, the late Sir Edmund Head, says so well in his preface to Viga Glum's Icelandic *Saga*, "The Sagas, of which this tale is one, were composed for the men who have left their mark in every corner of Europe; and whose language and laws are at this moment important elements in the speech and institutions of England, America, and Australia. There is no page of modern history in which the influence of the Norsemen and their conquests must not be taken into account—Russia, Constantinople, Greece, Palestine, Sicily, the coasts of Africa, Southern Italy, France, the Spanish Peninsula, England, Scotland, Ireland, and every rock and island round them, have been visited, and most of them at one time or the other ruled, by the men of Scandinavia. The motto on the sword of Roger Guiscard was a proud one:

Appulus et Calaber, Siculus mihi servit et Afer.

Every island, says Sir Edmund Head, and truly—for the name of almost every island on the coast of England, Scotland, and Eastern Ireland, ends in either *ey* or *ay* or *oe*, a Norse appellative, as is the word "island" itself—is a mark of its having been, at some time or other, visited by the Vikings of Scandinavia.

Norway, meanwhile, was convulsed by war; and what perhaps was of more immediate consequence, Svend Fork-beard, whom we Englishmen call Sweyn—the renegade from that Christian Faith which had been forced on him by his German conqueror, the Emperor Otto II.—with his illustrious son Cnut, whom we call Canute, were just calling together all the most daring spirits of the Baltic coasts for the subjugation of England; and when that great feat was performed, the Scandinavian emigration was paralysed, probably, for a time by the fearful wars at home. While the king of Sweden, and St. Olaf Tryggvason, king of Norway, were setting on Denmark during Cnut's pilgrimage to Rome, and Cnut, sailing with a mighty fleet to Norway, was driving St. Olaf into Russia, to return and fall in the fratricidal battle of Stiklestead—during, strangely enough, a total eclipse of the sun—Vinland was like enough to remain still uncolonised. After Cnut's short-lived triumph—king as he was of Denmark, Norway, England, and half Scotland, and what not of Wendish Folk inside the Baltic—the force of the Norsemen seems to have been exhausted in their native lands. Once more only, if I remember right, did "Lochlin," really and hopefully send forth her "mailed swarm" to conquer a foreign land; and with a result unexpected alike by them and by their enemies. Had it been otherwise, we might not have been here this day.

Let me sketch for you once more—though you have heard it, doubtless, many a time—the tale of that tremendous fortnight which settled the fate of Britain, and therefore of North America; which decided—just in those great times when the decision was to be made—whether we should be on a par with the other civilised nations of Europe, like them the "heirs of all the ages," with our share not only of Roman Christianity and Roman centralisation—a member of the great comity of European nations, held together in one Christian bond by the Pope—but heirs also of Roman civilisation, Roman literature, Roman Law; and therefore, in due time, of Greek philosophy and art. No less a question than this, it seems to me, hung in the balance during that fortnight of autumn, 1066.

Poor old Edward the Confessor, holy, weak, and sad, lay in his new choir of Westminster—where the wicked ceased from troubling, and the weary were at rest. The crowned ascetic had left no heir behind. England seemed as a corpse, to which all the eagles might gather together; and the South-English, in their utter need, had chosen for their king the ablest, and it may be the justest, man in Britain—Earl Harold Godwinsson: himself, like half the upper classes of England then, of the all-dominant Norse blood; for his mother was a Danish princess. Then out of Norway, with a mighty host, came Harold Hardraade, taller than all men, the ideal Viking of his time. Half-brother of the now dead St. Olaf, severely wounded when he was but fifteen, at Stiklestead, when Olaf fell, he had warred and plundered on many a coast. He had been away to Russia to King Jaroslaf; he had been in the Emperor's Varanger guard at Constantinople—and, it was whispered, had slain a lion there with his bare hands; he had carved his name and his comrades' in Runic characters—if you go to Venice you may see them at this day—on the loins of the great marble lion, which stood in his time not in Venice but in Athens. And now, king of Norway and conqueror, for the time, of Denmark, why should he not take England, as Sweyn and Canute took it sixty years before, when the flower of the English gentry perished at the fatal battle of Assingdune? If he and his half-barbarous host had conquered, the civilisation of Britain would have been thrown back, perhaps, for centuries. But it was not to be.

England *was* to be conquered by the Norman; but by the civilised, not the barbaric; by the Norse who had settled, but four generations before, in the North East of France under Rou, Rollo, Rolf the Ganger—so-called, they say, because his legs were so long that, when on horseback, he touched the ground and seemed to gang, or walk. He and his Norsemen had taken their share of France, and called it Normandy to this day; and meanwhile, with that docility and adaptability which marks so often truly great spirits, they had changed their creed, their language, their habits, and had become, from heathen and murderous Berserkers, the most truly civilised people of Europe, and—as was most natural then—the most faithful allies and servants of the Pope of Rome. So greatly had they changed, and so fast, that William Duke of Normandy, the great-great-grandson of Rolf the wild Viking, was perhaps the finest gentleman, as well as the most cultivated sovereign, and the greatest statesman and warrior in all Europe.

So Harold of Norway came with all his Vikings to Stamford Bridge by York; and took, by coming, only that which Harold of England promised him, namely, "forasmuch as he was taller than any other man, seven feet of English ground."

The story of that great battle, told with a few inaccuracies, but told as only great poets tell, you should read, if you have not read it already, in the "Heimskringla" of Snorri Sturluson, the Homer of the North:

> High feast that day held the birds of the air and
>   the beasts of the field,
> White-tailed erne and sallow glede,
> Dusky raven, with horny neb,
> And the gray deer the wolf of the wood.

The bones of the slain, men say, whitened the place for fifty years to come.

And remember, that on the same day on which

that fight befell—September 27, 1066—William, Duke of Normandy, with all his French-speaking Norsemen, was sailing across the British Channel, under the protection of a banner consecrated by the Pope, to conquer that England which the Norse-speaking Normans could not conquer.

And now King Harold showed himself a man. He turned at once from the North of England to the South. He raised the folk of the Southern, as he had raised those of the Central and Northern shires; and in sixteen days—after a march which in those times was a prodigious feat—he was entrenched upon the fatal down which men called Heathfield then, and Senlac, but Battle to this day—with William and his French Normans opposite him on Telham hill.

Then came the battle of Hastings. You all know what befell upon that day; and how the old weapon was matched against the new—the English axe against the Norman lance—and beaten only because the English broke their ranks. If you wish to refresh your memories, read the tale once more in Mr. Freeman's "History of England," or Professor Creasy's "Fifteen Decisive Battles of the World," or even, best of all, the late Lord Lytton's splendid romance of "Harold." And when you go to England, go, as some of you may have gone already, to Battle; and there from off the Abbey grounds, or from Mountjoye behind, look down off what was then "The Heathy Field," over the long slopes of green pasture and the rich hop-gardens, where were no hop-gardens then, and the flat tide-marshes winding between the wooded heights, towards the southern sea; and imagine for yourselves the feelings of an Englishman as he contemplates that broad green sloping lawn, on which was decided the destiny of his native land. Here, right beneath, rode Taillefer up the slope before them all, singing the song of Roland, tossing his lance in air and catching it as it fell, with all the Norse berserker spirit of his ancestors flashing out in him, at the thought of one fair fight, and then purgatory, or Valhalla—Taillefer perhaps preferred the latter. Yonder on the left, in that copse where the red-ochre gully runs, is Sanguelac, the drain of blood, into which (as the Bayeux tapestry, woven by Matilda's maids, still shows) the Norman knights fell, horse and man, till the gully was bridged with writhing bodies for those who rode after. Here, where you stand—the crest of the hill marks where it must have been—was the stockade on which depended the fate of England. Yonder, perhaps, stalked out one English squire or house-carle after another: tall men with long-handled battle-axes—one specially terrible, with a wooden helmet which no sword could pierce—who hewed and hewed down knight on knight, till they themselves were borne to earth at last. And here, among the trees and ruins of the garden, kept trim by those who know the treasure which they own, stood Harold's two standards of the fighting-man and the dragon of Wessex. And here, close by (for here, for many a century, stood the high altar of Battle Abbey, where monks sang masses for Harold's soul), upon this very spot the Swan-neck found her hero-lover's corpse. "Ah," says many an Englishman —and who will blame him for it—"how grand to have died beneath that standard on that day!" Yes, and how right. And yet how right, likewise, that the Norman's cry of *Dexaie!*—"God Help!"—and not the

English hurrah, should have won that day, till William rode up Mountjoye in the afternoon to see the English army, terrible even in defeat, struggling through copse and marsh away toward Brede, and, like retreating lions driven into their native woods, slaying more in the pursuit than they slew even in the fight.

But so it was to be; for so it ought to have been. You, my American friends, delight, as I have said already, in seeing the old places of the old country. Go, I beg you, and look at that old place, and if you be wise, you will carry back from it one lesson: That God's thoughts are not as our thoughts; nor His ways as our ways.

It was a fearful time which followed. I cannot but believe that our forefathers had been, in some way or other, great sinners, or two such conquests as Canute's and William's would not have fallen on them within the short space of sixty years. They did not want for courage, as Stamford Brigg and Hastings showed full well. English swine, their Norman conquerors called them often enough; but never English cowards. Their ruinous vice, if we are to trust the records of the time, was what the old monks called accidia—*ἀκηδία*—and ranked it as one of the seven deadly sins: a general careless, sleepy, comfortable habit of mind, which lets all go its way for good or evil—a habit of mind too often accompanied, as in the case of the Anglo-Danes, with self-indulgence, often coarse enough. Huge eaters and huger drinkers, fuddled with ale, were the men who went down at Hastings—though they went down like heroes—before the staid and sober Norman out of France.

But those were fearful times. As long as William

lived, ruthless as he was to all rebels, he kept order and did justice with a strong and steady hand; for he brought with him from Normandy the instincts of a truly great statesman. And in his sons' time matters grew worse and worse. After that, in the troubles of Stephen's reign, anarchy let loose tyranny in its most fearful form, and things were done which recall the cruelties of the old Spanish *conquistadores* in America. Scott's charming romance of "Ivanhoe" must be taken, I fear, as a too true picture of English society in the time of Richard I.

And what came of it all? What was the result of all this misery and wrong?

This, paradoxical as it may seem: That the Norman conquest was the making of the English people; of the Free Commons of England.

Paradoxical, but true. First, you must dismiss from your minds the too common notion that there is now, in England, a governing Norman aristocracy, or that there has been one, at least since the year 1215, when Magna Charta was won from the Norman John by Normans and by English alike. For the first victors at Hastings, like the first *conquistadores* in America, perished, as the monk chronicles point out, rapidly by their own crimes; and very few of our nobility can trace their names back to the authentic Battle Abbey roll. The great majority of the peers have sprung from, and all have intermarried with, the Commons; and the peerage has been from the first, and has become more and more as centuries have rolled on, the prize of success in life.

The cause is plain. The conquest of England by the Normans was not one of those conquests of a savage by a civilised race, or of a cowardly race by a brave race, which results in the slavery of the conquered, and leaves the gulf of caste between two races—master and slave. That was the case in France, and resulted, after centuries of oppression, in the great and dreadful revolution of 1793, which convulsed not only France but the whole civilised world. But caste, thank God, has never existed in England, since at least the first generation after the Norman conquest.

The vast majority, all but the whole population of England, have been always free; and free, as they are not where caste exists to change their occupations. They could intermarry, if they were able men, into the ranks above them; as they could sink, if they were unable men, into the ranks below them. Any man acquainted with the origin of our English surnames may verify this fact for himself, by looking at the names of a single parish or a single street of shops. There, jumbled together, he will find names marking the noblest Saxon or Angle blood—Kenward or Kenric, Osgood or Osborne, side by side with Cordery or Banister—now names of farmers in my own parish—or other Norman-French names which may be, like those two last, in Battle Abbey roll—and side by side the almost ubiquitous Brown, whose ancestor was probably some Danish or Norwegian house-carle, proud of his name Biorn the Bear, and the ubiquitous Smith or Smythe, the Smiter, whose forefather, whether he be now peasant or peer, assuredly handled the tongs and hammer at his own forge. This holds true equally in New England and in Old. When I search through (as I delight to do) your New England surnames, I find the same jumble of names—West Saxon, Angle, Danish, Norman, and French-Norman likewise, many of primæval and heathen antiquity, many of high nobility, all worked together, as at home, to form the Free Commoners of England.

If any should wish to know more on this curious and important subject, let me recommend them to study Ferguson's "Teutonic Name System," a book from which you will discover that some of our quaintest, and seemingly most plebeian surnames—many surnames, too, which are extinct in England, but remain in America—are really corruptions of good old Teutonic names, which our ancestors may have carried in the German Forest, before an Englishman set foot on British soil; from which he will rise with the comfortable feeling that we English-speaking men, from the highest to the lowest, are literally kinsmen. Nay, so utterly made up now is the old blood-feud between Norseman and Englishman, between the descendants of those who conquered and those who were conquered, that in the children of our Prince of Wales, after 800 years, the blood of William of Normandy is mingled with the blood of the very Harold who fell at Hastings. And so, by the bitter woes which followed the Norman conquest was the whole population, Dane, Angle, and Saxon, earl and churl, freeman and slave, crushed and welded together into one homogeneous mass, made just and merciful towards each other by the most wholesome of all teachings, a community of suffering; and if they had been, as I fear they were, a lazy and a sensual people, were taught

> That life is not as idle ore,
> But heated hot with burning fears,
> And bathed in baths of hissing tears,
> And battered with the strokes of doom
> To shape and use.

But how did these wild Vikings become Christian men? It is a long story. So stanch a race was sure to be converted only very slowly. Noble missionaries as Ansgar, Rembert, and Poppo, had worked for 150 years and more among the heathens of Denmark. But the patriotism of the Norseman always recoiled, even though in secret, from the fact that they were German monks, backed by the authority of the German emperor; and many a man, like Svend Fork-beard, father of the great Canute, though he had the Kaiser himself for godfather, turned heathen once more the moment he was free, because his baptism was the badge of foreign conquest, and neither pope nor kaiser should lord it over him, body or soul. St. Olaf, indeed, forced Christianity on the Norse at the sword's point, often by horrid cruelties, and perished in the attempt. But who forced it on the Norsemen of Scotland, England, Ireland, Neustria, Russia, and all the Eastern Baltic? It was absorbed and in most cases, I believe, gradually and willingly, as a gospel and good news to hearts worn out with the storm of their own passions. And whence came their Christianity? Much of it, as in the case of the Danes, and still more of the French Normans, came direct from Rome, the city which, let them defy its influence as they would, was still the fount of all theology, as well as of all civilisation. But I must believe that much of it came from that mysterious ancient Western Church, the Church of St. Patric, St. Bridget, St. Columba, which had covered with rude cells and chapels the rocky islets of the North Atlantic, even to Iceland itself. Even to Iceland; for when that island was first discovered, about A.D. 840, the Norsemen found in an isle, on the east and west and elsewhere, Irish books and bells and wooden crosses, and named that island Papey, the isle of the popes—some little colony of monks, who lived by fishing, and who are said to have left the land when the Norsemen settled in it. Let us believe, for it is consonant with reason and experience, that the sight of those poor monks, plundered and massacred again and again by the "mailed swarms of Lochlin," yet never exterminated, but springing up again in the same place, ready for fresh massacre, a sacred plant which God had planted, and which no rage of man could trample out—let us believe, I say, that that sight taught at last to the buccaneers of the old world that there was a purer manliness, a loftier heroism, than the ferocious self-assertion of the Berserker, even the heroism of humility, gentleness, self-restraint, self-sacrifice; that there was a strength which was made perfect in weakness; a glory, not of the sword but of the cross. We will believe that that was the lesson which the Norsemen learnt, after many a wild and blood-stained voyage, from the monks of Iona or of Derry, which caused the building of such churches as that which Sightrys, king of Dublin, raised about the year 1030, not in the Norse but in the Irish quarter of Dublin: a sacred token of amity between the new settlers and the natives on the ground of a common faith. Let us believe, too, that the influence of woman was not wanting in the good work—that the story of St. Margaret and Malcolm Canmore was repeated, though inversely, in the case of many a heathen Scandinavian jarl, who, marrying the princely daughter of some Scottish chieftain, found in her creed at last something more precious than herself; while his brother or his cousin became, at Dublin or

Wexford or Waterford, the husband of some saffron-robed Irish princess, "fair as an elf," as the old saying was; some "maiden of the three transcendent hues," of whom the old book of Linane says:

> Red as the blood which flowed from stricken deer,
> White as the snow on which that blood ran down,
> Black as the raven who drank up that blood;

—and possibly, as in the case of Brian Boru's mother, had given his fair-haired sister in marriage to some Irish prince, and could not resist the spell of their new creed, and the spell too, it may be, of some sister of theirs who had long given up all thought of earthly marriage to tend the undying fire of St. Bridget among the consecrated virgins of Kildare.

I am not drawing from mere imagination. That such things must have happened, and happened again and again, is certain to anyone who knows, even superficially, the documents of that time. And I doubt not that, in manners as well as in religion, the Norse were humanised and civilised by their contact with the Celts, both in Scotland and in Ireland. Both peoples had valour, intellect, imagination: but the Celt had that which the burly angular Norse character, however deep and stately, and however humorous, wanted; namely, music of nature, tenderness, grace, rapidity, playfulness; just the qualities, combining with the Scandinavian (and in Scotland with the Angle) elements of character which have produced, in Ireland and in Scotland, two schools of lyric poetry second to none in the world.

And so they were converted to what was then a dark and awful creed; a creed of ascetic self-torture and purgatorial fires for those who escape the still more dreadful, because endless, doom of the rest of the human race. But, because it was a sad creed, it suited better, men who had, when conscience re-awakened in them, but too good reason to be sad; and the minsters and cloisters which sprang up over the whole of Northern Europe, and even beyond it, along the dreary western shores of Greenland itself, are the symbols of a splendid repentance for their own sins and for the sins of their forefathers.

Gudruna herself, of whom I spoke just now, one of those old Norse heroines who helped to discover America, though a historic personage, is a symbolic one likewise, and the pattern of a whole class. She, too, after many journeys to Iceland, Greenland, and Winland, goes on a pilgrimage to Rome, to get, I presume, absolution from the Pope himself for all the sins of her strange, rich, stormy, wayward life.

Have you not read—many of you surely have—La Motte Fouqué's romance of "Sintram?" It embodies all that I would say. It is the spiritual drama of that early Middle Age; very sad, morbid if you will, but true to fact. The Lady Verena ought not, perhaps, to desert her husband, and shut herself up in a cloistor. But so she would have done in those old days. And who shall judge her harshly for so doing? When the brutality of the man seems past all cure, who shall blame the woman if she glides away into some atmosphere of peace and purity, to pray for him whom neither warnings nor caresses will amend? It is a sad book, "Sintram." And yet not too sad. For they were a sad people, those old Norse forefathers of ours. Their Christianity was sad; their minsters sad; there are few sadder, though few grander, buildings than a Norman church.

And yet, perhaps, their Christianity did not make them sad. It was but the other and the healthier side of that sadness which they had as heathens. Read which you will of the old sagas—heathen or half-Christian—the Eyrbiggia, Viga Glum, Burnt Niall, Grettir the Strong, and, above all, Snorri Sturluson's "Heimskringla" itself—and you will see at once how sad they are. There is, in the old sagas, none of that enjoyment of life which shines out everywhere in Greek poetry, even through its deepest tragedies. Not in complacency with Nature's beauty, but in the fierce struggle with her wrath, does the Norseman feel pleasure. Nature to him was not, as in Mr. Longfellow's exquisite poem,* the kind old nurse, to take him on her knee and whisper to him, ever anew, the story without an end. She was a weird witch-wife, mother of storm demons and frost giants, who must be fought with steadily, warily, wearily, over dreary heaths and snow-capped fells, and rugged nesses and tossing sounds, and away into the boundless sea—or who could live?—till he got hardened in the fight into ruthlessness of need and greed. The poor strip of flat strath, ploughed and re-ploughed again in the short summer days, would yield no more; or wet harvests spoiled the crops, or heavy snows starved the cattle. And so the Norseman launched his ships when the lands were sown in spring, and went forth to pillage or to trade, as luck would have, to summerted, as he himself called it; and came back, if he ever came, in autumn to the women to help at harvest-time, with blood upon his hand. But had he stayed at home, blood would have been there still. Three out of four of them had been

* On the Fiftieth Birthday of Agassiz.

mixed up in some man-slaying, or had some blood-feud to avenge among their own kin.

The whole of Scandinavia, Denmark, Sweden, Norway, Orkney, and the rest, remind me ever of that terrible picture of the great Norse painter, Tiddeman, in which two splendid youths, lashed together, in true Norse duel fashion by the waist, are hewing each other to death with the short axe, about some hot words over their ale. The loss of life, and that of the most gallant of the young, in those days must have been enormous. If the vitality of the race had not been even more enormous, they must have destroyed each other, as the Red Indians have done, off the face of the earth. They lived these Norsemen, not to live—they lived to die. For what cared they? Death—what was death to them? what it was to the Jomsburger Viking, who, when led out to execution, said to the headsman: "Die! with all pleasure. We used to question in Jomsburg whether a man felt when his head was off? Now I shall know; but if I do, take care, for I shall smite thee with my knife. And meanwhile, spoil not this long hair of mine; it is so beautiful."

But, oh! what waste! What might not these men have done if they had sought peace, not war; if they had learned a few centuries sooner to do justly, and love mercy, and walk humbly with their God?

And yet one loves them, blood-stained as they are. Your own poets, men brought up under circumstances, under ideas the most opposite to theirs, love them, and cannot help it. And why? It is not merely for their bold daring, it is not merely for their stern endurance; nor again that they had in them that shift and thrift, those steady and common-sense business habits, which made their noblest men not ashamed to go on voyages of merchandise. Nor is it, again, that grim humour—humour as of the modern Scotch—which so often flashes out into an actual jest, but more usually underlies unspoken all their deeds. Is it not rather that these men are our forefathers? that their blood runs in the veins of perhaps three men out of four in any general assembly, whether in America or in Britain? Startling as the assertion may be, I believe it to be strictly true.

Be that as it may, I cannot read the stories of your western men, the writings of Bret Harte, or Colonel John Hay, for instance, without feeling at every turn that there are the old Norse alive again, beyond the very ocean which they first crossed, 850 years ago.

Let me try to prove my point, and end with a story, as I began with one.

It is just thirty years before the Norman conquest of England, the evening of the battle of Sticklestead. St. Olaf's corpse is still lying unburied on the hillside. The reforming and Christian king has fallen in the attempt to force Christianity and despotism on the Conservative and half-heathen party—the free bonders or yeoman-farmers of Norway. Thormod, his poet—the man, as his name means, of thunder mood—who has been standing in the ranks, at last has an arrow in his left side. He breaks off the shaft, and thus sore wounded goes up, when all is lost, to a farm where is a great barn full of wounded. One Kimbe comes, a man out of the opposite or bonder part. "There is great howling and screaming in there," he says. "King Olaf's men fought bravely enough: but it is a shame brisk young lads cannot bear their wounds. On what side wert thou in the fight?" "On the best side," says the beaten Thormod. Kimbe sees that

Thormod has a good bracelet on his arm. "Thou art surely a king's man. Give me thy gold ring and I will hide thee, ere the bonders kill thee."

Thormod said, "Take it, if thou canst get it. I have lost that which is worth more;" and he stretched out his left hand, and Kimbe tried to take it. But Thormod, swinging his sword, cut off his hand; and it is said Kimbe behaved no better over his wound than those he had been blaming.

Then Thormod went into the barn; and after he had sung his song there in praise of his dead king, he went into an inner room, where was a fire, and water warming, and a handsome girl binding up men's wounds. And he sat down by the door; and one said to him, "Why art thou so dead pale? Why dost thou not call for the leech?" Then sung Thormod:

> "I am not blooming; and the fair
> And slender maiden loves to care
> For blooming youths. Few care for me,
> With Fenri's gold meal I can't fee;"

and so forth, improvising after the old Norse fashion.

Then Thormod got up and went to the fire, and stood and warmed himself. And the nurse-girl said to him, "Go out, man, and bring some of the split-firewood which lies outside the door." He went out and brought an armful of wood and threw it down. Then the nurse-girl looked him in the face, and said, "Dreadful pale is this man. Why art thou so?" Then sang Thormod:

> "Thou wonderest, sweet bloom, at me,
> A man so hideous to see.
> The arrow-drift o'ertook me, girl,
> A fine-ground arrow in the whirl
> Went through me, and I feel the dart
> Sits, lovely lass, too near my heart."

The girl said, "Let me see thy wound." Then Thormod sat down, and the girl saw his wounds, and that which was in his side, and saw that there was a piece of iron in it; but could not tell where it had gone. In a stone pot she had leeks and other herbs, and boiled them, and gave the wounded man of it to eat. But Thormod said, "Take it away; I have no appetite now for my broth." Then she took a great pair of tongs and tried to pull out the iron; but the wound was swelled, and there was too little to lay hold of. Now said Thormod, "Cut in so deep that thou canst get at the iron, and give me the tongs." She did as he said. Then took Thormod the gold bracelet off his hand and gave it the nurse-girl, and bade her do with it what she liked.

"It is a good man's gift," said he. "King Olaf gave me the ring this morning."

Then Thormod took the tongs and pulled the iron out. But on the iron was a barb, on which hung flesh from the heart, some red, some white. When he saw that, he said, "The king has fed us well. I am fat, even to the heart's roots." And so leant back and was dead.

CYRUS, THE SERVANT OF THE LORD.

CYRUS, THE SERVANT OF THE LORD.*

I WISH to speak to you to-night about one of those old despotic empires which were in every case the earliest known form of civilisation. Were I minded to play the cynic or the mountebank, I should choose some corrupt and effete despotism, already grown weak and ridiculous by its decay—as did at last the Roman and then the Byzantine Empire—and, after raising a laugh at the expense of the old system say: See what a superior people you are now—how impossible, under free and enlightened institutions, is anything so base and so absurd as went on, even in despotic France before the Revolution of 1793. Well, that would be on the whole true, thank God; but what need is there to say it?

Let us keep our scorn for our own weaknesses, our blame for our own sins, certain that we shall gain more instruction, though not more amusement, by hunting out the good which is in anything than by hunting out its evil. I have chosen, not the worst, but the best despotism which I could find in history, founded and ruled by a truly heroic personage,

* This lecture was given in America in 1874.

one whose name has become a proverb and a legend, that so I might lift up your minds, even by the contemplation of an old Eastern empire, to see that it, too, could be a work and ordinance of God, and its hero the servant of the Lord. For we are almost bound to call Cyrus, the founder of the Persian Empire, by this august title for two reasons—First, because the Hebrew Scriptures call him so; the next, because he proved himself to be such by his actions and their consequences—at least in the eyes of those who believe, as I do, in a far-seeing and far-reaching Providence, by which all human history is

> Bound by gold chains unto the throne of God.

His work was very different from any that need be done, or can be done, in these our days. But while we thank God that such work is now as unnecessary as impossible; we may thank God likewise that, when such work was necessary and possible, a man was raised up to do it: and to do it, as all accounts assert, better, perhaps, than it had ever been done before or since.

True, the old conquerors, who absorbed nation after nation, tribe after tribe, and founded empires on their ruins, are now, I trust, about to be replaced, throughout the world, as here and in Britain at home, by free self-governed peoples:

> The old order changeth, giving place to the new;
> And God fulfils Himself in many ways,
> Lest one good custom should corrupt the world.

And that custom of conquest and empire and transplantation did more than once corrupt the world. And yet in it, too, God may have more than once fulfilled

His own designs, as He did, if Scripture is to be believed, in Cyrus, well surnamed the Great, the founder of the Persian Empire some 2400 years ago. For these empires, it must be remembered, did at least that which the Roman Empire did among a scattered number of savage tribes, or separate little races, hating and murdering each other, speaking different tongues, and worshipping different gods, and losing utterly the sense of a common humanity, till they looked on the people who dwelt in the next valley as fiends, to be sacrificed, if caught, to their own fiends at home. Among such as these, empires did introduce order, law, common speech, common interest, the notion of nationality and humanity. They, as it were, hammered together the fragments of the human race till they had moulded them into one. They did it cruelly, clumsily, ill: but was there ever work done on earth, however noble, which was not—alas, alas!—done somewhat ill?

Let me talk to you a little about the old hero. He and his hardy Persians should be specially interesting to us. For in them first does our race, the Aryan race, appear in authentic history. In them first did our race give promise of being the conquering and civilising race of the future world. And to the conquests of Cyrus—so strangely are all great times and great movements of the human family linked to each other—to his conquests, humanly speaking, is owing the fact that you are here, and I am speaking to you at this moment.

It is an oft-told story: but so grand a one that I must sketch it for you, however clumsily, once more.

In that mountain province called Farsistan, north-east of what we now call Persia, the dwelling-place of the Persians, there dwelt, in the sixth and seventh centuries before Christ, a hardy tribe, of the purest blood of Iran, a branch of the same race as the Celtic, Teutonic, Greek, and Hindoo, and speaking a tongue akin to theirs. They had wandered thither, say their legends, out of the far north-east, from off some lofty plateau of Central Asia, driven out by the increasing cold, which left them but two months of summer to ten of winter.

They despised at first—would that they had despised always!—the luxurious life of the dwellers in the plains, and the effeminate customs of the Medes—a branch of their own race who had conquered and intermarried with the Turanian, or Finnish tribes; and adopted much of their creed, as well as of their morals, throughout their vast but short-lived Median Empire. "Soft countries," said Cyrus himself—so runs the tale—"gave birth to small men. No region produced at once delightful fruits and men of a war-like spirit." Letters were to them, probably, then unknown. They borrowed them in after years, as they borrowed their art, from Babylonians, Assyrians, and other Semitic nations whom they conquered. From the age of five to that of twenty, their lads were instructed but in two things—to speak the truth and to shoot with the bow. To ride was the third necessary art, introduced, according to Xenophon, after they had descended from their mountain fastnesses to conquer the whole East.

Their creed was simple enough. Ahura Mazda—Ormuzd, as he has been called since—was the one eternal Creator, the source of all light and life and good. He spake his word, and it accomplished the creation of heaven, before the water, before the earth, before the cow, before the tree, before the fire, before man the truthful, before the Devas and beasts of prey, before the whole existing universe ; before every good thing created by Ahura Mazda and springing from Truth.

He needed no sacrifices of blood. He was to be worshipped only with prayers, with offerings of the inspiring juice of the now unknown herb Homa, and by the preservation of the sacred fire, which, understand, was not he, but the symbol—as was light and the sun—of the good spirit—of Ahura Mazda. They had no images of the gods, these old Persians; no temples, no altars, so says Herodotus, and considered the use of them a sign of folly. They were, as has been well said of them, the Puritans of the old world. When they descended from their mountain fastnesses, they became the iconoclasts of the old world; and the later Isaiah, out of the depths of national shame, captivity, and exile, saw in them brother-spirits, the chosen of the Lord, whose hero Cyrus, the Lord was holding by His right hand, till all the foul superstitions and foul effeminacies of the rotten Semitic peoples of the East, and even of Egypt itself, should be crushed, though, alas! only for awhile, by men who felt that they had a commission from the God of light and truth and purity, to sweep out all that with the besom of destruction.

But that was a later inspiration. In earlier, and it may be happier, times the duty of the good man was to strive against all evil, disorder, uselessness, incompetence in their more simple forms. "He therefore is a holy man," says Ormuzd in the Zend-avesta, "who has built a dwelling on the earth, in which he maintains fire, cattle, his wife, his children, and flocks and herds; he who makes the earth produce barley, he who cultivates the fruits of the soil, cultivates purity; he advances the law of Ahura Mazda as much as if he had offered a hundred sacrifices."

To reclaim the waste, to till the land, to make a corner of the earth better than they found it, was to these men to rescue a bit of Ormuzd's world out of the usurped dominion of Ahriman; to rescue it from the spirit of evil and disorder for its rightful owner, the Spirit of Order and of Good.

For they believed in an evil spirit, these old Persians. Evil was not for them a lower form of good. With their intense sense of the difference between right and wrong it could be nothing less than hateful; to be attacked, exterminated, as a personal enemy, till it became to them at last impersonate and a person.

Zarathustra, the mystery of evil, weighed heavily on them and on their great prophet, Zoroaster—splendour of gold, as I am told his name signifies—who lived, no man knows clearly when or clearly where, but who lived and lives for ever, for his works follow him. He, too, tried to solve for his people the mystery of evil; and if he did not succeed, who has succeeded yet? Warring against Ormuzd, Ahura Mazda, was Ahriman, Angra Mainyus, literally the being of an evil mind, the ill-conditioned being. He was labouring perpetually to spoil the good work of Ormuzd alike in nature and in man. He was the cause of the fall of man, the tempter, the author of misery and death; he was eternal and uncreate as Ormuzd was. But that, perhaps, was a corruption of the purer and older Zoroastrian creed. With it, if Ahriman were eternal in the past, he would not be eternal in the future. Somehow, somewhen, somewhere, in the day when three prophets—the increasing light, the increasing truth, and the existing truth—should arise and give to mankind the last three books of the Zend-avesta, and convert all mankind to the pure creed, then evil should be conquered, the creation become pure again, and Ahriman vanish for ever; and, meanwhile, every good man was to fight valiantly for Ormuzd, his true lord, against Ahriman and all his works.

Men who held such a creed, and could speak truth and draw the bow, what might they not do when the hour and the man arrived? They were not a *big* nation. No; but they were a *great* nation, even while they were eating barley-bread and paying tribute to their conquerors the Medes, in the sterile valleys of Farsistan.

And at last the hour and the man came. The story is half legendary—differently told by different authors. Herodotus has one tale, Xenophon another. The first, at least, had ample means of information. Astyages is the old shah of the Median Empire, then at the height of its seeming might and splendour and effeminacy. He has married his daughter, the Princess Mandane, to Cambyses, seemingly a vassal-king or prince of the pure Persian blood. One night the old man is troubled with a dream. He sees a vine spring from his daughter, which overshadows all Asia. He sends for the Magi to interpret; and they tell him that Mandane will have a son who will reign in his stead. Having sons of his own, and fearing for the succession, he sends for Mandane, and, when her child is born, gives it to Harpagus, one of his courtiers, to be slain. The courtier relents, and hands it over to a herdsman, to be exposed on the mountains. The herdsman relents in turn, and brings the babe up as his own child.

When the boy, who goes by the name of Agradates, is grown, he is at play with the other herdboys, and they choose him for a mimic king. Some he makes his guards, some he bids build houses, some carry his messages. The son of a Mede of rank refuses, and Agradates has him seized by his guards and chastised with the whip. The ancestral instincts of command and discipline are showing early in the lad.

The young gentleman complains to his father, the father to the old king, who of course sends for the herdsman and his boy. The boy answers in a tone so exactly like that in which Xenophon's Cyrus would have answered, that I must believe that both Xenophon's Cyrus and Herodotus's Cyrus (like Xenophon's Socrates and Plato's Socrates) are real pictures of a real character; and that Herodotus's story, though Xenophon says nothing of it, is true.

He has done nothing, the noble boy says, but what was just. He had been chosen king in play, because the boys thought him most fit. The boy whom he had chastised was one of those who chose him. All the rest obeyed: but he would not, till at last he got his due reward. "If I deserve punishment for that," says the boy, "I am ready to submit."

The old king looks keenly and wonderingly at the young king, whose features seem somewhat like his own. Likely enough in those days, when an Iranian noble or prince would have a quite different cast of complexion and of face from a Turanian herdsman. A suspicion crosses him; and by threats of torture he gets the truth from the trembling herdsman.

To the poor wretch's rapture the old king lets him go unharmed. He has a more exquisite revenge to take, and sends for Harpagus, who likewise confesses the truth. The wily old tyrant has naught but gentle words. It is best as it is. He has been very sorry himself for the child, and Mandane's reproaches had gone to his heart. "Let Harpagus go home and send his son to be a companion to the new-found prince. To-night there will be great sacrifices in honour of the child's safety, and Harpagus is to be a guest at the banquet."

Harpagus comes; and after eating his fill, is asked how he likes the king's meat? He gives the usual answer; and a covered basket is put before him, out of which he is to take—in Median fashion—what he likes. He finds in it the head and hands and feet of his own son. Like a true Eastern he shows no signs of horror. The king asks him if he knew what flesh he had been eating. He answers that he knew perfectly. That whatever the king did pleased him.

Like an Eastern courtier, he knew how to dissemble, but not to forgive, and bided his time. The Magi, to their credit, told Astyages that his dream had been fulfilled, that Cyrus—as we must now call the foundling prince—had fulfilled it by becoming a king in play, and the boy is let to go back to his father and his hardy Persian life. But Harpagus does not leave him alone, nor perhaps, do his own thoughts. He has wrongs to avenge on his grandfather. And it seems not altogether impossible to the young mountaineer.

He has seen enough of Median luxury to despise it and those who indulge in it. He has seen his own grandfather with his cheeks rouged, his eyelids stained with antimony, living a womanlike life, shut up from all his subjects in the recesses of a vast seraglio.

He calls together the mountain rulers; makes friends with Tigranes, an Armenian prince, a vassal of the Mede, who has his wrongs likewise to avenge. And the two little armies of foot-soldiers—the Persians had no cavalry—defeat the innumerable horsemen of the Mede, take the old king, keep him in honourable captivity, and so change, one legend says, in a single battle, the fortunes of the whole East.

And then begins that series of conquests of which we know hardly anything, save the fact that they were made. The young mountaineer and his playmates, whom he makes his generals and satraps, sweep onward towards the West, teaching their men the art of riding, till the Persian cavalry becomes more famous than the Median had been. They gather to them, as a snowball gathers in rolling, the picked youth of every tribe whom they overcome. They knit these tribes to them in loyalty and affection by that righteousness—that truthfulness and justice—for which Isaiah in his grandest lyric strains has made them illustrious to all time; which Xenophon has celebrated in like manner in that exquisite book of his—the "Cyropædia." The great Lydian kingdom of Crœsus—Asia Minor as we call it now—goes down before them. Babylon itself goes down, after that world-famed siege which ended in Belshazzar's feast; and when Cyrus died—still in the prime of life, the legends seem to say—he left a coherent and well-organised empire, which stretched from the Mediterranean to Hindostan.

So runs the tale, which to me, I confess, sounds probable and rational enough. It may not do so to you; for it has not to many learned men. They are inclined to "relegate it into the region of myth;" in plain English, to call old Herodotus a liar, or at least a dupe. What means those wise men can have at this distance of more than 2000 years, of knowing more about the matter than Herodotus, who lived within 100 years of Cyrus, I for myself cannot discover. And I say this without the least wish to disparage these hypercritical persons. For there are —and more there ought to be, as long as lies and superstitions remain on this earth—a class of thinkers who hold in just suspicion all stories which savour of the sensational, the romantic, even the dramatic. They know the terrible uses to which appeals to the fancy and the emotions have been applied, and are still applied to enslave the intellects, the consciences, the very bodies of men and women. They dread so much from experience the abuse of that formula, that "a thing is so beautiful it must be true," that they are inclined to reply: "Rather let us say boldly, it is so beautiful that it cannot be true. Let us mistrust, or even refuse to believe *à priori*, and at first sight, all startling, sensational, even poetic tales, and accept nothing as history, which is not as dull as the ledger of a dry-goods' store." But I think that experience, both in nature and in society, are against that ditch-water philosophy. The weather, being governed by laws, ought always to be equable and normal, and yet you have whirlwinds, droughts, thunderstorms. The share-market, being governed by laws, ought to be always equable and normal, and yet you have startling transactions, startling panics, startling disclosures, and a whole sensational romance of commercial crime and folly. Which of us has lived to be fifty years old, without having witnessed in private life sensation tragedies, alas! sometimes too fearful to be told, or at least sensational romances, which we shall take care not to tell, because we shall not be believed? Let the ditch-water philosophy say what it will, human life is not a ditch, but a wild and roaring river, flooding its banks, and eating out new channels with many a landslip. It is a strange world, and man, a strange animal, guided, it is true, usually by most commonplace motives; but, for that reason, ready and glad at times to escape from them and their dulness and baseness; to give vent, if but for a moment, in wild freedom, to that demoniac element, which, as Goethe says, underlies his nature and all nature; and to prefer for an hour, to the normal and respectable ditch-water, a bottle of champagne or even a carouse on fire-water, let the consequences be what they may.

How else shall we explain such a phenomenon as those old crusades? Were they undertaken for any purpose, commercial or other? Certainly not for lightening an overburdened population. Nay, is not the history of your own Mormons, and their exodus into the far West, one of the most startling instances which the world has seen for several centuries, of the unexpected and incalculable forces which lie hid in man? Believe me, man's passions, heated to igniting point, rather than his prudence cooled down to freezing point, are the normal causes of all great human movement. And a truer law of social science than any that political economists are wont to lay down, is that old *Dov' é la donna?* of the Italian judge, who used to ask, as a preliminary to every case, civil or criminal, which was brought before him, *Dov' é la donna?* "Where is the lady?" certain, like a wise old gentleman, that a woman was most probably at the bottom of the matter.

Strangeness? Romance? Did any of you ever read—if you have not you should read—Archbishop Whately's "Historic Doubts about the Emperor Napoleon the First"? Therein the learned and witty Archbishop proved, as early as 1819, by fair use of the criticism of Mr. Hume and the Sceptic School, that the whole history of the great Napoleon ought to be treated by wise men as a myth and a romance, that there is little or no evidence of his having existed at all; and that the story of his strange successes and strange defeats was probably invented by our Government in order to pander to the vanity of the English nation.

I will say this, which Archbishop Whately, in a late edition, foreshadows, wittily enough—that if one or two thousand years hence, when the history of the late Emperor Napoleon the Third, his rise and fall, shall come to be subjected to critical analysis by future Philistine historians of New Zealand or Australia, it will be proved by them to be utterly mythical, incredible, monstrous—and that all the more, the more the actual facts remain to puzzle their unimaginative brains. What will they make two thousand years hence, of the landing at Boulogne with the tame eagle? Will not that, and stranger facts still, but just as true, be relegated to the region of myth, with the dream of Astyages, and the young and princely herdsman playing at king over his fellow-slaves?

But enough of this. To me these bits of romance often seem the truest, as well as the most important portions of history.

When old Herodotus tells me how, King Astyages having guarded the frontier, Harpagus sent a hunter to young Cyrus with a fresh-killed hare, telling him to open it in private; and how, sewn up in it was the letter, telling him that the time to rebel was come, I am inclined to say, That must be true. It is so beneath the dignity of history, so quaint and unexpected, that it is all the more likely *not* to have been invented.

So with that other story—How young Cyrus, giving out that his grandfather had made him general of the Persians, summoned them all, each man with a sickle in his hand, into a prairie full of thorns, and bade them clear it in one day; and how when they, like loyal men, had finished, he bade them bathe, and next day he took them into a great meadow and feasted them with corn and wine, and all that his father's farm would yield, and asked them which day they liked best; and, when they answered as was to be expected, how he opened his parable and told them, "Choose, then, to work for the Persians like slaves, or to be free with me."

Such a tale sounds to me true. It has the very savour of the parables of the Old Testament; as have, surely, the dreams of the old Sultan, with which the tale begins. Do they not put us in mind of the dreams of Nebuchadnezzar, in the Book of Daniel?

Such stories are actually so beautiful that they are very likely to be true. Understand me, I only say likely; the ditch-water view of history is not all wrong. Its advocates are right in saying great historic changes are not produced simply by one great person, by one remarkable event. They have been preparing, perhaps for centuries. They are the result of numberless forces, acting according to laws, which might have been foreseen, and will be foreseen, when the science of History is more perfectly understood.

For instance, Cyrus could not have conquered the Median Empire at a single blow, if first that empire had not been utterly rotten; and next, if he and his handful of Persians had not been tempered and sharpened, by long hardihood, to the finest cutting edge.

Yes, there were all the materials for the catastrophe—the cannon, the powder, the shot. But to say that the Persians must have conquered the Medes, even if Cyrus had never lived, is to say, as too many philosophers seem to me to say, that, given cannon, powder, and shot, it will fire itself off some day if we only leave it alone long enough.

It may be so. But our usual experience of Nature and Fact is, that spontaneous combustion is a rare and exceptional phenomenon; that if a cannon is to be fired, someone must arise and pull the trigger. And I believe that in Society and Politics, when a great event is ready to be done, someone must come and do it—do it, perhaps, half unwittingly, by some single rash act—like that first fatal shot fired by an electric spark.

But to return to Cyrus and his Persians.

I know not whether the "Cyropædia" is much read in your schools and universities. But it is one of the books which I should like to see, either in a translation or its own exquisite Greek, in the hands of every young man. It is not all fact. It is but a historic romance. But it is better than history. It is an ideal book, like Sidney's "Arcadia" or Spenser's "Fairy Queen"—the ideal self-education of an ideal hero. And the moral of the book—ponder it well, all young men who have the chance or the hope of exercising authority among your fellow-men—the noble and most Christian moral of that heathen book is this: that the path to solid and beneficent influence over our fellow-men lies, not through brute force, not through cupidity, but through the highest morality; through justice, truthfulness, humanity, self-denial, modesty, courtesy, and all which makes man or woman lovely in the eyes of mortals or of God.

Yes, the "Cyropædia" is a noble book, about a noble personage. But I cannot forget that there are nobler words by far concerning that same noble personage, in the magnificent series of Hebrew Lyrics, which begins "Comfort ye, comfort ye, my people, saith the Lord"—in which the inspired poet, watching the rise of Cyrus and his Puritans, and the fall of Babylon, and the idolatries of the East, and the coming deliverance of his own countrymen, speaks of the Persian hero in words so grand that they have been often enough applied, and with all fitness, to one greater than Cyrus, and than all men:

> Who raised up the righteous man from the East,
> And called him to attend his steps?
> Who subdued nations at his presence,
> And gave him dominion over kings?
> And made them like the dust before his sword,
> And the driven stubble before his bow?
> He pursueth them, he passeth in safety,
> By a way never trodden before by his feet.
> Who hath performed and made these things,
> Calling the generations from the beginning?
> I, Jehovah, the first and the last, I am the same.
>
> Behold my servant, whom I will uphold;
> My chosen, in whom my soul delighteth;

I will make my spirit rest upon him,
And he shall publish judgment to the nations.
He shall not cry aloud, nor clamour,
Nor cause his voice to be heard in the streets.
The bruised reed he shall not break,
And the smoking flax he shall not quench.
He shall publish justice, and establish it.
His force shall not be abated, nor broken,
Until he has firmly seated justice in the earth,
And the distant nations shall wait for his Law.
Thus saith the God, even Jehovah,
Who created the heavens, and stretched them out;
Who spread abroad the earth, and its produce,
I, Jehovah, have called thee for a righteous end,
And I will take hold of thy hand, and preserve thee,
And I will give thee for a covenant to the people,
And for a light to the nations;
To open the eyes of the blind,
To bring the captives out of prison,
And from the dungeon those who dwell in darkness.
I am Jehovah—that is my name;
And my glory will I not give to another,
Nor my praise to the graven idols.

Who saith to Cyrus—Thou art my shepherd,
And he shall fulfil all my pleasure:
Who saith to Jerusalem—Thou shalt be built;
And to the Temple—Thou shalt be founded.
Thus saith Jehovah to his anointed,
To Cyrus whom I hold fast by his right hand,
That I may subdue nations under him,
And loose the loins of kings;
That I may open before him the two-leaved doors,
And the gates shall not be shut;
I will go before thee
And bring the mountains low.
The gates of brass will I break in sunder,
And the bars of iron hew down.
And I will give thee the treasures of darkness,
And the hoards hid deep in secret places,
That thou mayest know that I am Jehovah.

I have surnamed thee, though thou knowest not me.
I am Jehovah, and none else;
Beside me there is no God.
I will gird thee, though thou hast not known me,
That they may know from the rising of the sun,
And from the west, that there is none beside me;
I am Jehovah, and none else;
Forming light and creating darkness;
Forming peace, and creating evil.
I, Jehovah, make all these.

This is the Hebrew prophet's conception of the great Puritan of the Old World who went forth with such a commission as this, to destroy the idols of the East, while

The isles saw that, and feared,
And the ends of the earth were afraid;
They drew near, they came together;
Everyone helped his neighbour,
And said to his brother, Be of good courage.

The carver encouraged the smith,
He that smoothed with the hammer
Him that smote on the anvil;
Saying of the solder, It is good;
And fixing the idol with nails, lest it be moved;

But all in vain; for as the poet goes on:

Bel bowed down, and Nebo stooped;
Their idols were upon the cattle,
A burden to the weary beast.
They stoop, they bow down together;
They could not deliver their own charge;
Themselves are gone into captivity.

And what, to return, what was the end of the great Cyrus and of his empire?

Alas, alas! as with all human glory, the end was not as the beginning.

We are scarce bound to believe positively the story how Cyrus made one war too many, and was cut off in the Scythian deserts, falling before the arrows of mere savages; and how their queen, Tomyris, poured blood down the throat of the dead corpse, with the words, "Glut thyself with the gore for which thou hast thirsted." But it may be true—for Xenophon states it expressly, and with detail—that Cyrus, from the very time of his triumph, became an Eastern despot, a sultan or a shah, living apart from his people in mysterious splendour, in the vast fortified palace which he built for himself; and imitating and causing his nobles and satraps to imitate, in all but vice and effeminacy, the very Medes whom he had conquered. And of this there is no doubt—that his sons and their empire ran rapidly through that same vicious circle of corruption to which all despotisms are doomed, and became within 250 years, even as the Medes, the Chaldeans, the Lydians, whom they had conquered, children no longer of Ahura Mazda, but of Ahriman, of darkness and not of light, to be conquered by Alexander and his Greeks even more rapidly and more shamefully than they had conquered the East.

This is the short epic of the Persian Empire, ending, alas! as all human epics are wont to end, sadly, if not shamefully.

But let me ask you, Did I say too much, when I said, that to these Persians we owe that we are here to-night?

I do not say that without them we should not have been here. God, I presume, when He is minded to do anything, has more than one way of doing it.

But that we are now the last link in a chain of causes and effects which reaches as far back as the emigration of the Persians southward from the plateau of Pamir, we cannot doubt.

For see. By the fall of Babylon and its empire the Jews were freed from their captivity—large numbers of them at least—and sent home to their own Jerusalem. What motives prompted Cyrus, and Darius after him, to do that deed?

Those who like to impute the lowest motives may say, if they will, that Daniel and the later Isaiah found it politic to worship the rising sun, and flatter the Persian conquerors: and that Cyrus and Darius in turn were glad to see Jerusalem rebuilt, as an impregnable frontier fortress between them and Egypt. Be it so; I, who wish to talk of things noble, pure, lovely, and of good report, would rather point you once more to the magnificent poetry of the later Isaiah which commences at the 40th chapter of the Book of Isaiah, and say—There, upon the very face of the document, stands written the fact that the sympathy between the faithful Persian and the faithful Jew—the two puritans of the Old World, the two haters of lies, idolatries, superstitions, was actually as intense as it ought to have been, as it must have been.

Be that as it may, the return of the Jews to Jerusalem preserved for us the Old Testament, while it restored to them a national centre, a sacred city, like that of Delphi to the Greeks, Rome to the Romans, Mecca to the Muslim, loyalty to which prevented their being utterly absorbed by the more civilised Eastern races among whom they had been scattered abroad as colonies of captives.

Then another, and a seemingly needful link of cause and effect ensued: Alexander of Macedon destroyed the Persian Empire, and the East became

Greek, and Alexandria, rather than Jerusalem, became the head-quarters of Jewish learning. But for that very cause, the Scriptures were not left inaccessible to the mass of mankind, like the old Pehlevi liturgies of the Zend-avesta, or the old Sanscrit Vedas, in an obsolete and hieratic tongue, but were translated into, and continued in, the then all but world-wide Hellenic speech, which was to the ancient world what French is to the modern.

Then the East became Roman, without losing its Greek speech. And under the wide domination of that later Roman Empire—which had subdued and organised the whole known world, save the Parthian descendants of those old Persians, and our old Teutonic forefathers in their German forests and on their Scandinavian shores—that Divine book was carried far and wide, East and West, and South, from the heart of Abyssinia to the mountains of Armenia, and to the isles of the ocean, beyond Britain itself to Ireland and to the Hebrides.

And that book—so strangely coinciding with the old creed of the earlier Persians—that book, long misunderstood, long overlain by the dust, and overgrown by the parasitic fungi of centuries, that book it was which sent to these trans-Atlantic shores the founders of your great nation. That book gave them their instinct of Freedom, tempered by reverence for Law. That book gave them their hatred of idolatry; and made them not only say but act upon their own words, with these old Persians and with the Jewish prophets alike, Sacrifice and burnt offering thou wouldst not; Then said we, Lo, we come. In the volume of the book it is written of us, that we come to do thy will, O God. Yes, long and fantastic is the chain of causes and effects, which links you here to the old heroes who came down from Central Asia, because the land had grown so wondrous cold, that there were ten months of winter to two of summer; and when simply after warmth and life, and food for them and for their flocks, they wandered forth to found and help to found a spiritual kingdom.

And even in their migration, far back in these dim and mystic ages, have we found the earliest link of the long chain? Not so. What if the legend of the change of climate be the dim recollection of an enormous physical fact? What if it, and the gradual depopulation of the whole north of Asia, be owing, as geologists now suspect, to the slow and age-long uprise of the whole of Siberia, thrusting the warm Arctic sea farther and farther to the northward, and placing between it and the Highlands of Thibet an ever-increasing breadth of icy land, destroying animals, and driving whole races southward, in search of the summer and the sun?

What if the first link in the chain, as yet conceivable by man, should be the cosmic changes in the distribution of land and water, which filled the mouths of the Siberian rivers with frozen carcases of woolly mammoth and rhinoceros; and those again, doubt it not, of other revolutions, reaching back and back, and on and on, into the infinite unknown? Why not? For so are all human destinies

> Bound with gold chains unto the throne of God.

ANCIENT CIVILISATION.

ANCIENT CIVILISATION.*

THERE is a theory abroad in the world just now about the origin of the human race, which has so many patent and powerful physiological facts to support it that we must not lightly say that it is absurd or impossible; and that is, that man's mortal body and brain were derived from some animal and ape-like creature. Of that I am not going to speak now. My subject is: How this creature called man, from whatever source derived, became civilised, rational, and moral. And I am sorry to say that there is tacked on by many to the first theory, another which does not follow from it, and which has really nothing to do with it, and it is this: That man, with all his wonderful and mysterious aspirations, always unfulfilled yet always precious, at once his torment and his joy, his very hope of everlasting life; that man, I say, developed himself, unassisted, out of a state of primæval brutishness, simply by calculations of pleasure and pain, by observing what actions would pay in the long run and what would not; and so learnt to conquer his selfishness by a more refined and extended selfishness, and exchanged his brutality for worldli-

* This lecture was given in America in 1874.

ness, and then, in a few instances, his worldliness for next-worldliness. I hope I need not say that I do not believe this theory. If I did, I could not be a Christian, I think, nor a philosopher either. At least, if I thought that human civilisation had sprung from such a dunghill as that, I should, in honour to my race, say nothing about it, here or elsewhere.

Why talk of the shame of our ancestors? I want to talk of their honour and glory. I want to talk, if I talk at all, about great times, about noble epochs, noble movements, noble deeds, and noble folk; about times in which the human race—it may be through many mistakes, alas! and sin, and sorrow, and bloodshed—struggled up one step higher on those great stairs which, as we hope, lead upward towards the far-off city of God; the perfect polity, the perfect civilisation, the perfect religion, which is eternal in the heavens.

Of great men, then, and noble deeds I want to speak. I am bound to do so first, in courtesy to my hearers. For in choosing such a subject I took for granted a nobleness and greatness of mind in them which can appreciate and enjoy the contemplation of that which is lofty and heroic, and that which is useful indeed, though not to the purses merely or the mouths of men, but to their intellects and spirits; that highest philosophy which, though she can (as has been sneeringly said of her) bake no bread, she—and she alone, can at least do this—make men worthy to eat the bread which God has given them.

I am bound to speak on such subjects, because I have never yet met, or read of, the human company who did not require, now and then at least, being reminded of such times and such personages—of whatsoever things are just, pure, true, lovely, and of good report, if there be any manhood and any praise to think, as St. Paul bids us all, of such things, that we may keep up in our minds as much as possible a lofty standard, a pure ideal, instead of sinking to the mere selfish standard which judges all things, even those of the world to come, by profit and by loss, and into that sordid frame of mind in which a man grows to believe that the world is constructed of bricks and timber, and kept going by the price of stocks.

We are all tempted, and the easier and more prosperous we are, the more we are tempted, to fall into that sordid and shallow frame of mind. Sordid even when its projects are most daring, its outward luxuries most refined; and shallow, even when most acute, when priding itself most on its knowledge of human nature, and of the secret springs which, so it dreams, move the actions and make the history of nations and of men. All are tempted that way, even the noblest-hearted. *Adhæsit pavimento venter,* says the old psalmist. I am growing like the snake, crawling in the dust, and eating the dust in which I crawl. I try to lift up my eyes to the heavens, to the true, the beautiful, the good, the eternal nobleness which was before all time, and shall be still when time has passed away. But to lift up myself is what I cannot do. Who will help me? Who will quicken me? as our old English tongue has it. Who will give me life? The true, pure, lofty human life which I did *not* inherit from the primæval ape, which the ape-nature in me is for ever trying to stifle, and make me that which I know too well I could so easily become —a cunninger and more dainty-featured brute? Death itself, which seems at times so fair, is fair because even it may raise me up and deliver me from the burden of this animal and mortal body:

> 'Tis life, not death for which I pant;
> 'Tis life, whereof my nerves are scant;
> More life, and fuller, that I want.

Man? I am a man not by reason of my bones and muscles, nerves and brain, which I have in common with apes and dogs and horses. I am a man—thou art a man or woman—not because we have a flesh—God forbid! but because there is a spirit in us, a divine spark and ray, which nature did not give, and which nature cannot take away. And therefore, while I live on earth, I will live to the spirit, not to the flesh, that I may be, indeed, a *man*; and this same gross flesh, this animal ape-nature in me, shall be the very element in me which I will renounce, defy, despise; at least, if I am minded to be, not a merely higher savage, but a truly higher civilised man. Civilisation with me shall mean, not more wealth, more finery, more self-indulgence—even more æsthetic and artistic luxury; but more virtue, more knowledge, more self-control, even though I earn scanty bread by heavy toil; and when I compare the Cæsar of Rome or the great king, whether of Egypt, Babylon, or Persia, with the hermit of the Thebaid, starving in his frock of camel's hair, with his soul fixed on the ineffable glories of the unseen, and striving, however wildly and fantastically, to become an angel and not an ape, I will say the hermit, and not the Cæsar, is the civilised man.

There are plenty of histories of civilisation and theories of civilisation abroad in the world just now, and which profess to show you how the primæval savage has, or at least may have, become the civilised man. For my part, with all due and careful consideration, I confess I attach very little value to any of them: and for this simple reason that we have no facts. The facts are lost.

Of course, if you assume a proposition as certainly true, it is easy enough to prove that proposition to be true, at least to your own satisfaction. If you assert with the old proverb, that you may make a silk purse out of a sow's ear, you will be stupider than I dare suppose anyone here to be, if you cannot invent for yourselves all the intermediate stages of the transformation, however startling. And, indeed, if modern philosophers had stuck more closely to this old proverb, and its defining verb "make," and tried to show how some person or persons—let them be who they may—men, angels, or gods—made the sow's ear into the silk purse, and the savage into the sage—they might have pleaded that they were still trying to keep their feet upon the firm ground of actual experience. But while their theory is, that the sow's ear grew into a silk purse of itself, and yet unconsciously and without any intention of so bettering itself in life, why, I think that those who have studied the history which lies behind them, and the poor human nature which is struggling, and sinning, and sorrowing, and failing around them, and which seems on the greater part of this planet going downwards and not upwards, and by no means bettering itself, save in the increase of opera-houses, liquor-bars, and gambling-tables, and that which pertaineth thereto; then we, I think, may be excused if we say with the old Stoics—ἐπέχω—I withhold my judgment. I know nothing about the matter yet; and you, oh my imaginative though learned friends, know I suspect very little either.

> Eldest of things, Divine Equality:

so sang poor Shelley, and with a certain truth. For if, as I believe, the human race sprang from a single pair, there must have been among their individual descendants an equality far greater than any which has been known on earth during historic times. But that equality was at best the infantile innocence of the primary race, which faded away in the race as quickly, alas! as it does in the individual child. Divine—therefore it was one of the first blessings which man lost; one of the last, I fear, to which he will return; that to which civilisation, even at its best yet known, has not yet attained, save here and there for short periods; but towards which it is striving as an ideal goal, and, as I trust, not in vain.

The eldest of things which we see actually as history is not equality, but an already developed hideous inequality, trying to perpetuate itself, and yet by a most divine and gracious law, destroying itself by the very means which it uses to keep itself alive.

"There were giants in the earth in those days. And Nimrod began to be a mighty one in the earth"—

> A mighty hunter; and his game was man.

No; it is not equality which we see through the dim mist of bygone ages.

What we do see is—I know not whether you will think me superstitious or old-fashioned, but so I hold—very much what the earlier books of the Bible show us under symbolic laws. Greek histories, Roman histories, Egyptian histories, Eastern histories, inscriptions, national epics, legends, fragments of legends—in the New World as in the Old—all tell the same story. Not the story without an end, but the story without a beginning. As in the Hindoo cosmogony, the world stands on an elephant, and the elephant on a tortoise, and the tortoise on—what? No man knows. I do not know. I only assert deliberately, waiting, as Napoleon says, till the world come round to me, that the tortoise does not stand—as is held by certain anthropologists, some honoured by me, some personally dear to me—upon the savages who chipped flints and fed on mammoth and reindeer in North-Western Europe, shortly after the age of ice, a few hundred thousand years ago. These sturdy little fellows—the kinsmen probably of the Esquimaux and Lapps—could have been but the *avant-couriers*, or more probably the fugitives from the true mass of mankind—spreading northward from the Tropics into climes becoming, after the long catastrophe of the age of ice, once more genial enough to support men who knew what decent comfort was, and were strong enough to get the same, by all means fair or foul. No. The tortoise of the human race does not stand on a savage. The savage may stand on an ape-like creature. I do not say that he does not. I do not say that he does. I do not know; and no man knows. But at least I say that the civilised man and his world stand not upon creatures like to any savage now known upon the earth. For first, it seems to be most unlikely; and next, and more important to an inductive philosopher, there is no proof of it. I see no savages becoming really civilised men—that is, not merely men who will ape the outside of our so-called civilisation, even absorb a few of our ideas; not merely that; but truly civilised men who will think for themselves, invent for themselves, act for themselves; and when the sacred lamp of light and truth has been passed into their hands, carry it on unextinguished, and transmit it to their successors without running back every moment to get it relighted by those from whom they received it: and who are bound—remember that —patiently and lovingly to relight it for them; to give freely to all their fellow-men of that which God has given to them and to their ancestors; and let God, not man, be judge of how much the Red Indian or the Polynesian, the Caffre or the Chinese, is capable of receiving and of using.

Moreover, in history there is no record, absolutely no record, as far as I am aware, of any savage tribe civilising itself. It is a bold saying. I stand by my assertion: most happy to find myself confuted, even in a single instance; for my being wrong would give me, what I can have no objection to possess, a higher opinion than I have now, of the unassisted capabilities of my fellow-men.

But civilisation must have begun somewhen, somewhere, with some person, or some family, or some nation; and how did it begin?

I have said already that I do not know. But I have had my dream—like the philosopher—and as I have not been ashamed to tell it elsewhere, I shall not be ashamed to tell it here. And it is this:

What if the beginnings of true civilisation in this unique, abnormal, diseased, unsatisfied, incomprehensible, and truly miraculous and supernatural race we call man, had been literally, and in actual fact, miraculous and supernatural likewise? What if that be the true key to the mystery of humanity and its origin? What if the few first chapters of the most ancient and most sacred book should point, under whatever symbols, to the actual and the only possible origin of civilisation, the education of a man, or a family by beings of some higher race than man? What if the old Puritan doctrine of Election should be even of a deeper and wider application than divines have been wont to think? What if individuals, if peoples, have been chosen out from time to time for a special illumination, that they might be the lights of the earth, and the salt of the world? What if they have, each in their turn, abused that divine teaching to make themselves the tyrants, instead of the ministers, of the less enlightened? To increase the inequalities of nature by their own selfishness, instead of decreasing them, into the equality of grace, by their own self-sacrifice? What if the Bible after all was right, and even more right than we were taught to think?

So runs my dream. If, after I have confessed to it, you think me still worth listening to, in this enlightened nineteenth century, I will go on.

At all events, what we see at the beginning of all known and half-known history, is not savagery, but high civilisation, at least of an outward and material kind. Do you demur? Then recollect, I pray you, that the three oldest peoples known to history on this planet are Egypt, China, Hindostan. The first glimpses of the world are always like those which the book of Genesis gives us; like those which your own continent gives us. As it was 400 years ago in America, so it was in North Africa and in Asia 4000 years ago, or 40,000 for aught I know. Nay, if anyone should ask—And why not 400,000 years ago, on Miocene continents long sunk beneath the Tropic sea? I for one have no rejoinder save—We have no proofs as yet.

There loom up, out of the darkness of legend, into the as yet dim dawn of history, what the old Arabs call Races of pre-Adamite Sultans—colossal monarchies, with fixed and often elaborate laws, customs, creeds; with aristocracies, priesthoods—seemingly always of a superior and conquering race; with a mass of common folk, whether free or half-free, composed of older conquered races; of imported slaves too, and their descendants.

But whence comes the royal race, the aristocracy, the priesthood? You inquire, and you find that they usually know not themselves. They are usually—I had almost dared to say, always—foreigners. They have crossed the neighbouring mountains. They have come by sea, like Dido to Carthage, like Manco Cassac and Mama Bello to America, and they have sometimes forgotten when. At least they are wiser, stronger, fairer, than the aborigines. They are to them—as Jacques Cartier was to the Indians of Canada—as gods. They are not sure that they are not descended from gods. They are the Children of the Sun, or what not. The children of light, who ray out such light as they have, upon the darkness of their subjects. They are at first, probably, civilisers, not conquerors. For, if tradition is worth anything—and we have nothing else to go upon—they are at first few in number. They come as settlers, or even as single sages. It is, in all tradition, not the many who influence the few, but the few who influence the many.

So aristocracies, in the true sense, are formed.

But the higher calling is soon forgotten. The purer light is soon darkened in pride and selfishness, luxury and lust; as in Genesis, the sons of God see the daughters of men, that they are fair; and they take them wives of all that they choose. And so a mixed race springs up and increases, without detriment at first to the commonwealth. For, by a well-known law of heredity, the cross between two races, probably far apart, produces at first a progeny possessing the forces, and, alas! probably the vices of both. And when the sons of God go in to the daughters of men, there are giants in the earth in those days, men of renown. The Roman Empire, remember, was never stronger than when the old Patrician blood had mingled itself with that of every nation round the Mediterranean.

But it does not last. Selfishness, luxury, ferocity, spread from above, as well as from below. The just aristocracy of virtue and wisdom becomes an unjust one of mere power and privilege; that again, one of mere wealth, corrupting and corrupt; and is destroyed, not by the people from below, but by the monarch from above. The hereditary bondsmen may know

> Who would be free,
> Himself must strike the blow.

But they dare not, know not how. The king must do it for them. He must become the State. "Better one tyrant," as Voltaire said, "than many." Better stand in fear of one lion far away, than of many wolves, each in the nearest wood. And so arise those truly monstrous Eastern despotisms, of which modern Persia is, thank God, the only remaining specimen; for Turkey and Egypt are too amenable of late years to the influence of the free nations to be counted as despotisms pure and simple—despotisms in which men, instead of worshipping a God-man, worship the hideous counterfeit, a *Man*-god—a poor human being endowed by public opinion with the powers of deity, while he is the slave of all the weaknesses of humanity. But such, as an historic fact, has been the last stage of every civilisation—even that of Rome, which ripened itself upon this earth the last in ancient times, and, I had almost said, until this very day, except among the men who speak Teutonic tongues, and who have preserved through all temptations, and reasserted through all dangers, the free ideas which have been our sacred heritage ever since Tacitus beheld us, with respect and awe, among our German forests, and saw in us the future masters of the Roman Empire.

Yes, it is very sad, the past history of mankind. But shall we despise those who went before us, and on whose accumulated labours we now stand?

Shall we not reverence our spiritual ancestors? Shall we not show our reverence by copying them, at least whenever, as in those old Persians, we see in them manliness and truthfulness, hatred of idolatries, and devotion to the God of light and life and good? And shall we not feel pity, instead of contempt, for their ruder forms of government, their ignorances, excesses, failures—so excusable in men who, with little or no previous teaching, were trying to solve for themselves for the first time the deepest social and political problems of humanity.

Yes, those old despotisms we trust are dead, and never to revive. But their corpses are the corpses, not of our enemies, but of our friends and predecessors, slain in the world-old fight of Ormuzd against

Ahriman—light against darkness, order against disorder. Confusedly they fought, and sometimes ill: but their corpses piled the breach and filled the trench for us, and over their corpses we step on to what should be to us an easy victory—what may be to us, yet, a shameful ruin.

For if we be, as we are wont to boast, the salt of the earth and the light of the world, what if the salt should lose its savour? What if the light which is in us should become darkness? For myself, when I look upon the responsibilities of the free nations of modern times, so far from boasting of that liberty in which I delight—and to keep which I freely, too, could die—I rather say, in fear and trembling, God help us on whom He has laid so heavy a burden as to make us free; responsible, each individual of us, not only to ourselves, but to Him and all mankind. For if we fall we shall fall I know not whither, and I dare not think.

How those old despotisms, the mighty empires of old time, fell, we know, and we can easily explain. Corrupt, luxurious, effeminate, eaten out by universal selfishness and mutual fear, they had at last no organic coherence. The moral anarchy within showed through, at last burst through, the painted skin of prescriptive order which held them together. Some braver and abler, and usually more virtuous people, often some little, hardy, homely mountain tribe, saw that the fruit was ripe for gathering; and, caring naught for superior numbers—and saying with German Alaric when the Romans boasted of their numbers, "The thicker the hay the easier it is mowed"—struck one brave blow at the huge inflated wind-bag—as Cyrus and his handful of Persians struck at the Medes; as

Alexander and his handful of Greeks struck afterwards at the Persians—and behold, it collapsed upon the spot. And then the victors took the place of the conquered; and became in their turn an aristocracy, and then a despotism; and in their turn rotted down and perished. And so the vicious circle repeated itself, age after age, from Egypt and Assyria to Mexico and Peru.

And therefore, we, free peoples as we are, have need to watch, and sternly watch, ourselves. Equality of some kind or other is, as I said, our natural and seemingly inevitable goal. But which equality? For there are two—a true one and a false; a noble and a base; a healthful and a ruinous. There is the truly divine equality, and there is the brute equality of sheep and oxen, and of flies and worms. There is the equality which is founded on mutual envy. The equality which respects others, and the equality which asserts itself. The equality which longs to raise all alike, and the equality which desires to pull down all alike. The equality which says: Thou art as good as I, and it may be better too, in the sight of God. And the equality which says: I am as good as thou, and will therefore see if I cannot master thee.

Side by side, in the heart of every free man, and every free people, are the two instincts struggling for the mastery, called by the same name, but bearing the same relation to each other as Marsyas to Apollo, the Satyr to the God. Marsyas and Apollo, the base and the noble, are, as in the old Greek legend, contending for the prize. And the prize is no less a one than all free people of this planet.

In proportion as that nobler idea conquers, and men unite in the equality of mutual respect and mutual service, they move one step farther towards realising on earth that Kingdom of God of which it is written: "The despots of the nations exercise dominion over them, and they that exercise authority over them are called benefactors. But he that will be great among you let him be the servant of all."

And in proportion as that base idea conquers, and selfishness, not self-sacrifice, is the ruling spirit of a State, men move on, one step forward, towards realising that kingdom of the devil upon earth, "Every man for himself and the devil take the hindmost." Only, alas! in that evil equality of envy and hate, there is no hindmost, and the devil takes them all alike.

And so is a period of discontent, revolution, internecine anarchy, followed by a tyranny endured, as in old Rome, by men once free, because tyranny will at least do for them what they were too lazy and greedy and envious to do for themselves.

And all because they have forgot
What 'tis to be a man—to curb and spurn
The tyrant in us: the ignobler self
Which boasts, not loathes, its likeness to the brute;
And owns no good save ease, no ill save pain,
No purpose, save its share in that wild war
In which, through countless ages, living things
Compete in internecine greed. Ah, loving God,
Are we as creeping things, which have no lord?
That we are brutes, great God, we know too well;
Apes daintier-featured; silly birds, who flaunt
Their plumes, unheeding of the fowler's step;
Spiders, who catch with paper, not with webs;
Tigers, who slay with cannon and sharp steel,
Instead of teeth and claws:—all these we are.
Are we no more than these, save in degree?
Mere fools of nature, puppets of strong lusts,
Taking the sword, to perish by the sword

Upon the universal battle-field,
Even as the things upon the moor outside?

The heath eats up green grass and delicate herbs;
The pines eat up the heath; the grub the pine;
The finch the grub; the hawk the silly finch;
And man, the mightiest of all beasts of prey,
Eats what he lists. The strong eat up the weak;
The many eat the few; great nations, small;
And he who cometh in the name of all
Shall, greediest, triumph by the greed of all,
And, armed by his own victims, eat up all.
While ever out of the eternal heavens
Looks patient down the great magnanimous God,
Who, Master of all worlds, did sacrifice
All to Himself? Nay: but Himself to all;
Who taught mankind, on that first Christmas Day,
What 'tis to be a man—to give, not take;
To serve, not rule; to nourish, not devour;
To lift, not crush; if need, to die, not live.

"He that cometh in the name of all"—the popular military despot—the "saviour of his country"—he is our internecine enemy on both sides of the Atlantic, whenever he rises—the inaugurator of that Imperialism, that Cæsarism into which Rome sank, when not her liberties merely, but her virtues, were decaying out of her—the sink into which all wicked States, whether republics or monarchies, are sure to fall, simply because men must eat and drink for to-morrow they die. The Military and Bureaucratic Despotism which keeps the many quiet, as in old Rome, by *panem et circenses*—bread and games—or, if need be, Pilgrimages; that the few may make money, eat, drink, and be merry, as long as it can last. That, let it ape as it may—as did the Cæsars of old Rome at first—as another Emperor did even in our own days—the forms of dead freedom, really upholds an artificial luxury by brute force; and consecrates the basest of all aristocracies, the aristocracy of the money-bag, by the divine sanction of the bayonet.

That at all risks, even at the price of precious blood, the free peoples of the earth must ward off from them; for, makeshift and stop-gap as it is, it does not even succeed in what it tries to do. It does not last. Have we not seen that it does not, cannot last? How can it last? This falsehood, like all falsehoods, must collapse at one touch of Ithuriel's spear of truth and fact. And—

"Then saw I the end of these men. Namely, how Thou dost set them in slippery places, and casteth them down. Suddenly do they perish, and come to a fearful end. Yea, like as a dream when one awaketh, so shalt Thou make their image to vanish out of the city."

Have we not seen that too, though, thank God, neither in England nor in the United States?

And then? What then? None knows, and none can know.

The future of France and Spain, the future of the Tropical Republics of Spanish America, is utterly blank and dark; not to be prophesied, I hold, by mortal man, simply because we have no like cases in the history of the past whereby to judge the tendencies of the present. Will they revive? Under the genial influences of free institutions will the good seed which is in them take root downwards, and bear fruit upwards? and make them all what that fair France has been, in spite of all her faults, so often in past years—a joy and an inspiration to all the nations round? Shall it be thus? God grant it may; but He, and He alone, can tell. We only stand by, watching, if we be wise, with pity and with fear, the working out of a tremendous new social problem, which must affect the future of the whole civilised world.

For if the agonising old nations fail to regenerate themselves, what can befall? What, when even Imperialism has been tried and failed, as fail it must? What but that lower depth within the lowest deep?

> That last dread mood
> Of sated lust, and dull decrepitude.
> No law, no art, no faith, no hope, no God.
> When round the freezing founts of life in peevish ring,
> Crouched on the bare-worn sod,
> Babbling about the unreturning spring,
> And whining for dead creeds, which cannot save,
> The toothless nations shiver to their grave.

And we, who think we stand, let us take heed lest we fall. Let us accept, in modesty and in awe, the responsibility of our freedom, and remember that that freedom can be preserved only in one old-fashioned way. Let us remember that the one condition of a true democracy is the same as the one condition of a true aristocracy, namely, virtue. Let us teach our children, as grand old Lilly taught our forefathers 300 years ago—"It is virtue, gentlemen, yea, virtue that maketh gentlemen; that maketh the poor rich, the subject a king, the lowborn noble, the deformed beautiful. These things neither the whirling wheel of fortune can overturn, nor the deceitful cavillings of worldlings separate, neither sickness abate, nor age abolish."

Yes. Let us teach our children thus on both sides of the Atlantic. For if they—which God forbid—should grow corrupt and weak by their own sins, there is no hardier race now left on earth to conquer our descendants and bring them back to reason, as those old Jews were brought by bitter shame and woe. And all that is before them and the whole civilised world, would be long centuries of anarchy such as the world has not seen for ages—a true Ragnarok, a twilight of the very gods, an age such as the wise woman foretold in the old Voluspà.

When brethren shall be
Each other's bane,
And sisters' sons rend
The ties of kin.
Hard will be that age,
An age of bad women,
An axe-age, a sword-age,
Shields oft cleft in twain,
A storm-age, a wolf-age,
Ere earth meet its doom.

So sang, 2000 years ago, perhaps, the great unnamed prophetess, of our own race, of what might be, if we should fail mankind and our own calling and election.

God grant that day may never come. But God grant, also, that if that day does come, then may come true also what that wise Vala sang, of the day when gods, and men, and earth should be burnt up with fire.

When slaked Surtur's flame is,
Still the man and the maider
Hight Valour and Life,
Shall keep themselves hid
In the wood of remembrance.
The dew of the dawning
For food it shall serve them:
From them spring new peoples.

New peoples. For after all is said, the ideal form of human society is democracy.

A nation—and, were it even possible, a whole world—of free men, lifting free foreheads to God and Nature; calling no man master—for one is their master, even God; knowing and obeying their duties towards the Maker of the Universe, and therefore to each other, and that not from fear, nor calculation of profit or loss, but because they loved and liked it, and had seen the beauty of righteousness and trust and peace; because the law of God was in their hearts, and needing at last, it may be, neither king nor priest, for each man and each woman, in their place, were kings and priests to God. Such a nation—such a society—what nobler conception of mortal existence can we form? Would not that be, indeed, the kingdom of God come on earth?

And tell me not that that is impossible—too fair a dream to be ever realised. All that makes it impossible is the selfishness, passions, weaknesses, of those who would be blest were they masters of themselves, and therefore of circumstances; who are miserable because, not being masters of themselves, they try to master circumstance, to pull down iron walls with weak and clumsy hands, and forget that he who would be free from tyrants must first be free from his worst tyrant, self.

But tell me not that the dream is impossible. It is so beautiful that it must be true. If not now, nor centuries hence, yet still hereafter. God would never, as I hold, have inspired man with that rich imagination had He not meant to translate, some day, that imagination into fact.

The very greatness of the idea, beyond what a

single mind or generation can grasp, will ensure failure on failure—follies, fanaticisms, disappointments, even crimes, bloodshed, hasty furies, as of children baulked of their holiday.

But it will be at last fulfilled, filled full, and perfected; not perhaps here, or among our peoples, or any people which now exist on earth: but in some future civilisation—it may be in far lands beyond the sea—when all that you and we have made and done shall be as the forest-grown mounds of the old nameless civilisers of the Mississippi valley.*

* This lecture and the two preceding ones, being published after the author's death, have not had the benefit of his corrections.

RONDELET,

THE HUGUENOT NATURALIST.

RONDELET,*

THE HUGUENOT NATURALIST.†

"Apollo, god of medicine, exiled from the rest of the earth, was straying once across the Narbonnaise in Gaul, seeking to fix his abode there. Driven from Asia, from Africa, and from the rest of Europe, he wandered through all the towns of the province in search of a place propitious for him and for his disciples. At last he perceived a new city, constructed from the ruins of Maguelonne, of Lattes, and of Substantion. He contemplated long its site, its aspect, its neighbourhood, and resolved to establish on this hill of Montpellier a temple for himself and his priests. All smiled on his desires. By the genius of the soil, by the character of the inhabitants, no town is more fit for the culture of letters, and above all of medicine. What site is more delicious and more lovely? A heaven

* A Life of Rondelet, by his pupil Laurent Joubert, is to be found appended to his works; and with an account of his illness and death, by his cousin, Claude Formy, which is well worth the perusal of any man, wise or foolish. Many interesting details beside, I owe to the courtesy of Professor Planchon, of Montpellier, author of a discourse on "Rondelet et ses Disciples," which appeared, with a learned and curious Appendix, in the "Montpellier Médical" for 1866.

† This lecture was given at Cambridge in 1869.

pure and smiling; a city built with magnificence; men born for all the labours of the intellect. All around vast horizons and enchanting sites—meadows, vines, olives, green champaigns; mountains and hills, rivers, brooks, lagoons, and the sea. Everywhere a luxuriant vegetation—everywhere the richest production of the land and the water. Hail to thee, sweet and dear city! Hail, happy abode of Apollo, who spreadest afar the light of the glory of thy name!"

"This fine tirade," says Dr. Maurice Raynaud—from whose charming book on the "Doctors of the Time of Molière" I quote—"is not, as one might think, the translation of a piece of poetry. It is simply part of a public oration by François Fanchon, one of the most illustrious chancellors of the faculty of medicine of Montpellier in the seventeenth century." "From time immemorial," he says, "'the faculty' of Montpellier had made itself remarkable by a singular mixture of the sacred and the profane. The theses which were sustained there began by an invocation to God, the Blessed Virgin, and St. Luke, and ended by these words: 'This thesis will be sustained in the sacred Temple of Apollo.'"

But however extravagant Chancellor Fanchon's praises of his native city may seem, they are really not exaggerated. The Narbonnaise, or Languedoc, is perhaps the most charming district of charming France. In the far north-east gleam the white Alps; in the far south-west the white Pyrenees; and from the purple glens and yellow downs of the Cevennes on the north-west, the Herault slopes gently down towards the "Etangs," or great salt-water lagoons, and the vast alluvial flats of the Camargue, the field of Caius Marius, where still run herds of half-wild horses, descended from some ancient Roman stock; while beyond all glitters the blue Mediterranean. The great almond orchards, each one sheet of rose-colour in spring; the mulberry orchards, the oliveyards, the vineyards, cover every foot of available upland soil: save where the rugged and arid downs are sweet with a thousand odoriferous plants, from which the bees extract the famous white honey of Narbonne. The native flowers and shrubs, of a beauty and richness rather Eastern than European, have made the "Flora Montpeliensis," and with it the names of Rondelet and his disciples, famous among botanists; and the strange fish and shells upon its shores afforded Rondelet materials for his immortal work upon the "Animals of the Sea." The innumerable wild fowl of the Bouches du Rhône; the innumerable songsters and other birds of passage, many of them unknown in these islands, and even in the north of France itself, which haunt every copse of willow and aspen along the brook-sides; the gaudy and curious insects which thrive beneath that clear, fierce, and yet bracing sunlight; all these have made the district of Montpellier a home prepared by Nature for those who study and revere her.

Neither was Chancellor Fanchon misled by patriotism, when he said the pleasant people who inhabit that district are fit for all the labours of the intellect. They are a very mixed race, and, like most mixed races, quick-witted, and handsome also. There is probably much Roman blood among them, especially in the towns; for Languedoc, or Gallia Narbonnensis, as it was called of old, was said to be more Roman than Rome itself. The Roman remains are more perfect and more interesting—so the late Dr. Whewell used to say—than any to be seen now in Italy; and the old capital, Narbonne itself, was a complete museum of Roman antiquities ere Francis I. destroyed it, in order to fortify the city upon a modern system against the invading armies of Charles V. There must be much Visigothic blood likewise in Languedoc: for the Visigothic Kings held their courts there from the fifth century, until the time that they were crushed by the invading Moors. Spanish blood, likewise, there may be; for much of Languedoc was held in the early Middle Age by those descendants of Eudes of Aquitaine who established themselves as kings of Majorca and Arragon; and Languedoc did not become entirely French till 1349, when Philip le Bel bought Montpellier of those potentates. The Moors, too, may have left some traces of their race behind. They held the country from about A.D. 713 to 758, when they were finally expelled by Charles Martel and Eudes. One sees to this day their towers of meagre stonework, perched on the grand Roman masonry of those old amphitheatres, which they turned into fortresses. One may see, too—so tradition holds—upon those very amphitheatres the stains of the fires with which Charles Martel smoked them out; and one may see, too, or fancy that one sees, in the aquiline features, the bright black eyes, the lithe and graceful gestures, which are so common in Languedoc, some touch of the old Mahommedan race, which passed like a flood over that Christian land.

Whether or not the Moors left behind any traces of their blood, they left behind, at least, traces of their learning; for the university of Montpellier claimed to have been founded by Moors at a date of altogether abysmal antiquity. They looked upon the Arabian physicians of the Middle Age, on Avicenna and

Averrhoes, as modern innovators, and derived their parentage from certain mythic doctors of Cordova, who, when the Moors were expelled from Spain in the eighth century, fled to Montpellier, bringing with them traditions of that primæval science which had been revealed to Adam while still in Paradise; and founded Montpellier, the mother of all the universities in Europe. Nay, some went farther still, and told of Bengessaus and Ferragius, the physicians of Charlemagne, and of Marilephus, chief physician of King Chilperic, and even—if a letter of St. Bernard's was to be believed—of a certain bishop who went as early as the second century to consult the doctors of Montpellier; and it would have been in vain to reply to them that in those days, and long after them, Montpellier was not yet built. The facts are said to be: that as early as the beginning of the thirteenth century Montpellier had its schools of law, medicine, and arts, which were erected into a university by Pope Nicholas IV. in 1289.

The university of Montpellier, like—I believe—most foreign ones, resembled more a Scotch than an English university. The students lived, for the most part, not in colleges, but in private lodgings, and constituted a republic of their own, ruled by an abbé of the scholars, one of themselves, chosen by universal suffrage. A terror they were often to the respectable burghers, for they had all the right to carry arms; and a plague likewise, for, if they ran in debt, their creditors were forbidden to seize their books, which, with their swords, were generally all the property they possessed. If, moreover, anyone set up a noisy or unpleasant trade near their lodgings, the scholars could compel the town authorities to turn him out.

They were most of them, probably, mere boys of from twelve to twenty, living poorly, working hard, and—those at least of them who were in the colleges—cruelly beaten daily, after the fashion of those times; but they seem to have comforted themselves under their troubles by a good deal of wild life out of school, by rambling into the country on the festivals of the saints, and now and then by acting plays; notably, that famous one which Rabelais wrote for them in 1531: "The moral comedy of the man who had a dumb wife;" which "joyous *patelinage*" remains unto this day in the shape of a well-known comic song. That comedy young Rondelet must have seen acted. The son of a druggist, spicer, and grocer—the three trades were then combined—in Montpellier, and born in 1507, he had been destined for the cloister, being a sickly lad. His uncle, one of the canons of Maguelonne, near by, had even given him the revenues of a small chapel—a job of nepotism which was common enough in those days. But his heart was in science and medicine. He set off, still a mere boy, to Paris to study there; and returned to Montpellier, at the age of eighteen, to study again.

The next year, 1530, while still a scholar himself, he was appointed procurator of the scholars—a post which brought him in a small fee on each matriculation—and that year he took a fee, among others, from one of the most remarkable men of that or of any age, François Rabelais himself.

And what shall I say of him?—who stands alone, like Shakespeare, in his generation; possessed of colossal learning—of all science which could be gathered in his days—of practical and statesmanlike wisdom—of knowledge of languages, ancient and modern, beyond all his compeers—of eloquence, which when he speaks of pure and noble things becomes heroic, and, as it were, inspired—of scorn for meanness, hypocrisy, ignorance—of esteem, genuine and earnest, for the Holy Scriptures, and for the more moderate of the Reformers who were spreading the Scriptures in Europe,—and all this great light wilfully hidden, not under a bushel, but under a dunghill. He is somewhat like Socrates in face, and in character likewise; in him, as in Socrates, the demigod and the satyr, the man and the ape, are struggling for the mastery. In Socrates, the true man conquers, and comes forth high and pure; in Rabelais, alas! the victor is the ape, while the man himself sinks down in cynicism, sensuality, practical jokes, foul talk. He returns to Paris, to live an idle, luxurious life; to die —says the legend—saying, "I go to seek a great perhaps," and to leave behind him little save a school of Pantagruelists—careless young gentlemen, whose ideal was to laugh at everything, to believe in nothing, and to gratify their five senses like the brutes which perish. There are those who read his books to make them laugh; the wise man, when he reads them, will be far more inclined to weep. Let any young man who may see these words remember, that in him, as in Rabelais, the ape and the man are struggling for the mastery. Let him take warning by the fate of one who was to him as a giant to a pigmy; and think of Tennyson's words—

> Arise, and fly
> The reeling faun, the sensual feast;
> Strive upwards, working out the beast,
> And let the ape and tiger die.

But to return. Down among them there at Montpellier, like a brilliant meteor, flashed this wonderful Rabelais, in the year 1530. He had fled, some say, for his life. Like Erasmus, he had no mind to be a martyr, and he had been terrified at the execution of poor Louis de Berquin, his friend, and the friend of Erasmus likewise. This Louis de Berquin, a man well known in those days, was a gallant young gentleman and scholar, holding a place in the court of Francis I., who had translated into French the works of Erasmus, Luther, and Melancthon, and had asserted that it was heretical to invoke the Virgin Mary instead of the Holy Spirit, or to call her our Hope and our Life, which titles—Berquin averred—belonged alone to God. Twice had the doctors of the Sorbonne, with that terrible persecutor, Noel Beda, at their head, seized poor Berquin, and tried to burn his books and him; twice had that angel in human form, Marguerite d'Angoulême, sister of Francis I., saved him from their clutches; but when Francis—taken prisoner at the battle of Pavia—at last returned from his captivity in Spain, the suppression of heresy and the burning of heretics seemed to him and to his mother, Louise of Savoy, a thank-offering so acceptable to God, that Louis Berquin—who would not, in spite of the entreaties of Erasmus, purchase his life by silence—was burnt at last on the Place de Grêve, being first strangled, because he was of gentle blood.

Montpellier received its famous guest joyfully. Rabelais was now forty-two years old, and a distinguished savant; so they excused him his three years' undergraduate's career, and invested him at once with the red gown of the bachelors. That red gown—or, rather, the ragged phantom of it—is still shown at Montpellier, and must be worn by each bachelor when he takes his degree. Unfortunately, antiquarians assure us that the precious garment has been renewed again and again—the students having clipped bits of it away for relics, and clipped as earnestly from the new gowns as their predecessors had done from the authentic original.

Doubtless, the coming of such a man among them to lecture on the Aphorisms of Hippocrates, and the Ars Parva of Galen, not from the Latin translations then in use, but from original Greek texts, with comments and corrections of his own, must have had a great influence on the minds of the Montpellier students; and still more influence—and that not altogether a good one—must Rabelais's lighter talk have had, as he lounged—so the story goes—in his dressing-gown upon the public place, picking up quaint stories from the cattle-drivers off the Cevennes, and the villagers who came in to sell their olives and their grapes, their vinegar and their vine-twig faggots, as they do unto this day. To him may be owing much of the sound respect for natural science, and much, too, of the contempt for the superstition around them, which is notable in that group of great naturalists who were boys in Montpellier at that day. Rabelais seems to have liked Rondelet, and no wonder: he was a cheery, lovable, honest little fellow, very fond of jokes, a great musician and player on the violin, and who, when he grew rich, liked nothing so well as to bring into his house any buffoon or strolling-player to make fun for him. Vivacious he was, hot-tempered, forgiving, and with a power of learning and a power of work which were prodigious, even in those hard-working days. Rabelais chaffs Rondelet, under the name of Rondibilis; for, indeed, Rondelet grew up into a very round, fat, little man; but Rabelais puts excellent sense into his mouth, cynical enough, and too cynical, but both learned and humorous; and, if he laughs at him for being shocked at the offer of a fee, and taking it, nevertheless, kindly enough, Rondelet is not the first doctor who has done that, neither will he be the last.

Rondelet, in his turn, put on the red robe of the bachelor, and received, on taking his degree, his due share of fisticuffs from his dearest friends, according to the ancient custom of the University of Montpellier. He then went off to practise medicine in a village at the foot of the Alps, and, half-starved, to teach little children. Then he found he must learn Greek; went off to Paris a second time, and alleviated his poverty there somewhat by becoming tutor to a son of the Viscomte de Turenne. There he met Gonthier of Andernach, who had taught anatomy at Louvain to the great Vesalius, and learned from him to dissect. We next find him setting up as a medical man amid the wild volcanic hills of the Auvergne, struggling still with poverty, like Erasmus, like George Buchanan, like almost every great scholar in those days; for students then had to wander from place to place, generally on foot, in search of new teachers, in search of books, in search of the necessaries of life; undergoing such an amount of bodily and mental toil as makes it wonderful that all of them did not—as some of them doubtless did—die under the hard training, or, at best, desert the penurious Muses for the paternal shop or plough.

Rondelet got his doctorate in 1537, and next year fell in love with and married a beautiful young girl called Jeanne Sandre, who seems to have been as poor as he.

But he had gained, meanwhile, a powerful patron; and the patronage of the great was then as necessary to men of letters as the patronage of the public is now. Guillaume Pellicier, Bishop of Maguelonne—or rather then of Montpellier itself, whither he had persuaded Paul II. to transfer the ancient see—was a model of the literary gentleman of the sixteenth century; a savant, a diplomat, a collector of books and manuscripts, Greek, Hebrew, and Syriac, which formed the original nucleus of the present library of the Louvre; a botanist, too, who loved to wander with Rondelet collecting plants and flowers. He retired from public life to peace and science at Montpellier, when to the evil days of his master, Francis I., succeeded the still worse days of Henry II., and Diana of Poitiers. That Jezebel of France could conceive no more natural or easy way of atoning for her own sins than that of hunting down heretics, and feasting her wicked eyes—so it is said—upon their dying torments. Bishop Pellicier fell under suspicion of heresy: very probably with some justice. He fell, too, under suspicion of leading a life unworthy of a celibate churchman, a fault which—if it really existed—was, in those days, pardonable enough in an orthodox prelate, but not so in one whose orthodoxy was suspected. And for awhile Pellicier was in prison. After his release he gave himself up to science, with Rondelet and the school of disciples who were growing up around him. They rediscovered together the Garum, that classic sauce, whose praises had been sung of old by Horace, Martial, and Ausonius; and so child-like, superstitious if you will, was the reverence in the sixteenth century for classic antiquity, that when Pellicier and Rondelet discovered that the Garum was made from the fish called Picarel—called Garon by the fishers of Antibes, and Giroli at Venice, both these last names corruptions of the Latin Gerres—then did the two fashionable poets of France, Étienne Dolet and Clement Marot, think it not unworthy of their muse to sing the praises of the sauce which Horace had sung of old. A proud day, too, was it for Pellicier and Rondelet, when wandering somewhere in the marshes of the Camargue, a scent of garlic caught the nostrils of the gentle bishop, and in the lovely pink flowers of the water-germander he recognised the Scordium of the ancients. "The discovery," says Professor Planchon, "made almost as much noise as that of the famous Garum; for at that moment of naïve fervour on behalf of antiquity, to re-discover a plant of Dioscorides or of Pliny was a good fortune and almost an event."

I know not whether, after his death, the good bishop's bones reposed beneath some gorgeous tomb, bedizened with the incongruous half-Pagan statues of the Renaissance; but this at least is certain, that Rondelet's disciples imagined for him a monument more enduring than of marble or of brass, more graceful and more curiously wrought than all the sculptures of Torrigiano or Cellini, Baccio Bandinelli or Michael Angelo himself. For they named a lovely little lilac snapdragon, *Linaria Domini Pellicerii*—"Lord Pellicier's toad-flax;" and that name it will keep, we may believe, as long as winter and summer shall endure.

But to return. To this good Patron—who was the Ambassador at Venice—the newly-married Rondelet determined to apply for employment; and to Venice he would have gone, leaving his bride behind, had he not been stayed by one of those angels who sometimes walk the earth in women's shape. Jeanne Sandre had an elder sister, Catharine, who had brought her up. She was married to a wealthy man, but she had no children of her own. For four years she and her good husband had let the Rondelets lodge with them, and now she was a widow, and to part with them was more than she could bear. She carried Rondelet off from the students who were seeing him safe out of the city, brought him back, settled on him the same day half her fortune, and soon after settled on him the whole, on the sole condition that she should live with him and her sister. For years afterwards she watched over the pretty young wife and her two girls and three boys—the three boys, alas! all died young—and over Rondelet himself, who, immersed in books and experiments, was utterly careless about money; and was to them all a mother—advising, guiding, managing, and regarded by Rondelet with genuine gratitude as his guardian angel.

Honour and good fortune, in a worldly sense, now poured in upon the druggist's son. Pellicier, his own bishop, stood godfather to his first-born daughter. Montluc, Bishop of Valence, and that wise and learned statesman, the Cardinal of Tournon, stood godfathers a few years later to his twin boys; and what was of still more solid worth to him, Cardinal Tournon took him to Antwerp, Bordeaux, Bayonne, and more than once to Rome; and in these Italian journeys of his he collected many facts for the great work of his life, that "History of Fishes" which he dedicated, naturally enough, to the cardinal. This book with its plates is, for the time, a masterpiece of accuracy. Those who are best acquainted with the subject say, that it is up to the present day a key to the whole ichthyology of the Mediterranean. Two other men, Belon and Salviani, were then at work on the same subject, and published their books almost at the same time; a circumstance which caused, as was natural, a three-cornered duel between the supporters of the three naturalists, each party accusing the other of plagiarism. The simple fact seems to be that the almost simultaneous appearance of the three books in 1554–55 is one of those coincidences inevitable at moments when many minds are stirred in the same direction by the same great thoughts—coincidences which have happened in our own day on questions of geology, biology, and astronomy; and which, when the facts have been carefully examined, and the first flush of natural jealousy has cooled down, have proved only that there were more wise men than one in the world at the same time.

And this sixteenth century was an age in which the minds of men were suddenly and strangely turned to examine the wonders of nature with an earnestness, with a reverence, and therefore with an accuracy, with which they had never been investigated before. "Nature," says Professor Planchon, "long veiled in mysticism and scholasticism, was opening up infinite vistas. A new superstition, the exaggerated worship of the ancients, was nearly hindering this movement of thought towards facts. Nevertheless, Learning did her work. She rediscovered, reconstructed, purified, commented on the texts of ancient authors. Then came in observation, which showed that more was to be seen in one blade of grass than in any page of

Pliny. Rondelet was in the middle of this crisis a man of transition, while he was one of progress. He reflected the past; he opened and prepared the future. If he commented on Dioscorides, if he remained faithful to the theories of Galen, he founded in his 'History of Fishes' a monument which our century respects. He is above all an inspirer, an initiator; and if he wants one mark of the leader of a school, the foundation of certain scientific doctrines, there is in his speech what is better than all systems, the communicative power which urges a generation of disciples along the path of independent research, with Reason for guide, and Faith for aim."

Around Rondelet, in those years, sometimes indeed in his house—for professors in those days took private pupils as lodgers—worked the group of botanists whom Linnæus calls "the Fathers," the authors of the descriptive botany of the sixteenth century. Their names, and those of their disciples and their disciples again, are household words in the mouth of every gardener, immortalised, like good Bishop Pellicier, in the plants that have been named after them. The Lobelia commemorates Lobel, one of Rondelet's most famous pupils, who wrote those "Adversaria" which contain so many curious sketches of Rondelet's botanical expeditions, and who inherited his botanical (as Joubert his biographer inherited his anatomical) manuscripts. The Magnolia commemorates the Magnols; the Sarracenia, Sarrasin of Lyons; the Bauhinia, Jean Bauhin; the Fuchsia, Bauhin's earlier German master, Leonard Fuchs; and the Clusia—the received name of that terrible "Matapalo" or "Scotch attorney," of the West Indies, which kills the hugest tree, to become as huge a tree itself—immortalises the great Clusius, Charles de l'Escluse, citizen of Arras, who, after studying civil law at Louvain, philosophy at Marburg, and theology at Wittemberg under Melancthon, came to Montpellier in 1551, to live in Rondelet's own house, and become the greatest botanist of his age.

These were Rondelet's palmy days. He had got a theatre of anatomy built at Montpellier, where he himself dissected publicly. He had, says tradition, a little botanic garden, such as were springing up then in several universities, specially in Italy. He had a villa outside the city, whose tower, near the modern railway station, still bears the name of the "Mas de Rondelet." There, too, may be seen the remnants of the great tanks, fed with water brought through earthen pipes from the Fountain of Albe, wherein he kept the fish whose habits he observed. Professor Planchon thinks that he had salt-water tanks likewise; and thus he may have been the father of all "Aquariums." He had a large and handsome house in the city itself, a large practice as physician in the country round; money flowed in fast to him, and flowed out fast likewise. He spent much upon building, pulling down, rebuilding, and sent the bills in seemingly to his wife and to his guardian angel Catharine. He himself had never a penny in his purse: but earned the money, and let his ladies spend it; an equitable and pleasant division of labour which most married men would do well to imitate. A generous, affectionate, careless little man, he gave away, says his pupil and biographer, Joubert, his valuable specimens to any savant who begged for them, or left them about to be stolen by visitors, who, like too many collectors in all ages, possessed light fingers and lighter consciences. So pacific was he meanwhile, and so brave withal, that even in the fearful years of "The Troubles," he would never carry sword, nor even tuck or dagger: but went about on the most lonesome journeys as one who wore a charmed life, secure in God and in his calling, which was to heal, and not to kill.

These were the golden years of Rondelet's life; but trouble was coming on him, and a stormy sunset after a brilliant day. He lost his sister-in-law, to whom he owed all his fortunes, and who had watched ever since over him and his wife like a mother; then he lost his wife herself under most painful circumstances; then his best-beloved daughter. Then he married again, and lost the son who was born to him; and then came, as to many of the best in those days, even sorer trials, trials of the conscience, trials of faith.

For in the meantime Rondelet had become a Protestant, like many of the wisest men round him; like, so it would seem from the event, the majority of the university and the burghers of Montpellier. It is not to be wondered at. Montpellier was a sort of halfway resting-place for Protestant preachers, whether fugitive or not, who were passing from Basle, Geneva, or Lyons, to Marguerite of Navarre's little Protestant court at Pau or at Nerac, where all wise and good men, and now and then some foolish and fanatical ones, found shelter and hospitality. Thither Calvin himself had been, passing probably through Montpellier, and leaving —as such a man was sure to leave—the mark of his foot behind him. At Lyons, no great distance up the Rhone, Marguerite had helped to establish an organised Protestant community; and when in 1536 she herself had passed through Montpellier, to visit her brother at Valence, and Montmorency's camp at Avignon, she took with her doubtless Protestant chaplains of her own, who spoke wise words—it may be that she spoke wise words herself—to the ardent and inquiring students of Montpellier. Moreover, Rondelet and his disciples had been for years past in constant communication with the Protestant savants of Switzerland and Germany, among whom the knowledge of nature was progressing as it never had progressed before. For—it is a fact always to be remembered—it was only in the free air of Protestant countries the natural sciences could grow and thrive. They sprung up, indeed, in Italy after the restoration of Greek literature in the fifteenth century; but they withered there again only too soon under the blighting upas shade of superstition. Transplanted to the free air of Switzerland, of Germany, of Britain, and of Montpellier, then half Protestant, they developed rapidly and surely, simply because the air was free; to be checked again in France by the return of superstition with despotism superadded, until the eve of the great French Revolution.

So Rondelet had been for some years Protestant. He had hidden in his house for a long while a monk who had left his monastery. He had himself written theological treatises: but when his Bishop Pellicier was imprisoned on a charge of heresy, Rondelet burnt his manuscripts, and kept his opinions to himself. Still he was a suspected heretic, at last seemingly a notorious one; for only the year before his death, going to visit patients at Perpignan, he was waylaid by the Spaniards, and had to get home through by-passes of the Pyrenees, to avoid being thrown into the Inquisition.

And those were times in which it was necessary for

a man to be careful, unless he had made up his mind to be burned. For more than thirty years of Rondelet's life the burning had gone on in his neighbourhood; intermittently it is true: the spasms of superstitious fury being succeeded, one may charitably hope, by pity and remorse; but still the burnings had gone on. The Benedictine monk of St. Maur, who writes the history of Languedoc, says, quite *en passant*, how someone was burnt at Toulouse in 1553, luckily only in effigy, for he had escaped to Geneva: but he adds, "next year they burned several heretics," it being not worth while to mention their names. In 1556 they burned alive at Toulouse Jean Escalle, a poor Franciscan monk, who had found his order intolerable; while one Pierre de Lavaur, who dared preach Calvinism in the streets of Nismes, was hanged and burnt. So had the score of judicial murders been increasing year by year, till it had to be, as all evil scores have to be in this world, paid off with interest, and paid off especially against the ignorant and fanatic monks who for a whole generation, in every university and school in France, had been howling down sound science, as well as sound religion; and at Montpellier in 1560–61, their debt was paid them in a very ugly way. News came down to the hot southerners of Languedoc of the so-called conspiracy of Amboise.—How the Duc de Guise and the Cardinal de Lorraine had butchered the best blood in France under the pretence of a treasonable plot; how the King of Navarre and the Prince de Condé had been arrested; then how Condé and Coligny were ready to take up arms at the head of all the Huguenots of France, and try to stop this life-long torturing, by sharp shot and cold steel; then how in six months' time the king would assemble a general council to settle the question between Catholics and Huguenots. The Huguenots, guessing how that would end, resolved to settle the question for themselves. They rose in one city after another, sacked the churches, destroyed the images, put down by main force superstitious processions and dances; and did many things only to be excused by the exasperation caused by thirty years of cruelty. At Montpellier there was hard fighting, murders—so say the Catholic historians—of priests and monks, sack of the new cathedral, destruction of the noble convents which lay in a ring round Montpellier. The city and the university were in the hands of the Huguenots, and Montpellier became Protestant on the spot.

Next year came the counter-blow. There were heavy battles with the Catholics all round the neighbourhood, destruction of the suburbs, threatened siege and sack, and years of misery and poverty for Montpellier and all who were therein.

Horrible was the state of France in those times of the wars of religion which began in 1562; the times which are spoken of usually as "The Troubles," as if men did not wish to allude to them too openly. Then, and afterwards in the wars of the League, deeds were done for which language has no name. The population decreased. The land lay untilled. The fair face of France was blackened with burnt homesteads and ruined towns. Ghastly corpses dangled in rows upon the trees, or floated down the blood-stained streams. Law and order were at an end. Bands of robbers prowled in open day, and bands of wolves likewise. But all through the horrors of the troubles we catch sight of the little fat doctor riding all unarmed to see his patients throughout Languedoc; going vast distances, his biographers say, by means of regular relays of horses, till he too broke down. Well, for him, perhaps, that he broke down when he did; for capture and recapture, massacre and pestilence, were the fate of Montpellier and the surrounding country, till the better times of Henry IV. and the Edict of Nantes in 1598, when liberty of worship was given to the Protestants for awhile.

In the burning summer of 1566, Rondelet went a long journey to Toulouse, seemingly upon an errand of charity, to settle some law affairs for his relations. The sanitary state of the southern cities is bad enough still. It must have been horrible in those days of barbarism and misrule. Dysentery was epidemic at Toulouse then, and Rondelet took it. He knew from the first that he should die. He was worn out, it is said, by over-exertion; by sorrow for the miseries of the land; by fruitless struggles to keep the peace, and to strive for moderation in days when men were all immoderate. But he rode away a day's journey—he took two days over it, so weak he was—in the blazing July sun, to a friend's sick wife at Realmont, and there took to his bed, and died a good man's death. The details of his death and last illness were written and published by his cousin Claude Formy; and well worth reading they are to any man who wishes to know how to die. Rondelet would have no tidings of his illness sent to Montpellier. He was happy, he said, in dying away from the tears of his household, and "safe from insult." He dreaded, one may suppose, lest priests and friars should force their way to his bedside, and try to extort some recantation from the great savant, the honour and glory of their city. So they sent for no priest to Realmont; but round his bed a knot of Calvinist gentlemen and ministers read the Scriptures, and sang David's psalms, and prayed; and Rondelet prayed with them through long agonies, and so went home to God.

The Benedictine monk-historian of Languedoc, in all his voluminous folios, never mentions, as far as I can find, Rondelet's existence. Why should he? The man was only a druggist's son and a heretic, who healed diseases, and collected plants, and wrote a book on fish. But the learned men of Montpellier, and of all Europe, had a very different opinion of him. His body was buried at Realmont; but before the schools of Toulouse they set up a white marble slab, and an inscription thereon setting forth his learning and his virtues; and epitaphs on him were composed by the learned throughout Europe, not only in French and Latin, but in Greek, Hebrew, and even Chaldee.

So lived and so died a noble man; more noble, to my mind, than many a victorious warrior, or successful statesman, or canonised saint. To know facts, and to heal diseases, were the two objects of his life. For them he toiled, as few men have toiled; and he died in harness, at his work—the best death any man can die.

VESALIUS THE ANATOMIST.

VESALIUS THE ANATOMIST.*

I CANNOT begin a sketch of the life of this great man better than by trying to describe a scene so picturesque, so tragic in the eyes of those who are wont to mourn over human follies, so comic in the eyes of those who prefer to laugh over them, that the reader will not be likely to forget either it or the actors in it.

It is a darkened chamber in the College of Alcala, in the year 1562, where lies, probably in a huge four-post bed, shrouded in stifling hangings, the heir-apparent of the greatest empire in the then world, Don Carlos, only son of Philip II. and heir-apparent of Spain, the Netherlands, and all the Indies. A short sickly boy of sixteen, with a bull head, a crooked shoulder, a short leg, and a brutal temper, he will not be missed by the world if he should die. His profligate career seems to have brought its own punishment. To the scandal of his father, who tolerated no one's vices save his own, as well as to the scandal of the university authorities of Alcala, he has been scouring the streets at the head of the most profligate students, insulting women, even ladies of rank, and amenable only to his

* This lecture was given at Cambridge in 1869.

lovely young stepmother, Elizabeth of Valois, Isabel de la Paz, as the Spaniards call her, the daughter of Catherine de Medicis, and sister of the King of France. Don Carlos should have married her, had not his worthy father found it more advantageous for the crown of Spain, as well as more pleasant for him, Philip, to marry her himself. Whence came heart-burnings, rage, jealousies, romances, calumnies, of which two last—in as far at least as they concern poor Elizabeth—no wise man now believes a word.

Going on some errand on which he had no business—there are two stories, neither of them creditable nor necessary to repeat—Don Carlos has fallen downstairs and broken his head. He comes, by his Portuguese mother's side, of a house deeply tainted with insanity; and such an injury may have serious consequences. However, for nine days the wound goes on well, and Don Carlos, having had a wholesome fright, is, according to Doctor Olivarez, the *medico de camara*, a very good lad, and lives on chicken broth and dried plums. But on the tenth day comes on numbness of the left side, acute pains in the head, and then gradually shivering, high fever, erysipelas. His head and neck swell to an enormous size; then comes raging delirium, then stupefaction, and Don Carlos lies as one dead.

A modern surgeon would, probably, thanks to that training of which Vesalius may be almost called the father, have had little difficulty in finding out what was the matter with the luckless lad, and little difficulty in removing the evil, if it had not gone too far. But the Spanish physicians were then, as many of them are said to be still, as far behind the world in surgery as in other things; and indeed surgery itself was then in its infancy, because men, ever since the early Greek schools of Alexandria had died out, had been for centuries feeding their minds with anything rather than with facts. Therefore the learned morosophs who were gathered round Don Carlos's sick bed had become, according to their own confession, utterly confused, terrified, and at their wits' end.

It is the 7th of May, the eighteenth day after the accident, according to Olivarez's story: he and Dr Vega have been bleeding the unhappy prince, enlarging the wound twice, and torturing him seemingly on mere guesses. "I believe," says Olivarez, "that all was done well: but as I have said, in wounds in the head there are strange labyrinths." So on the 7th they stand round the bed in despair. Don Garcia de Toledo, the prince's faithful governor, is sitting by him, worn out with sleepless nights, and trying to supply to the poor boy that mother's tenderness which he has never known. Alva, too, is there, stern, self-compressed, most terrible, and yet most beautiful. He has a God on earth, and that is Philip his master; and though he has borne much from Don Carlos already, and will have to bear more, yet the wretched lad is to him as a son of God, a second deity, who will by right divine succeed to the inheritance of the first; and he watches this lesser deity struggling between life and death with an intensity of which we, in these less loyal days, can form no notion. One would be glad to have a glimpse of what passed through that mind, so subtle and so ruthless, so disciplined and so loyal withal: but Alva was a man who was not given to speak his mind, but to act it.

One would wish, too, for a glimpse of what was passing through the mind of another man, who has been daily in that sick chamber, according to Olivarez's statement, since the first of the month: but he is one who has had, for some years past, even more reason than Alva for not speaking his mind. What he looked like we know well, for Titian has painted him from the life—a tall, bold, well-dressed man, with a noble brain, square and yet lofty, short curling locks and beard, an eye which looks as though it feared neither man nor fiend—and it has had good reason to fear both—and features which would be exceeding handsome, but for the defiant snub-nose. That is Andreas Vesalius, of Brussels, dreaded and hated by the doctors of the old school—suspect, moreover, it would seem to inquisitors and theologians, possibly to Alva himself; for he has dared to dissect human bodies; he has insulted the mediævalists at Paris, Padua, Bologna, Pisa, Venice, in open theatre; he has turned the heads of all the young surgeons in Italy and France; he has written a great book, with prints in it, designed, some say, by Titian —they were actually done by another Netherlander, John of Calcar, near Cleves—in which he has dared to prove that Galen's anatomy was at fault throughout, and that he had been describing a monkey's inside when he had pretended to be describing a man's; and thus, by impudence and quackery, he has wormed himself—this Netherlander, a heretic at heart, as all Netherlanders are, to God as well as to Galen—into the confidence of the late Emperor Charles V., and gone campaigning with him as one of his physicians, anatomising human bodies even on the battle-field, and defacing the likeness of Deity; and worse than that, the most religious King Philip is deceived by him likewise, and keeps him in Madrid in wealth and honour; and now, in the prince's extreme danger, the king has actually sent for him, and bidden him try his skill—a man who knows nothing save about bones and muscles and the outside of the body, and is unworthy the name of a true physician.

One can conceive the rage of the old Spanish pedants at the Netherlander's appearance, and still more at what followed, if we are to believe Hugo Bloet of Delft, his countryman and contemporary.* Vesalius, he says, saw that the surgeons had bound up the wound so tight that an abscess had formed outside the skull, which could not break: he asserted that the only hope lay in opening it; and did so, Philip having given leave, "by two cross-cuts. Then the lad returned to himself, as if awakened from a profound sleep, affirming that he owed his restoration to life to the German doctor."

Dionysius Daza, who was there with the other physicians and surgeons, tells a different story: "The most learned, famous, and rare Baron Vesalius," he says, advised that the skull should be trepanned; but his advice was not followed.

Olivarez's account agrees with that of Daza. They had opened the wounds, he says, down to the skull before Vesalius came. Vesalius insisted that the injury lay inside the skull, and wished to pierce it. Olivarez spends much labour in proving that Vesalius had "no

* I owe this account of Bloet's—which appears to me the only one trustworthy—to the courtesy and erudition of Professor Henry Morley, who finds it quoted from Bloet's "Acroama," in the "Observationum Medicarum Rariorum," lib. vii., of John Theodore Schenk. Those who wish to know several curious passages of Vesalius's life, which I have not inserted in this article, would do well to consult one by Professor Morley, "Anatomy in Long Clothes," in "Fraser's Magazine" for November, 1853. May I express a hope, which I am sure will be shared by all who have read Professor Morley's biographies of Jerome Carden and of Cornelius Agrippa, that he will find leisure to return to the study of Vesalius's life; and will do for him what he has done for the two just-mentioned writers?

great foundation for his opinion:" but confesses that he never changed that opinion to the last, though all the Spanish doctors were against him. Then on the 6th, he says, the Bachelor Torres came from Madrid, and advised that the skull should be laid bare once more; and on the 7th, there being still doubt whether the skull was not injured, the operation was performed —by whom it is not said—but without any good result, or, according to Olivarez, any discovery, save that Vesalius was wrong, and the skull uninjured.

Whether this second operation of the 7th of May was performed by Vesalius, and whether it was that of which Bloet speaks, is an open question. Olivarez's whole relation is apologetic, written to justify himself and his seven Spanish colleagues, and to prove Vesalius in the wrong. Public opinion, he confesses, had been very fierce against him. The credit of Spanish medicine was at stake: and we are not bound to believe implicitly a paper drawn up under such circumstances for Philip's eye. This, at least, we gather: that Don Carlos was never trepanned, as is commonly said; and this, also, that whichever of the two stories is true, equally puts Vesalius into direct, and most unpleasant, antagonism to the Spanish doctors.*

But Don Carlos still lay senseless; and yielding to popular clamour, the doctors called in the aid of a certain Moorish doctor, from Valencia, named Priotarete, whose unguents, it was reported, had achieved many miraculous cures. The unguent, however, to the

* Olivarez's "Relacion" is to be found in the Granvelle State Papers. For the general account of Don Carlos's illness, and of the miraculous agencies by which his cure was said to have been effected, the general reader should consult Miss Frere's "Biography of Elizabeth of Valois," vol. i. pp. 307–19.

horror of the doctors, burned the skull till the bone was as black as the colour of ink; and Olivarez declares he believes it to have been a preparation of pure caustic. On the morning of the 9th of May, the Moor and his unguents were sent away, "and went to Madrid, to send to heaven Hernando de Vega, while the prince went back to our method of cure."

Considering what happened on the morning of the 10th of May, we should now presume that the second opening of the abscess, whether by Vesalius or some-one else, relieved the pressure on the brain; that a critical period of exhaustion followed, probably prolonged by the Moor's premature caustic, which stopped the suppuration: but that God's good handiwork, called nature, triumphed at last; and that therefore it came to pass that the prince was out of danger within three days of the operation. But he was taught, it seems, to attribute his recovery to a very different source from that of a German knife. For on the morning of the 9th, when the Moor was gone, and Don Carlos lay seemingly lifeless, there descended into his chamber a *Deus e machinâ*, or rather a whole pantheon of greater or lesser deities, who were to effect that which medical skill seemed not to have effected. Philip sent into the prince's chamber several of the precious relics which he usually carried about with him. The miraculous image of the Virgin of Atocha, in embroidering garments for whom, Spanish royalty, male and female, has spent so many an hour ere now, was brought in solemn procession and placed on an altar at the foot of the prince's bed; and in the afternoon there entered, with a procession likewise, a shrine containing the bones of a holy anchorite, one Fray Diego, "whose life and miracles," says Olivarez, "are so notorious:" and the bones of St. Justus and St. Pastor, the tutelar saints of the university of Alcala. Amid solemn litanies the relics of Fray Diego were laid upon the prince's pillow, and the sudarium, or mortuary cloth, which had covered his face, was placed upon the prince's forehead.

Modern science might object that the presence of so many personages, however pious or well intentioned, in a sick chamber on a hot Spanish May day, especially as the bath had been, for some generations past, held in religious horror throughout Spain, as a sign of Moorish and Mussulman tendencies, might have somewhat interfered with the chances of the poor boy's recovery. Nevertheless the event seems to have satisfied Philip's highest hopes; for that same night (so Don Carlos afterwards related) the holy monk Diego appeared to him in a vision, wearing the habit of St. Francis, and bearing in his hand a cross of reeds tied with a green band. The prince stated that he first took the apparition to be that of the blessed St. Francis; but not seeing the stigmata, he exclaimed, "How? Dost thou not bear the marks of the wounds?" What he replied Don Carlos did not recollect; save that he consoled him, and told him that he should not die of that malady.

Philip had returned to Madrid, and shut himself up in grief in the great Jeronymite monastery. Elizabeth was praying for her step-son before the miraculous images of the same city. During the night of the 9th of May prayers went up for Don Carlos in all the churches of Toledo, Alcala, and Madrid. Alva stood all that night at the bed's foot. Don Garcia de Toledo sat in the arm-chair, where he had now sat night and day for more than a fortnight. The good preceptor, Honorato Juan, afterwards Bishop of Osma, wrestled in prayer for the lad the whole night through. His prayer was answered: probably it had been answered already, without his being aware of it. Be that as it may, about dawn Don Carlos's heavy breathing ceased; he fell into a quiet sleep; and when he awoke all perceived at once that he was saved.

He did not recover his sight, seemingly on account of the erysipelas, for a week more. He then opened his eyes upon the miraculous image of Atocha, and vowed that, if he recovered, he would give to the Virgin, at four different shrines in Spain, gold plate of four times his weight; and silver plate of seven times his weight, when he should rise from his couch. So on the 6th of June he rose, and was weighed in a fur coat and a robe of damask, and his weight was three arrobas and one pound—seventy-six pounds in all. On the 14th of June he went to visit his father at the episcopal palace; then to all the churches and shrines in Alcala, and of course to that of Fray Diego, whose body it is said he contemplated for some time with edifying devotion. The next year saw Fray Diego canonised as a saint, at the intercession of Philip and his son; and thus Don Carlos re-entered the world, to be a terror and a torment to all around him, and to die—not by Philip's cruelty, as his enemies reported too hastily indeed, yet excusably, for they knew him to be capable of any wickedness—but simply of constitutional insanity.

And now let us go back to the history of "that most learned, famous, and rare Baron Vesalius," who had stood by and seen all these things done; and try if we cannot, after we have learned the history of his early life, guess at some of his probable meditations on this celebrated clinical case; and guess also how those meditations may have affected seriously the events of his after life.

Vesalius (as I said) was a Netherlander, born at Brussels in 1513 or 1514. His father and grandfather had been medical men of the highest standing in a profession which then, as now, was commonly hereditary. His real name was Wittag, an ancient family of Wesel, on the Rhine, from which town either he or his father adopted the name of Vesalius, according to the classicising fashion of those days. Young Vesalius was sent to college at Louvain, where he learned rapidly. At sixteen or seventeen he knew not only Latin, but Greek enough to correct the proofs of Galen, and Arabic enough to become acquainted with the works of the Mussulman physicians. He was a physicist too, and a mathematician, according to the knowledge of those times; but his passion—the study to which he was destined to devote his life—was anatomy.

Little or nothing (it must be understood) had been done in anatomy since the days of Galen of Pergamos, in the second century after Christ, and very little even by him. Dissection was all but forbidden among the ancients. The Egyptians, Herodotus tells us, used to pursue with stones and curses the embalmers as soon as they had performed their unpleasant office; and though Herophilus and Erasistratus are said to have dissected many subjects under the protection of Ptolemy Soter in Alexandria itself: yet the public feeling of the Greeks as well as of the Romans continued the same as that of the ancient Egyptians; and Galen was fain—as Vesalius proved—to supplement his ignorance of the human frame by describing that of an ape. Dissection was equally forbidden among the Mussulmans; and the great Arabic physicians could do no more than comment on Galen. The same prejudice extended through the Middle Age. Medical men were all clerks, *clerici*, and as such forbidden to shed blood. The only dissection, as far as I am aware, made during the Middle Age was one by Mundinus in 1306; and his subsequent commentaries on Galen—for he dare allow his own eyes to see no more than Galen had seen before him—constituted the best anatomical manual in Europe till the middle of the fifteenth century.

Then, in Italy at least, the classic Renaissance gave fresh life to anatomy as to all other sciences. Especially did the improvements in painting and sculpture stir men up to a closer study of the human frame. Leonardo da Vinci wrote a treatise on muscular anatomy. The artist and the sculptor often worked together, and realised that sketch of Michael Angelo's in which he himself is assisting Fallopius, Vesalius's famous pupil, to dissect. Vesalius soon found that his thirst for facts could not be slaked by the theories of the Middle Age; so in 1530 he went off to Montpellier, where Francis I. had just founded a medical school, and where the ancient laws of the city allowed the faculty each year the body of a criminal. From thence, after becoming the fellow-pupil and the friend of Rondelet, and probably also of Rabelais and those other luminaries of Montpellier, of whom I spoke in my essay on Rondelet, he returned to Paris to study under old Sylvius, whose real name was Jacques Dubois, *alias* Jock o' the Wood; and to learn less—as he complains himself—in an anatomical theatre than a butcher might learn in his shop.

Were it not that the whole question of dissection is one over which it is right to draw a reverent veil, as a thing painful, however necessary and however innocent, it would be easy to raise ghastly laughter in many a reader by the stories which Vesalius himself tells of his struggles to learn anatomy. How old Sylvius tried to demonstrate the human frame from a bit of a dog, fumbling in vain for muscles which he could not find, or which ought to have been there, according to Galen, and were not; while young Vesalius, as soon as the old pedant's back was turned, took his place, and, to the delight of the students, found for him—provided it were there—what he could not find himself;—how he went body-snatching and gibbet-robbing, often at the danger of his life, as when he and his friend were nearly torn to pieces by the cannibal dogs who haunted the Butte de Montfaucon, or place of public execution;—how he acquired, by a long and dangerous process, the only perfect skeleton then in the world, and the hideous story of the robber to whom it had belonged—all these horrors those who list may read for themselves elsewhere. I hasten past them with this remark—that to have gone through the toils, dangers, and disgusts which Vesalius faced, argued in a superstitious and cruel age like his, no common physical and moral courage, and a deep conscience that he was doing right, and must do it at all risks in the face of a generation which, peculiarly reckless of human life and human agony, allowed that frame which it called the image of God to be tortured, maimed, desecrated in every way while alive; and yet—straining at the gnat after having swallowed the camel—forbade it to be examined when dead, though for the purpose of alleviating the miseries of mankind.

The breaking out of war between Francis I. and Charles V. drove Vesalius back to his native country and Louvain; and in 1535 we hear of him as a surgeon in Charles V.'s army. He saw, most probably, the Emperor's invasion of Provence, and the disastrous retreat from before Montmorency's fortified camp at Avignon, through a country in which that crafty general had destroyed every article of human food, except the half-ripe grapes. He saw, perhaps, the Spanish soldiers, poisoned alike by the sour fruit and by the blazing sun, falling in hundreds along the white roads which led back into Savoy, murdered by the peasantry whose homesteads had been destroyed, stifled by the weight of their own armour, or desperately putting themselves, with their own hands, out of a world which had become intolerable. Half the army perished. Two thousand corpses lay festering between Aix and Fréjus alone. If young Vesalius needed "subjects," the ambition and the crime of man found enough for him in those blazing September days.

He went to Italy, probably with the remnants of the army. Where could he have rather wished to find himself? He was at last in the country where the human mind seemed to be growing young once more; the country of revived arts, revived sciences, learning, languages; and—though, alas! only for awhile—of revived free thought, such as Europe had not seen since the palmy days of Greece. Here at least he would be appreciated; here at least he would be allowed to think and speak: and he was appreciated. The Italian cities, who were then, like the Athenians of old, "spending their time in nothing else save to hear or to tell something new," welcomed the brave young Fleming and his novelties. Within two years he was professor of anatomy at Padua, then the first school in the world; then at Bologna and at Pisa at the same time; last of all at Venice, where Titian painted that portrait of him which remains unto this day.

These years were for him a continual triumph; everywhere, as he demonstrated on the human body, students crowded his theatre, or hung round him as he walked the streets; professors left their own chairs—their scholars having deserted them already—to go and listen humbly or enviously to the man who could give them what all brave souls throughout half Europe were craving for, and craving in vain—facts. And so, year after year, was realised that scene which stands engraved in the frontispiece of his great book—where, in the little quaint Cinquecento theatre, saucy scholars, reverend doctors, gay gentlemen, and even cowled monks, are crowding the floor, peeping over each other's shoulders, hanging on the balustrades; while in the centre, over his "subject"—which one of those same cowled monks knew but too well—stands young Vesalius, upright, proud, almost defiant, as one who knows himself safe in the impregnable citadel of fact; and in his hand the little blade of steel, destined—because wielded in obedience to the laws of nature, which are the laws of God—to work more benefit for the human race than all the swords which were drawn in those days, or perhaps in any other, at the bidding of most Catholic Emperors and most Christian Kings.

Those were indeed days of triumph for Vesalius; of triumph deserved, because earned by patient and accurate toil in a good cause: but Vesalius, being but a mortal man, may have contracted in those same days a temper of imperiousness and self-conceit, such as he showed afterwards when his pupil Fallopius dared to add fresh discoveries to those of his master. And yet, in spite of all Vesalius knew, how little he knew! How humbling to his pride it would have been had he known then—perhaps he does know now—that he had actually again and again walked, as it were, round and round the true theory of the circulation of the blood, and yet never seen it; that that discovery which, once made, is intelligible, as far as any phenomenon is intelligible, to the merest peasant, was reserved for another century, and for one of those Englishmen on whom Vesalius would have looked as semi-barbarians.

To make a long story short: three years after the publication of his famous book, "De Corporis Humani Fabrica," he left Venice to cure Charles V., at Regensburg, and became one of the great Emperor's physicians.

This was the crisis of Vesalius's life. The medicine with which he had worked the cure was China—Sarsaparilla, as we call it now—brought home from the then newly-discovered banks of the Paraguay and Uruguay, where its beds of tangled vine, they say, tinge the clear waters a dark-brown like that of peat, and convert whole streams into a healthful and pleasant tonic. On the virtues of this China (then supposed to be a root) Vesalius wrote a famous little book, into which he contrived to interweave his opinions on things in general, as good Bishop Berkeley did afterwards into his essay on the virtues of tar-water. Into this book, however, Vesalius introduced—as Bishop Berkeley did not—much, and perhaps too much, about himself; and much, though perhaps not too much, about poor old Galen, and his substitution of an ape's inside for that of a human being. The storm which had been long gathering burst upon him. The old school, trembling for their time-honoured reign, bespattered, with all that pedantry, ignorance, and envy could suggest, the man who dared not only to revolutionise surgery, but to interfere with the privileged mysteries of medicine; and, over and above, to become a greater favourite at the court of the greatest of monarchs. While such as Eustachius, himself an able discoverer, could join in the cry, it is no wonder if a lower soul, like that of Sylvius, led it open-mouthed. He was a mean, covetous, bad man, as George Buchanan well knew; and, according to his nature, he wrote a furious book —"Ad Vesani calumnias depulsandas." The punning change of Vesalius into Vesanus (madman) was but a fair and gentle stroke for a polemic, in days in which those who could not kill their enemies with steel or powder, held themselves justified in doing so, if possible, by vituperation, calumny, and every engine of moral torture. But a far more terrible weapon, and one which made Vesalius rage, and it may be for once in his life tremble, was the charge of impiety and heresy. The Inquisition was a very ugly place. It was very easy to get into it, especially for a Netherlander: but not so easy to get out. Indeed Vesalius must have trembled, when he saw his master, Charles V., himself take fright, and actually call on the theologians of Salamanca to decide whether it was lawful to dissect a human body. The monks, to their honour, used their common sense, and answered Yes. The deed was so plainly useful that it must be lawful likewise. But Vesalius did not feel that he had triumphed. He dreaded, possibly, lest the storm should only have blown over for a time. He fell, possibly, into hasty disgust at the folly of mankind, and despair of arousing them to use their common sense, and acknowledge their true interest and their true benefactors. At all events, he threw into the fire—so it is said—all his unpublished manuscripts, the records of long years of observation, and renounced science thenceforth.

We hear of him after this at Brussels, and at Basle likewise—in which latter city, in the company of physicians, naturalists, and Grecians, he must have breathed awhile a freer air. But he seems to have returned thence to his old master Charles V., and to have finally settled at Madrid as a court surgeon to Philip II., who sent him, but too late, to extract the lance splinters from the eye of the dying Henry II.

He was now married to a lady of rank from Brussels, Anne van Hamme by name; and their daughter married in time Philip II.'s grand falconer, who was doubtless a personage of no small social rank. Vesalius was well off in worldly things; somewhat fond, it is said, of good living and of luxury; inclined, it may be, to say, "Let us eat and drink, for to-morrow we die," and to sink more and more into the mere worldling, unless some shock should awake him from his lethargy.

And the awakening shock did come. After eight years of court life, he resolved, early in the year 1564, to go on a pilgrimage to Jerusalem.

The reasons for so strange a determination are wrapped in mystery and contradiction. The common story was that he had opened a corpse to ascertain the cause of death, and that, to the horror of the bystanders, the heart was still seen to beat; that his enemies accused him to the Inquisition, and that he was condemned to death, a sentence which was commuted to that of going on pilgrimage. But here, at the very outset, accounts differ. One says that the victim was a nobleman, name not given; another that it was a lady's maid, name not given. It is most improbable, if not impossible, that Vesalius, of all men, should have mistaken a living body for a dead one; while it is most probable, on the other hand, that his medical enemies would gladly raise such a calumny against him, when he was no longer in Spain to contradict it. Meanwhile Llorente, the historian of the Inquisition, makes no mention of Vesalius having been brought before its tribunal, while he does mention Vesalius's residence at Madrid. Another story is, that he went abroad to escape the bad temper of his wife; another that he wanted to enrich himself. Another story—and that not an unlikely one—is, that he was jealous of the rising reputation of his pupil Fallopius, then professor of anatomy at Venice. This distinguished surgeon, as I said before, had written a book, in which he added to Vesalius's discoveries, and corrected certain of his errors. Vesalius had answered him hastily and angrily, quoting his anatomy from memory; for, as he himself complained, he could not in Spain obtain a subject for dissection; not even, he said, a single skull. He had sent his book to Venice to be published, and had heard, seemingly, nothing of it. He may have felt that he was falling behind in the race of science, and that it was impossible for him to carry on his studies in Madrid; and so, angry with his own laziness and luxury, he may have felt the old sacred fire flash up in him, and have determined to go to Italy and become a student and a worker once more.

The very day that he set out, Clusius of Arras, then probably the best botanist in the world, arrived at Madrid; and, asking the reason of Vesalius's departure, was told by their fellow-countryman, Charles de Tisnacq, procurator for the affairs of the Netherlands, that Vesalius had gone of his own free will, and with all facilities which Philip could grant him, in performance of a vow which he had made during a dangerous illness. Here, at least, we have a drop of information, which seems taken from the stream sufficiently near to the fountain-head: but it must be recollected that De Tisnacq lived in dangerous times, and may have found it necessary to walk warily in them; that through him had been sent, only the year before, that famous letter from William of Orange, Horn, and Egmont, the fate whereof may be read in Mr. Motley's fourth chapter; that the crisis of the Netherlands which sprung out of that letter was coming fast; and that, as De Tisnacq was on friendly terms with Egmont, he may have felt his head at times somewhat loose on his shoulders; especially if he had heard Alva say, as he wrote, "that every time he saw the despatches of those three señors, they moved his choler so, that if he did not take much care to temper it, he would seem a frenzied man." In such times, De Tisnacq may have thought good to return a diplomatic answer to a fellow-countryman concerning a third fellow-countryman, especially when that countryman, as a former pupil of Melancthon at Wittemberg, might himself be under suspicion of heresy, and therefore of possible treason.

Be this as it may, one cannot but suspect some strain of truth in the story about the Inquisition; for, whether or not Vesalius operated on Don Carlos, he had seen with his own eyes that miraculous Virgin of Atocha at the bed's foot of the prince. He had heard his recovery attributed, not to the operation, but to the intercession of Fray, now Saint Diego;* and he must have had his thoughts thereon, and may, in an unguarded moment, have spoken them.

For he was, be it always remembered, a Netherlander. The crisis of his country was just at hand. Rebellion was inevitable, and, with rebellion, horrors unutterable; and, meanwhile, Don Carlos had set his mad brain on having the command of the Netherlands. In his rage at not having it, as all the world knows, he nearly killed Alva with his own hands, some two years after. If it be true that Don Carlos felt a debt of gratitude to Vesalius, he may (after his wont) have poured out to him some wild confidence about the Netherlands, to have even heard which would be a crime in Philip's eyes. And if this be but a fancy, still Vesalius was, as I just said, a Netherlander, and one of a brain and a spirit to which Philip's doings, and the air of the Spanish court, must have been growing ever more and more intolerable. Hundreds of his country folk, perhaps men and women whom he had known, were being racked, burnt alive, buried alive, at the bidding of a jocular ruffian, Peter Titelmann, the chief inquisitor. The "day of the *mau-*

* In justice to poor Doctor Olivarez, it must be said that, while he allows all force to the intercession of the Virgin and of Fray Diego, and of "many just persons," he cannot allow that there was any "miracle properly so called," because the prince was cured according to "natural order," and by "experimental remedies" of the physicians.

brulez," and the wholesale massacre which followed it, had happened but two years before; and, by all the signs of the times, these murders and miseries were certain to increase. And why were all these poor wretches suffering the extremity of horror, but because they would not believe in miraculous images, and bones of dead friars, and the rest of that science of unreason and unfact, against which Vesalius had been fighting all his life, consciously or not, by using reason and observing fact? What wonder if, in some burst of noble indignation and just contempt, he forgot a moment that he had sold his soul, and his love of science likewise, to be a luxurious, yet uneasy, hanger-on at the tyrant's court; and spoke unadvisedly some word worthy of a German man?

As to the story of his unhappy quarrels with his wife, there may be a grain of truth in it likewise. Vesalius's religion must have sat very lightly on him. The man who had robbed churchyards and gibbets from his youth was not likely to be much afraid of apparitions and demons. He had handled too many human bones to care much for those of saints. He was probably, like his friends of Basle, Montpellier, and Paris, somewhat of a heretic at heart, probably somewhat of a pagan, while his lady, Anne van Hamme, was probably a strict Catholic, as her father, being a councillor and master of the exchequer at Brussels, was bound to be; and freethinking in the husband, crossed by superstition in the wife, may have caused in them that wretched *vie à part*, that want of any true communion of soul, too common to this day in Catholic countries.

Be these things as they may—and the exact truth of them will now be never known—Vesalius set out to Jerusalem in the spring of 1564. On his way he visited his old friends at Venice to see about his book against Fallopius. The Venetian republic received the great philosopher with open arms. Fallopius was just dead; and the senate offered their guest the vacant chair of anatomy. He accepted it: but went on to the East.

He never occupied that chair; wrecked upon the Isle of Zante, as he was sailing back from Palestine, he died miserably of fever and want, as thousands of pilgrims returning from the Holy Land had died before him. A goldsmith recognised him; buried him in a chapel of the Virgin; and put up over him a simple stone, which remained till late years; and may remain, for aught I know, even now.

So perished, in the prime of life, "a martyr to his love of science," to quote the words of M. Burggraeve of Ghent, his able biographer and commentator, "the prodigious man, who created a science at an epoch when everything was still an obstacle to his progress; a man whose whole life was a long struggle of knowledge against ignorance, of truth against lies."

Plaudite: Exeat: with Rondelet and Buchanan. And whensoever this poor foolish world needs three such men, may God of His great mercy send them.

PARACELSUS.

PARACELSUS.*

I told you of Vesalius and Rondelet as specimens of the men who three hundred years ago were founding the physical science of the present day, by patient investigation of facts. But such an age as this would naturally produce men of a very different stamp, men who could not imitate their patience and humility; who were trying for royal roads to knowledge, and to the fame and wealth which might be got out of knowledge; who meddled with vain dreams about the occult sciences, alchemy, astrology, magic, the cabala, and so forth, who were reputed magicians, courted and feared for awhile, and then, too often, died sad deaths.

Such had been, in the century before, the famous Dr. Faust—Faustus, who was said to have made a compact with Satan—actually one of the inventors of printing—immortalised in Goethe's marvellous poem.

Such, in the first half of the sixteenth century, was Cornelius Agrippa—a doctor of divinity and a knight-at-arms; secret-service diplomatist to the Emperor Maximilian in Austria; astrologer, though unwilling, to his daughter Margaret, Regent of the Low Countries;

* This lecture was given at Cambridge in 1869, and has not had the benefit of the author's corrections for the press.

writer on the occult sciences and of the famous "De Vanitate Scientiarum," and what not? who died miserably at the age of forty-nine, accused of magic by the Dominican monks from whom he had rescued a poor girl, who they were torturing on a charge of witchcraft; and by them hunted to death; nor to death only, for they spread the fable—such as you may find in Delrio the Jesuit's "Disquisitions on Magic"*—that his little pet black dog was a familiar spirit, as Butler has it in "Hudibras":

> Agrippa kept a Stygian pug
> I' the garb and habit of a dog—
> That was his taste; and the cur
> Read to th' occult philosopher,
> And taught him subtly to maintain
> All other sciences are vain.

Such also was Jerome Cardan, the Italian scholar and physician, the father of algebraic science (you all recollect Cardan's rule), believer in dreams, prognostics, astrology; who died, too, miserably enough, in old age.

Cardan's sad life, and that of Cornelius Agrippa, you can, and ought to read for yourselves, in two admirable biographies, as amusing as they are learned, by Professor Morley, of the London University. I have not chosen either of them as a subject for this lecture, because Mr. Morley has so exhausted what is to be known about them, that I could tell you nothing which I had not stolen from him.

But what shall I say of the most famous of these men—Paracelsus? whose name you surely know. He too has been immortalised in a poem which you all ought to have read, one of Robert Browning's earliest and one of his best creations.

* Delrio's book, a famous one in its day, was published about 1612.

I think we must accept as true Mr. Browning's interpretation of Paracelsus's character. We must believe that he was at first an honest and high-minded, as he was certainly a most gifted, man; that he went forth into the world, with an intense sense of the worthlessness of the sham knowledge of the pedants and quacks of the schools; an intense belief that some higher and truer science might be discovered, by which diseases might be actually cured, and health, long life, happiness, all but immortality, be conferred on man; an intense belief that he, Paracelsus, was called and chosen by God to find out that great mystery, and be a benefactor to all future ages. That fixed idea might degenerate—did, alas! degenerate—into wild self-conceit, rash contempt of the ancients, violent abuse of his opponents. But there was more than this in Paracelsus. He had one idea to which, if he had kept true, his life would have been a happier one—the firm belief that all pure science was a revelation from God; that it was not to be obtained at second or third hand, by blindly adhering to the words of Galen or Hippocrates or Aristotle, and putting them (as the scholastic philosophers round him did) in the place of God: but by going straight to nature at first hand, and listening to what Bacon calls "the voice of God revealed in facts." True and noble is the passage with which he begins his "Labyrinthus Medicorum," one of his attacks on the false science of his day,

"The first and highest book of all healing," he says, "is called wisdom, and without that book no man will carry out anything good or useful . . . And that book is God Himself. For in Him alone who hath created all things, the knowledge and principle of all things dwells . . . without Him all is folly. As the sun shines on us from above, so He must pour into us from above all arts whatsoever. Therefore the root of all learning and cognition is, that we should seek first the kingdom of God—the kingdom of God in which all sciences are founded. . . . If any man think that nature is not founded on the kingdom of God, he knows nothing about it. All gifts," he repeats again and again, confused and clumsily (as is his wont), but with a true earnestness, "are from God."

The true man of science, with Paracelsus, is he who seeks first the kingdom of God in facts, investigating nature reverently, patiently, in faith believing that God, who understands His own work best, will make him understand it likewise. The false man of science is he who seeks the kingdom of this world, who cares nothing about the real interpretation of facts: but is content with such an interpretation as will earn him the good things of this world—the red hat and gown, the ambling mule, the silk clothes, the partridges, capons, and pheasants, the gold florins chinking in his palm. At such pretenders Paracelsus sneered, at last only too fiercely, not only as men whose knowledge consisted chiefly in wearing white gloves, but as rogues, liars, villains, and every epithet which his very racy vocabulary, quickened (it is to be feared) by wine and laudanum, could suggest. With these he contrasts the true men of science. It is difficult for us now to understand how a man setting out in life with such pure and noble views should descend at last (if indeed he did descend) to be a quack and a conjuror—and die under the imputation that

> Bombastes kept a devil's bird
> Hid in the pommel of his sword,

and have, indeed, his very name, Bombast, used to

this day as a synonym of loud, violent, and empty talk. To understand it at all, we must go back and think a little over these same occult sciences which were believed in by thousands during the fifteenth and sixteenth centuries.

The reverence for classic antiquity, you must understand, which sprang up at the renaissance in the fifteenth century, was as indiscriminating as it was earnest. Men caught the trash as well as the jewels. They put the dreams of the Neoplatonists, Iamblicus, Porphyry, or Plotinus, or Proclus, on the same level as the sound dialectic philosophy of Plato himself. And these Neoplatonists were all, more or less, believers in magic—Theurgy, as it was called—in the power of charms and spells, in the occult virtues of herbs and gems, in the power of adepts to evoke and command spirits, in the significance of dreams, in the influence of the stars upon men's characters and destinies. If the great and wise philosopher Iamblicus believed such things, why might not the men of the sixteenth century?

And so grew up again in Europe a passion for what were called the Occult sciences. It had always been haunting the European imagination. Mediæval monks had long ago transformed the poet Virgil into a great necromancer. And there were immense excuses for such a belief. There was a mass of collateral evidence that the occult sciences were true, which it was impossible then to resist. Races far more ancient, learned, civilised, than any Frenchman, German, Englishman, or even Italian, in the fifteenth century had believed in these things. The Moors, the best physicians of the Middle Ages, had their heads full, as the "Arabian Nights" prove, of enchanters, genii, peris, and what not? The Jewish rabbis had their Cabala, which sprang up in Alexandria, a system of philosophy founded on the mystic meaning of the words and the actual letters of the text of Scripture, which some said was given by the angel Ragiel to Adam in Paradise, by which Adam talked with angels, the sun and moon, summoned spirits, interpreted dreams, healed and destroyed; and by that book of Ragiel, as it was called, Solomon became the great magician and master of all the spirits and their hoarded treasures.

So strong, indeed, was the belief in the mysteries of the Cabala, that Reuchlin, the restorer of Hebrew learning in Germany, and Pico di Mirandola, the greatest of Italian savants, accepted them; and not only Pope Leo X. himself, but even statesmen and warriors received with delight Reuchlin's cabalistic treatise, "De Verbo Mirifico," on the mystic word "Schemhamphorash"—that hidden name of God, which whosoever can pronounce aright is, for the moment, lord of nature and of all dæmons.

Amulets, too, and talismans; the faith in them was exceeding ancient. Solomon had his seal, by which he commanded all dæmons; and there is a whole literature of curious nonsense, which you may read if you will, about the Abraxas and other talismans of the Gnostics in Syria; and another, of the secret virtues which were supposed to reside in gems: especially in the old Roman and Greek gems, carved into intaglios with figures of heathen gods and goddesses. Lapidaria, or lists of these gems and their magical virtues, were not uncommon in the Middle Ages. You may read a great deal that is interesting about them at the end of Mr. King's book on gems.

Astrology too; though Pico di Mirandola might

set himself against the rest of the world, few were found daring enough to deny so ancient a science. Luther and Melancthon merely followed the regular tradition of public opinion when they admitted its truth. It sprang probably from the worship of the Seven Planets by the old Chaldees. It was brought back from Babylon by the Jews after the Captivity, and spread over all Europe—perhaps all Asia likewise.

The rich and mighty of the earth must needs have their nativities cast, and consult the stars; and Cornelius Agrippa gave mortal offence to the Queen-Dowager of France (mother of Francis I.) because, when she compelled him to consult the stars about Francis's chance of getting out of his captivity in Spain after the battle of Pavia, he wrote and spoke his mind honestly about such nonsense.

Even Newton seems to have hankered after it when young. Among his MSS. in Lord Portsmouth's library at Hurstbourne are whole folios of astrologic calculations. It went on till the end of the seventeenth century, and died out only when men had begun to test it, and all other occult sciences, by experience, and induction founded thereon.

Countless students busied themselves over the transmutation of metals. As for magic, necromancy, pyromancy, geomancy, coscinomancy, and all the other mancies—there was then a whole literature about them. And the witch-burning inquisitors like Sprenger, Bodin, Delrio, and the rest, believed as firmly in the magic powers of the poor wretches whom they tortured to death, as did, in many cases, the poor wretches themselves.

Everyone, almost, believed in magic. Take two cases. Read the story which Benvenuto Cellini, the sculptor, tells in his life (everyone should read it) of the magician whom he consults in the Coliseum at Rome, and the figure which he sees as he walks back with the magician, jumping from roof to roof along the tiles of the houses.

And listen to this story, which Mr. Froude has dug up in his researches. A Church commissioner at Oxford, at the beginning of the Reformation, being unable to track an escaped heretic, "caused a figure to be made by an expert in astronomy;" by which it was discovered that the poor wretch had fled in a tawny coat and was making for the sea. Conceive the respected head of your College—or whoever he may be—in case you slept out all night without leave, going to a witch to discover whether you had gone to London or to Huntingdon, and then writing solemnly to inform the Bishop of Ely of his meritorious exertions!

In such a mad world as this was Paracelsus born. The son of a Swiss physician, but of noble blood, Philip Aureolus Theophrastus was his Christian name, Bombast von Hohenheim his surname, which last word he turned, after the fashion of the times, into Paracelsus. Born in 1493 at Einsiedeln (the hermitage), in Schweiz, which is still a famous place of pilgrimage, he was often called Eremita—the hermit. Erasmus, in a letter still extant, but suspected not to be genuine, addressed him by that name.

How he passed the first thirty-three years of his life it is hard to say. He used to boast that he had wandered over all Europe, been in Sweden, Italy, in Constantinople, and perhaps in the far East, with barber-surgeons, alchemists, magicians, haunting mines, and forges of Sweden and Bohemia, especially those which the rich merchants of that day had in the Tyrol.

It was from that work, he said, that he learnt what he knew: from the study of nature and of facts. He had heard all the learned doctors and professors; he had read all their books, and they could teach him nothing. Medicine was his monarch, and no one else. He declared that there was more wisdom under his bald pate than in Aristotle and Galen, Hippocrates and Rhasis. And fact seemed to be on his side. He re-appeared in Germany about 1525, and began working wondrous cures. He had brought back with him from the East an arcanum, a secret remedy, and laudanum was its name. He boasted, says one of his enemies, that he could raise the dead to life with it; and so the event all but proved. Basle was then the university where free thought and free creeds found their safest home; and hither Œcolampadius the reformer invited young Paracelsus to lecture on medicine and natural science.

It would have been well for him, perhaps, had he never opened his lips. He might have done good enough to his fellow-creatures by his own undoubted powers of healing. He cured John Frobenius, the printer, Erasmus's friend, at Basle, when the doctors were going to cut his leg off. His fame spread far and wide. Round Basle and away into Alsace he was looked on, even an enemy says, as a new Æsculapius.

But these were days in which in a university everyone was expected to talk and teach, and so Paracelsus began lecturing; and then the weakness which was mingled with his strength showed itself. He began by burning openly the books of Galen and Avicenna, and declared that all the old knowledge was useless. Doctors and students alike must begin over again with him. The dons were horrified. To burn Galen and Avicenna was as bad as burning the Bible. And more horrified still were they when Paracelsus began lecturing, not in the time-honoured dog-Latin, but in good racy German, which everyone could understand. They shuddered under their red gowns and hats. If science was to be taught in German, farewell to the Galenists' formulas, and their lucrative monopoly of learning. Paracelsus was bold enough to say that he wished to break up their monopoly; to spread a popular knowledge of medicine. "How much," he wrote once, "would I endure and suffer, to see every man his own shepherd—his own healer." He laughed to scorn their long prescriptions, used the simplest drugs, and declared Nature, after all, to be the best physician—as a dog, he says, licks his wound well again without our help; or as the broken rib of the ox heals of its own accord.

Such a man was not to be endured. They hated him, he says, for the same reason that they hated Luther, for the same reason that the Pharisees hated Christ. He met their attacks with scorn, rage, and language as coarse and violent as their own. The coarseness and violence of those days seem incredible to us now; and, indeed, Paracelsus, as he confessed himself, was, though of gentle blood, rough and unpolished; and utterly, as one can see from his writings, unable to give and take, to conciliate—perhaps to pardon. He looked impatiently on these men who were (not unreasonably) opposing novelties which they could not understand, as enemies of God, who were balking him in his grand plan for regenerating science and alleviating the woes of humanity, and he outraged their prejudices instead of soothing them.

Soon they had their revenge. Ugly stories were whispered about. Oporinus, the printer, who had lived with him for two years, and who left him, it is said, because he thought Paracelsus concealed from him unfairly the secret of making laudanum, told how Paracelsus was neither more nor less than a sot, who came drunk to his lectures, used to prime himself with wine before going to his patients, and sat all night in pothouses swilling with the boors.

Men looked coldly on him—longed to be rid of him. And they soon found an opportunity. He took in hand some Canon of the city from whom it was settled beforehand that he was to receive a hundred florins. The priest found himself cured so suddenly and easily that, by a strange logic, he refused to pay the money, and went to the magistrates. They supported him, and compelled Paracelsus to take six florins instead of the hundred. He spoke his mind fiercely to them. I believe, according to one story, he drew his long sword on the Canon. His best friends told him he must leave the place; and within two years, seemingly, after his first triumph at Basle, he fled from it a wanderer and a beggar.

The rest of his life is a blank. He is said to have recommenced his old wanderings about Europe, studying the diseases of every country, and writing his books, which were none of them published till after his death. His enemies joyfully trampled on the fallen man. He was a "dull rustic, a monster, an atheist, a quack, a maker of gold, a magician." When he was drunk, one Wetter, his servant, told Erastus (one of his enemies) that he used to offer to call up legions of devils to prove his skill, while Wetter, in abject terror of his spells, entreated him to leave the fiends alone—that he had sent his book by a fiend to the spirit of Galen in hell, and challenged him to say which was the better system, his or Paracelsus', and what not?

His books were forbidden to be printed. He himself was refused a hearing, and it was not till after ten years of wandering that he found rest and protection in a little village of Carinthia.

Three years afterwards he died in the hospital of St. Sebastian at Salzburg, in the Tyrol. His death was the signal for empirics and visionaries to foist on the public book after book on occult philosophy, written in his name—of which you may see ten folios—not more than a quarter, I believe, genuine. And these foolish books, as much as anything, have helped to keep up the popular prejudice against one who, in spite of all his faults was a true pioneer of science.* I believe (with those moderns who have tried to do him justice) that under all his verbiage and confusion there was a vein of sound scientific, experimental common sense.

When he talks of astronomy as necessary to be known by a physician, it seems to me that he laughs at astrology, properly so called; that is, that the stars influence the character and destiny of man. Mars, he says, did not make Nero cruel. There would have

* For a true estimate of Paracelsus you must read "Für Philippus Aureolus Theophrastus von Hohenheim," by that great German physician and savant, Professor Marx, of Göttingen; also a valuable article founded on Dr. Marx's views in the "Nouveau Biographie Universelle;" and also—which is within the reach of all—Professor Maurice's article on Paracelsus in Vol. II. of his history of "Moral and Metaphysical Philosophy." But the best key to Paracelsus is to be found in his own works.

been long-lived men in the world if Saturn had never ascended the skies; and Helen would have been a wanton, though Venus had never been created. But he does believe that the heavenly bodies, and the whole skies, have a physical influence on climate, and on the health of men.

He talks of alchemy, but he means by it, I think, only that sound science which we call chemistry, and at which he worked, wandering, he says, among mines and forges, as a practical metallurgist.

He tells us—what sounds startling enough—that magic is the only preceptor which can teach the art of healing; but he means, it seems to me, only an understanding of the invisible processes of nature, in which sense an electrician or a biologist, a Faraday or a Darwin, would be a magician; and when he compares medical magic to the Cabalistic science, of which I spoke just now (and in which he seems to have believed), he only means, I think, that as the Cabala discovers hidden meaning and virtues in the text of Scripture, so ought the man of science to find them in the book of nature. But this kind of talk, wrapt up too in the most confused style, or rather no style at all, is quite enough to account for ignorant and envious people accusing him of magic, saying that he had discovered the philosopher's stone, and the secret of Hermes Trismegistus; that he must make gold, because, though he squandered all his money, he had always money in hand; and that he kept a "devil's-bird," a familiar spirit, in the pommel of that famous long sword of his, which he was only too ready to lug out on provocation—the said spirit, Agoth by name, being probably only the laudanum bottle with which he worked so many wondrous cures, and of which, to judge from his writings, he took only too freely himself.

But the charm of Paracelsus is in his humour, his mother-wit. He was blamed for consorting with boors in pot-houses; blamed for writing in racy German, instead of bad school-Latin: but you can hardly read a chapter, either of his German or his dog-Latin, without finding many a good thing—witty and weighty, though often not a little coarse. He talks in parables. He draws illustrations, like Socrates of old, from the commonest and the oddest matters to enforce the weightiest truths. "Fortune and misfortune," he says, for instance nobly enough, "are not like snow and wind, they must be deduced and known from the secrets of nature. Therefore misfortune is ignorance, fortune is knowledge. The man who walks out in the rain is not unfortunate if he gets a ducking.

"Nature," he says again, "makes the text, and the medical man adds the gloss; but the two fit each other no better than a dog does a bath; and again, when he is arguing against the doctors who hated chemistry—"Who hates a thing which has hurt nobody? Will you complain of a dog for biting you, if you lay hold of his tail? Does the emperor send the thief to the gallows, or the thing which he has stolen? The thief, I think. Therefore science should not be despised on account of some who know nothing about it." You will say the reasoning is not very clear, and indeed the passage, like too many more, smacks strongly of wine and laudanum. But such is his quaint racy style. As humorous a man, it seems to me, as you shall meet with for many a day; and where there is humour there is pretty sure to be imagination, tenderness, and depth of heart.

As for his notions of what a man of science should be, the servant of God, and of Nature—which is the work of God—using his powers not for money, not for ambition, but in love and charity, as he says, for the good of his fellow-man—on that matter Paracelsus is always noble. All that Mr. Browning has conceived on that point, all the noble speeches which he has put into Paracelsus's mouth, are true to his writings. How can they be otherwise, if Mr. Browning set them forth—a genius as accurate and penetrating as he is wise and pure?

But was Paracelsus a drunkard after all?

Gentlemen, what concern is that of yours or mine? I have gone into the question, as Mr. Browning did, cannot say, and don't care to say.

Oporinus, who slandered him so cruelly, recanted when Paracelsus was dead, and sang his praises—too late. But I do not read that he recanted the charge of drunkenness. His defenders allow it, only saying that it was the fault not of him alone, but of all Germans. But if so, why was he specially blamed for what certainly others did likewise? I cannot but fear from his writings, as well as from common report, that there was something wrong with the man. I say only something. Against his purity there never was a breath of suspicion. He was said to care nothing for women; and even that was made the subject of brutal jests and lies. But it may have been that, worn out with toil and poverty, he found comfort in that laudanum which he believed to be the arcanum—the very elixir of life; that he got more and more into the habit of exciting his imagination with the narcotic, and then, it may be, when the fit of depression followed, he strung his nerves up again by wine. It may have been so. We have had, in the last generation, an exactly similar case in a philosopher, now I trust in heaven, and to whose genius I owe too much to mention his name here.

But that Paracelsus was a sot I cannot believe. That face of his, as painted by the great Tintoretto, is not the face of a drunkard, quack, bully, but of such a man as Browning has conceived. The great globular brain, the sharp delicate chin, is not that of a sot. Nor are those eyes, which gleam out from under the deep compressed brow, wild, intense, hungry, homeless, defiant, and yet complaining, the eyes of a sot—but rather the eyes of a man who struggles to tell a great secret, and cannot find words for it, and yet wonders why men cannot understand, will not believe what seems to him as clear as day—a tragical face, as you well can see.

God keep us all from making our lives a tragedy by one great sin. And now let us end this sad story with the last words which Mr. Browning puts into the mouth of Paracelsus, dying in the hospital at Salzburg, which have come literally true:

> Meanwhile, I have done well though not all well.
> As yet men cannot do without contempt;
> 'Tis for their good; and therefore fit awhile
> That they reject the weak and scorn the false,
> Rather than praise the strong and true in me:
> But after, they will know me. If I stoop
> Into a dark tremendous sea of cloud,
> It is but for a time. I press God's lamp
> Close to my breast; its splendour, soon or late,
> Will pierce the gloom. I shall emerge one day.

GEORGE BUCHANAN, SCHOLAR.

GEORGE BUCHANAN, SCHOLAR.

The scholar, in the sixteenth century, was a far more important personage than now. The supply of learned men was very small, the demand for them very great. During the whole of the fifteenth, and a great part of the sixteenth century, the human mind turned more and more from the scholastic philosophy of the Middle Ages to that of the Romans and the Greeks; and found more and more in old Pagan Art an element which Monastic Art had not, and which was yet necessary for the full satisfaction of their craving after the Beautiful. At such a crisis of thought and taste, it was natural that the classical scholar, the man who knew old Rome, and still more old Greece, should usurp the place of the monk, as teacher of mankind; and that scholars should form, for awhile, a new and powerful aristocracy, limited and privileged, and all the more redoubtable, because its power lay in intellect, and had been won by intellect alone.

Those who, whether poor or rich, did not fear the monk and priest, at least feared the "scholar," who held, so the vulgar believed, the keys of that magic lore by which the old necromancers had built cities like Rome, and worked marvels of mechanical and chemical skill, which the degenerate modern could never equal.

If the "scholar" stopped in a town, his hostess probably begged of him a charm against toothache or rheumatism. The penniless knight discoursed with him on alchemy, and the chances of retrieving his fortune by the art of transmuting metals into gold. The queen or bishop worried him in private about casting their nativities, and finding their fates among the stars. But the statesman, who dealt with more practical matters, hired him as an advocate and rhetorician, who could fight his master's enemies with the weapons of Demosthenes and Cicero. Wherever the scholar's steps were turned, he might be master of others, as long as he was master of himself. The complaints which he so often uttered concerning the cruelty of fortune, the fickleness of princes and so forth, were probably no more just then than such complaints are now. Then, as now, he got his deserts; and the world bought him at his own price. If he chose to sell himself to this patron and to that, he was used and thrown away: if he chose to remain in honourable independence, he was courted and feared.

Among the successful scholars of the sixteenth century, none surely is more notable than George Buchanan. The poor Scotch widow's son, by force of native wit, and, as I think, by force of native worth, fights his way upward, through poverty and severest persecution, to become the correspondent and friend of the greatest literary celebrities of the Continent, comparable, in their opinion, to the best Latin poets of antiquity; the preceptor of princes; the counsellor and spokesman of Scotch statesmen in the most dangerous of times; and leaves behind him political treatises, which have influenced not only the history of his own country, but that of the civilised world.

Such a success could not be attained without making enemies, perhaps without making mistakes. But the more we study George Buchanan's history, the less we shall be inclined to hunt out his failings, the more inclined to admire his worth. A shrewd, sound-hearted, affectionate man, with a strong love of right and scorn of wrong, and a humour withal which saved him—except on really great occasions—from bitterness, and helped him to laugh where narrower natures would have only snarled,—he is, in many respects, a type of those Lowland Scots, who long preserved his jokes, genuine or reputed, as a common household book.* A schoolmaster by profession, and struggling for long years amid the temptations which, in those days, degraded his class into cruel and sordid pedants, he rose from the mere pedagogue to be, in the best sense of the word, a courtier: "One," says Daniel Heinsius, "who seemed not only born for a court, but born to amend it. He brought to his queen that at which she could not wonder enough. For, by affecting a certain liberty in censuring morals, he avoided all offence, under the cloak of simplicity." Of him and his compeers, Turnebus, and Muretus, and their friend Andrea Govea, Ronsard, the French court poet, said that they had nothing of the pedagogue about them but the gown and cap. "Austere in face, and rustic in his looks," says David Buchanan, "but most polished in style and speech; and continually, even in serious conversation,

* So says Dr. Irving, writing in 1817. I have, however, tried in vain to get a sight of this book. I need not tell Scotch scholars how much I am indebted throughout this article to Mr. David Irving's erudite second edition of Buchanan's Life.

jesting most wittily." "Rough-hewn, slovenly, and rude," says Peacham, in his "Compleat Gentleman," speaking of him, probably, as he appeared in old age, "in his person, behaviour, and fashion; seldom caring for a better outside than a rugge-gown girt close about him: yet his inside and conceipt in poesie was most rich, and his sweetness and facilitie in verse most excellent." A typical Lowland Scot, as I said just now, he seems to have absorbed all the best culture which France could afford him, without losing the strength, honesty, and humour which he inherited from his Stirlingshire kindred.

The story of his life is easily traced. When an old man, he himself wrote down the main events of it, at the request of his friends; and his sketch has been filled out by commentators, if not always favourable, at least erudite. Born in 1506, at the Moss, in Killearn —where an obelisk to his memory, so one reads, has been erected in this century—of a family "rather ancient than rich," his father dead in the prime of manhood, his grandfather a spendthrift, he and his seven brothers and sisters were brought up by a widowed mother, Agnes Heriot—of whom one wishes to know more; for the rule that great sons have great mothers probably holds good in her case. George gave signs, while at the village school, of future scholarship; and when he was only fourteen, his uncle James sent him to the University of Paris. Those were hard times; and the youths, or rather boys, who meant to become scholars, had a cruel life of it, cast desperately out on the wide world to beg and starve, either into self-restraint and success, or into ruin of body and soul. And a cruel life George had. Within two years he was down in a severe illness, his uncle dead, his supplies stopped; and the boy of sixteen got home, he does not tell how. Then he tried soldiering; and was with Albany's French Auxiliaries at the ineffectual attack on Wark Castle. Marching back through deep snow, he got a fresh illness, which kept him in bed all winter. Then he and his brother were sent to St. Andrew's, where he got his B.A. at nineteen. The next summer he went to France once more; and "fell," he says, "into the flames of the Lutheran sect, which was then spreading far and wide." Two years of penury followed; and then three years of school-mastering in the College of St. Barbe, which he has immortalised—at least, for the few who care to read modern Latin poetry—in his elegy on "The Miseries of a Parisian Teacher of the Humanities." The wretched regent-master, pale and suffering, sits up all night preparing his lecture, biting his nails and thumping his desk; and falls asleep for a few minutes, to start up at the sound of the four-o'clock bell, and be in school by five, his Virgil in one hand, and his rod in the other, trying to do work on his own account at old manuscripts, and bawling all the while at his wretched boys, who cheat him, and pay each other to answer to truants' names. The class is all wrong. "One is barefoot, another's shoe is burst, another cries, another writes home. Then comes the rod, the sound of blows, and howls; and the day passes in tears." "Then mass, then another lesson, then more blows; there is hardly time to eat." I have no space to finish the picture of the stupid misery which, Buchanan says, was ruining his intellect, while it starved his body. However, happier days came. Gilbert Kennedy, Earl of Cassilis, who seems to have been a noble young gentleman, took him as his tutor for the next five years; and with him he went back to Scotland.

But there his plain speaking got him, as it did more than once afterward, into trouble. He took it into his head to write, in imitation of Dunbar, a Latin poem, in which St. Francis asks him in a dream to become a Gray Friar, and Buchanan ânswered in language which had the unpleasant fault of being too clever, and—to judge from contemporary evidence—only too true. The friars said nothing at first; but when King James made Buchanan tutor to one of his natural sons, they, "men professing meekness, took the matter somewhat more angrily than befitted men so pious in the opinion of the people." So Buchanan himself puts it: but, to do the poor friars justice, they must have been angels, not men, if they did not writhe somewhat under the scourge which he had laid on them. To be told that there was hardly a place in heaven for monks, was hard to hear and bear. They accused him to the king of heresy; but not being then in favour with James, they got no answer, and Buchanan was commanded to repeat the castigation. Having found out that the friars were not to be touched with impunity, he wrote, he says, a short and ambiguous poem. But the king, who loved a joke, demanded something sharp and stinging, and Buchanan obeyed by writing, but not publishing, "The Franciscans," a long satire, compared to which the "Somnium" was bland and merciful. The storm rose. Cardinal Beaton, Buchanan says, wanted to buy him of the king, and then, of course, burn him, as he had just burnt five poor souls; so, knowing James's avarice, he fled to England, through freebooters and pestilence.

There he found, he says, "men of both factions being burned on the same day and in the same fire" —a pardonable exaggeration—"by Henry VIII., in his old age more intent on his own safety than on the purity of religion. So to his beloved France he went again, to find his enemy Beaton ambassador at Paris. The capital was too hot to hold him; and he fled south to Bordeaux, to Andrea Govea, the Portuguese principal of the College of Guienne. As Professor of Latin at Bordeaux, we find him presenting a Latin poem to Charles V.; and indulging that fancy of his for Latin poetry which seems to us nowadays a childish pedantry, which was then—when Latin was the vernacular tongue of all scholars—a serious, if not altogether a useful, pursuit. Of his tragedies, so famous in their day—the "Baptist," the "Medea," the "Jephtha," and the "Alcestis"—there is neither space nor need to speak here, save to notice the bold declamations in the "Baptist" against tyranny and priestcraft; and to notice also that these tragedies gained for the poor Scotsman, in the eyes of the best scholars of Europe, a credit amounting almost to veneration. When he returned to Paris, he found occupation at once; and, as his Scots biographers love to record, "three of the most learned men in the world taught humanity in the same college," viz. Turnebus, Muretus, and Buchanan.

Then followed a strange episode in his life. A university had been founded at Coimbra, in Portugal, and Andrea Govea had been invited to bring thither what French savants he could collect. Buchanan went to Portugal with his brother Patrick, two more Scotsmen, Dempster and Ramsay, and a goodly company of French scholars, whose names and histories may be read in the erudite pages of Dr. Irving, went likewise. All prospered in the new Temple of the Muses for a year or so. Then its high-priest, Govea, died; and, by a peripeteia too common in those days and countries, Buchanan and two of his friends migrated unwillingly from the Temple of the Muses for that of Moloch, and found themselves in the Inquisition.

Buchanan, it seems, had said that St. Augustine was more of a Lutheran than a Catholic on the question of the mass. He and his friends had eaten flesh in Lent; which, he says, almost everyone in Spain did. But he was suspected, and with reason, as a heretic; the Gray Friars formed but one brotherhood throughout Europe; and news among them travelled surely if not fast, so that the story of the satire written in Scotland had reached Portugal. The culprits were imprisoned, examined, bullied—but not tortured—for a year and a half. At the end of that time, the proofs of heresy, it seems, were insufficient; but lest, says Buchanan with honest pride, "they should get the reputation of having vainly tormented a man not altogether unknown," they sent him for some months to a monastery, to be instructed by the monks. "The men," he says, "were neither inhuman nor bad, but utterly ignorant of religion;" and Buchanan solaced himself during the intervals of their instructions, by beginning his Latin translation of the Psalms.

At last he got free, and begged leave to return to France; but in vain. And so, wearied out, he got on board a Candian ship at Lisbon, and escaped to England. But England, he says, during the anarchy of Edward VI.'s reign, was not a land which suited him; and he returned to France, to fulfil the hopes which he had expressed in his charming

"Desiderium Lutitiæ," and the still more charming, because more simple, "Adventus in Galliam," in which he bids farewell, in most melodious verse, to "the hungry moors of wretched Portugal, and her clods fertile in naught but penury."

Some seven years succeeded of schoolmastering and verse-writing: the Latin paraphrase of the Psalms; another of the "Alcestis" of Euripides; an Epithalamium on the marriage of poor Mary Stuart, noble and sincere, however fantastic and pedantic, after the manner of the times; "Pomps," too, for her wedding, and for other public ceremonies, in which all the heathen gods and goddesses figure; epigrams, panegyrics, satires, much of which latter productions he would have consigned to the dust-heap in his old age, had not his too fond friends persuaded him to republish the follies and coarsenesses of his youth. He was now one of the most famous scholars in Europe, and the intimate friend of all the great literary men. Was he to go on to the end, die, and no more? Was he to sink into the mere pedant; or, if he could not do that, into the mere court versifier?

The wars of religion saved him, as they saved many another noble soul, from that degradation. The events of 1560–62 forced Buchanan, as they forced many a learned man besides, to choose whether he would be a child of light or a child of darkness; whether he would be a dilettante classicist, or a preacher—it might be a martyr—of the Gospel. Buchanan may have left France in "The Troubles" merely to enjoy in his own country elegant and learned repose. He may have fancied that he had found it, when he saw himself, in spite of his public profession of adherence to the Reformed Kirk, reading

Livy every afternoon with his exquisite young sovereign; master, by her favour, of the temporalities of Crossraguel Abbey, and by the favour of Murray, Principal of St. Leonard's College in St. Andrew's. Perhaps he fancied at times that "to-morrow was to be as to-day, and much more abundant;" that thenceforth he might read his folio, and write his epigram, and joke his joke, as a lazy comfortable pluralist, taking his morning stroll out to the corner where poor Wishart had been burned, above the blue sea and the yellow sands, and looking up to the castle tower from whence his enemy Beaton's corpse had been hung out; with the comfortable reflection that quieter times had come, and that whatever evil deeds Archbishop Hamilton might dare, he would not dare to put the Principal of St. Leonard's into the "bottle dungeon."

If such hopes ever crossed Geordie's keen fancy, they were disappointed suddenly and fearfully. The fire which had been kindled in France was to reach to Scotland likewise. "Revolutions are not made with rose-water;" and the time was at hand when all good spirits in Scotland, and George Buchanan among them, had to choose, once and for all, amid danger, confusion, terror, whether they would serve God or Mammon; for to serve both would be soon impossible.

Which side, in that war of light and darkness, George Buchanan took, is notorious. He saw then, as others have seen since, that the two men in Scotland who were capable of being her captains in the strife were Knox and Murray; and to them he gave in his allegiance heart and soul.

This is the critical epoch in Buchanan's life. By his conduct to Queen Mary he must stand or fall.

It is my belief that he will stand. It is not my intention to enter into the details of a matter so painful, so shocking, so prodigious; and now that that question is finally set at rest, by the writings both of Mr. Froude and Mr. Burton, there is no need to allude to it further, save where Buchanan's name is concerned. One may now have every sympathy with Mary Stuart; one may regard with awe a figure so stately, so tragic, in one sense so heroic,—for she reminds one rather of the heroine of an old Greek tragedy, swept to her doom by some irresistible fate, than of a being of our own flesh and blood, and of our modern and Christian times. One may sympathise with the great womanhood which charmed so many while she was alive; which has charmed, in later years, so many noble spirits who have believed in her innocence, and have doubtless been elevated and purified by their devotion to one who seemed to them an ideal being. So far from regarding her as a hateful personage, one may feel oneself forbidden to hate a woman whom God may have loved, and may have pardoned, to judge from the punishment so swift, and yet so enduring, which He inflicted. At least, he must so believe who holds that punishment is a sign of mercy; that the most dreadful of all dooms is impunity. Nay, more, those "Casket" letters and sonnets may be a relief to the mind of one who believes in her guilt on other grounds; a relief when one finds in them a tenderness, a sweetness, a delicacy, a magnificent self-sacrifice, however hideously misplaced, which shows what a womanly heart was there; a heart which, joined to that queenly brain, might have made her a blessing and a glory to Scotland, had not the whole character been warped and ruinate from childhood, by an education so abominable, that anyone who knows what words she must have heard, what scenes she must have beheld in France, from her youth up, will wonder that she sinned so little: not that she sinned so much. One may feel, in a word, that there is every excuse for those who have asserted Mary's innocence, because their own high-mindedness shrank from believing her guilty: but yet Buchanan, in his own place and time, may have felt as deeply that he could do no otherwise than he did.

The charges against him, as all readers of Scotch literature know well, may be reduced to two heads. 1st. The letters and sonnets were forgeries. Maitland of Lethington may have forged the letters; Buchanan, according to some, the sonnets. Whoever forged them, Buchanan made use of them in his Detection, knowing them to be forged. 2nd. Whether Mary was innocent or not, Buchanan acted a base and ungrateful part in putting himself in the forefront amongst her accusers. He had been her tutor, her pensioner. She had heaped him with favours; and, after all, she was his queen, and a defenceless woman: and yet he returned her kindness, in the hour of her fall, by invectives fit only for a rancorous and reckless advocate, determined to force a verdict by the basest arts of oratory.

Now as to the Casket letters. I should have thought they bore in themselves the best evidence of being genuine. I can add nothing to the arguments of Mr. Froude and Mr. Burton, save this: that no one clever enough to be a forger would have put together documents so incoherent, and so incomplete. For the evidence of guilt which they contain is, after all, slight and indirect, and, moreover, superfluous altogether; seeing that Mary's guilt was open and palpable, before the supposed discovery of the letters, to every person at home and abroad who had any knowledge of the facts. As for the alleged inconsistency of the letters with proven facts: the answer is, that whosoever wrote the letters would be more likely to know facts which were taking place around them than any critic could be one hundred or three hundred years afterwards. But if these mistakes as to facts actually exist in them, they are only a fresh argument for their authenticity. Mary, writing in agony and confusion, might easily make a mistake: forgers would only take too good care to make none.

But the strongest evidence in favour of the letters and sonnets, in spite of the arguments of good Dr. Whittaker and other apologists for Mary, is to be found in their tone. A forger in those coarse days would have made Mary write in some Semiramis or Roxana vein, utterly alien to the tenderness, the delicacy, the pitiful confusion of mind, the conscious weakness, the imploring and most feminine trust which makes the letters, to those who—as I do—believe in them, more pathetic than any fictitious sorrows which poets could invent. More than one touch, indeed, of utter self-abasement, in the second letter, is so unexpected, so subtle, and yet so true to the heart of woman, that—as has been well said—if it was invented there must have existed in Scotland an earlier Shakespeare; who yet has died without leaving any other sign, for good or evil, of his dramatic genius.

As for the theory (totally unsupported) that Buchanan forged the poem usually called the "Sonnets;" it is paying old Geordie's genius, however versatile it may have been, too high a compliment to believe that he could have written both them and the Detection; while it is paying his shrewdness too low a compliment to believe that he could have put into them, out of mere carelessness or stupidity, the well-known line, which seems incompatible with the theory both of the letters and of his own Detection; and which has ere now been brought forward as a fresh proof of Mary's innocence.

And, as with the letters, so with the sonnets: their delicacy, their grace, their reticence, are so many arguments against their having been forged by any Scot of the sixteenth century, and least of all by one in whose character—whatever his other virtues may have been—delicacy was by no means the strongest point.

As for the complaint that Buchanan was ungrateful to Mary, it must be said: That even if she, and not Murray, had bestowed on him the temporalities of Crossraguel Abbey four years before, it was merely fair pay for services fairly rendered; and I am not aware that payment, or even favours, however gracious, bind any man's soul and conscience in questions of highest morality and highest public importance. And the importance of that question cannot be exaggerated. At a moment when Scotland seemed struggling in death-throes of anarchy, civil and religious, and was in danger of becoming a prey either to England or to France, if there could not be formed out of the heart of her a people, steadfast, trusty, united, strong politically because strong in the fear of God and the desire of righteousness—at such a moment as this, a crime had been committed, the like of which had not been heard in Europe since the tragedy of Joan of Naples. All Europe stood aghast. The honour of the Scottish nation was at stake. More than Mary or Bothwell were known to be implicated in the deed; and—as Buchanan puts it in the opening of his "De Jure Regni"—"The fault of some few was charged upon all; and the common hatred of a particular person did redound to the whole nation; so that even such as were remote from any suspicion were inflamed by the infamy of men's crimes."*

To vindicate the national honour, and to punish the guilty, as well as to save themselves from utter anarchy, the great majority of the Scotch nation had taken measures against Mary which required explicit justification in the sight of Europe, as Buchanan frankly confesses in the opening of his "De Jure Regni." The chief authors of those measures had been summoned, perhaps unwisely and unjustly, to answer for their conduct to the Queen of England. Queen Elizabeth—a fact which was notorious enough then, though it has been forgotten till the last few years—was doing her utmost to shield Mary. Buchanan was deputed, it seems, to speak out for the people of Scotland; and certainly never people had an abler apologist. If he spoke fiercely, savagely, it must be remembered that he spoke of a fierce and savage matter; if he used—and it may be abused—all the arts of oratory, it must be remembered that he was fighting for the honour, and it may be for the national life, of his country, and striking—as men in such cases have a right to strike—as hard as he could. If he makes no secret of his indignation, and even contempt, it must be remembered that indignation and contempt may well have been real with him, while they were

* From the quaint old translation of 1721, by "A Person of Honour of the Kingdom of Scotland."

real with the soundest part of his countrymen; with that reforming middle class, comparatively untainted by French profligacy, comparatively undebauched by feudal subservience, which has been the leaven which has leavened the whole Scottish people in the last three centuries with the elements of their greatness. If, finally, he heaps up against the unhappy Queen charges which Mr. Burton thinks incredible, it must be remembered that, as he well says, these charges give the popular feeling about Queen Mary; and it must be remembered also, that that popular feeling need not have been altogether unfounded. Stories which are incredible, thank God, in these milder days, were credible enough then, because, alas! they were so often true. Things more ugly than any related of poor Mary were possible enough—as no one knew better than Buchanan—in that very French court in which Mary had been brought up; things as ugly were possible in Scotland then, and for at least a century later; and while we may hope that Buchanan has overstated his case, we must not blame him too severely for yielding to a temptation common to all men of genius when their creative power is roused to its highest energy by a great cause and a great indignation.

And that the genius was there, no man can doubt; one cannot read that "hideously eloquent" description of Kirk o' Field, which Mr. Burton has well chosen as a specimen of Buchanan's style, without seeing that we are face to face with a genius of a very lofty order: not, indeed, of the loftiest—for there is always in Buchanan's work, it seems to me, a want of unconsciousness, and a want of tenderness—but still a genius worthy to be placed beside those ancient writers from whom he took his manner. Whether or not we agree with his contemporaries, who say that he equalled Virgil in Latin poetry, we may place him fairly as a prose writer by the side of Demosthenes, Cicero, or Tacitus. And so I pass from this painful subject; only quoting—if I may be permitted to quote—Mr. Burton's wise and gentle verdict on the whole. "Buchanan," he says, "though a zealous Protestant, had a good deal of the Catholic and sceptical spirit of Erasmus, and an admiring eye for everything that was great and beautiful. Like the rest of his countrymen, he bowed himself in presence of the lustre that surrounded the early career of his mistress. More than once he expressed his pride and reverence in the inspiration of a genius deemed by his contemporaries to be worthy of the theme. There is not, perhaps, to be found elsewhere in literature so solemn a memorial of shipwrecked hopes, of a sunny opening and a stormy end, as one finds in turning the leaves of the volume which contains the beautiful epigram "Nympha Caledoniæ" in one part, the "Detectio Mariæ Reginæ" in another; and this contrast is, no doubt, a faithful parallel of the reaction in the popular mind. This reaction seems to have been general, and not limited to the Protestant party; for the conditions under which it became almost a part of the creed of the Church of Rome to believe in her innocence had not arisen."

If Buchanan, as some of his detractors have thought, raised himself by subserviency to the intrigues of the Regent Murray, the best heads in Scotland seem to have been of a different opinion. The murder of Murray did not involve Buchanan's fall. He had avenged it, as far as pen could do it, by that "Admonition Direct to the Trew Lordis," in which he showed himself as great a master of Scottish, as he was of Latin prose. His satire of the "Chameleon," though its publication was stopped by Maitland, must have been read in manuscript by many of those same "True Lords;" and though there were nobler instincts in Maitland than any Buchanan gave him credit for, the satire breathed an honest indignation against that wily turncoat's misgoings, which could not but recommend the author to all honest men. Therefore it was, I presume, and not because he was a rogue, and a hired literary spadassin, that to the best heads in Scotland he seemed so useful, it may be so worthy, a man, that he be provided with continually increasing employment. As tutor to James I.; as director, for a short time, of the chancery; as keeper of the privy seal, and privy councillor; as one of the commissioners for codifying the laws, and again—for in the semi-anarchic state of Scotland, government had to do everything in the way of organisation—in the committee for promulgating a standard Latin grammar; in the committee for reforming the University of St. Andrew's: in all these Buchanan's talents were again and again called for; and always ready. The value of his work, especially that for the reform of St. Andrew's, must be judged by Scotsmen, rather than by an Englishman; but all that one knows of it justifies Melville's sentence in the well-known passage in his memoirs, wherein he describes the tutors and household of the young king. "Mr. George was a Stoic philosopher, who looked not far before him;" in plain words, a high-minded and right-minded man, bent on doing the duty which lay nearest him. The worst that can be said against him during these times is, that his name appears with the sum of £100 against it, as one of those "who were to be entertained in Scotland by pensions out of England;" and Ruddiman, of course, comments on the fact by saying that Buchanan "was at length to act under the threefold character of malcontent, reformer, and pensioner:" but it gives no proof whatsoever that Buchanan ever received any such bribe; and in the very month, seemingly, in which that list was written —10th March, 1579—Buchanan had given a proof to the world that he was not likely to be bribed or bought, by publishing a book, as offensive probably to Queen Elizabeth as it was to his own royal pupil; namely, his famous "De Jure Regni apud Scotos," the very primer, according to many great thinkers, of constitutional liberty. He dedicates that book to King James, "not only as his monitor, but also as an importunate and bold exactor, which in these his tender and flexible years may conduct him in safety past the rocks of flattery." He has complimented James already on his abhorrence of flattery, "his inclination far above his years for undertaking all heroical and noble attempts, his promptitude in obeying his instructors and governors, and all who give him sound admonition, and his judgment and diligence in examining affairs, so that no man's authority can have much weight with him unless it be confirmed by probable reasons." Buchanan may have thought that nine years of his stern rule had eradicated some of James's ill conditions; the petulance which made him kill the Master of Mar's sparrow, in trying to wrest it out of his hand; the carelessness with which —if the story told by Chytræus, on the authority of Buchanan's nephew, be true—James signed away his crown to Buchanan for fifteen days, and only discovered his mistake by seeing Buchanan act in open court the character of King of Scots. Buchanan had at last made him a scholar; he may have fancied that he had made him likewise a manful man: yet he may have dreaded that, as James grew up, the old inclinations would return in stronger and uglier shapes, and that flattery might be, as it was after all, the cause of James's moral ruin. He at least will be no flatterer. He opens the dialogue which he sends to the king, with a calm but distinct assertion of his mother's guilt, and a justification of the conduct of men who were now most of them past helping Buchanan, for they were laid in their graves; and then goes on to argue fairly, but to lay down firmly, in a sort of Socratic dialogue, those very principles by loyalty to which the House of Hanover has reigned, and will reign, over these realms. So with his History of Scotland; later antiquarian researches have destroyed the value of the earlier portions of it: but they have surely increased the value of those later portions, in which Buchanan inserted so much which he had already spoken out in his Detection of Mary. In that book also *liberavit animam suam*; he spoke his mind fearless of consequences, in the face of a king who he must have known—for Buchanan was no dullard—regarded him with deep dislike, who might in a few years be able to work his ruin.

But those few years were not given to Buchanan. He had all but done his work, and he hastened to get it over before the night should come wherein no man can work. One must be excused for telling—one would not tell it in a book intended to be read only by Scotsmen, who know or ought to know the tale already—how the two Melvilles and Buchanan's nephew

Thomas went to see him in Edinburgh, in September, 1581, hearing that he was ill, and his History still in the press; and how they found the old sage, true to his schoolmaster's instincts, teaching the Hornbook to his servant-lad; and how he told them that doing that was "better than stealing sheep, or sitting idle, which was as bad," and showed them that dedication to James I., in which he holds up to his imitation as a hero whose equal was hardly to be found in history, that very King David whose liberality to the Romish Church provoked James's witticism that "David was a sair saint for the crown." Andrew Melville, so James Melville says, found fault with the style. Buchanan replied that he could do no more for thinking of another thing, which was to die. They then went to Arbuthnot's printing-house, and inspected the history, as far as that terrible passage concerning Rizzio's burial, where Mary is represented as "laying the miscreant almost in the arms of Maud de Valois, the late queen." Alarmed, and not without reason, at such plain speaking, they stopped the press, and went back to Buchanan's house. Buchanan was in bed. "He was going," he said, "the way of welfare." They asked him to soften the passage; the king might prohibit the whole work. "Tell me, man," said Buchanan, "if I have told the truth." They could not, or would not, deny it. "Then I will abide his feud, and all his kin's; pray, pray to God for me, and let Him direct all." "So," says Melville, "before the printing of his chronicle was ended, this most learned, wise, and godly man ended his mortal life."

Camden has a hearsay story—written, it must be remembered, in James I.'s time—that Buchanan, on his death-bed, repented of his harsh words against

Queen Mary; and an old Lady Rosyth is said to have said that when she was young a certain David Buchanan recollected hearing some such words from George Buchanan's own mouth. Those who will, may read what Ruddiman and Love have said, and oversaid, on both sides of the question: whatever conclusion they come to, it will probably not be that to which George Chalmers comes in his life of Ruddiman: that "Buchanan, like other liars, who, by the repetition of falsehoods are induced to consider the fiction as truth, had so often dwelt with complacency on the forgeries of his Detections, and the figments of his History, that he at length regarded his fictions and his forgeries as most authentic facts."

At all events his fictions and his forgeries had not paid him in that coin which base men generally consider the only coin worth having, namely, the good things of this life. He left nothing behind him—if at least Dr. Irving has rightly construed the "Testament Dative" which he gives in his appendix—save arrears to the sum of £100 of his Crossraguel pension. We may believe as we choose the story in Mackenzie's "Scotch Writers," that when he felt himself dying, he asked his servant Young about the state of his funds, and finding he had not enough to bury himself withal, ordered what he had to be given to the poor, and said that if they did not choose to bury him they might let him lie where he was, or cast him in a ditch, the matter was very little to him. He was buried, it seems, at the expense of the city of Edinburgh, in the Greyfriars' Churchyard—one says in a plain turf grave—among the marble monuments which covered the bones of worse or meaner men; and whether or not the "Throughstone" which, "sunk under the ground in the Greyfriars," was raised and cleaned by the Council of Edinburgh in 1701, was really George Buchanan's, the reigning powers troubled themselves little for several generations where he lay.

For Buchanan's politics were too advanced for his age. Not only Catholic Scotsmen, like Blackwood, Winzet, and Ninian, but Protestants, like Sir Thomas Craig and Sir John Wemyss, could not stomach the "De Jure Regni." They may have had some reason on their side. In the then anarchic state of Scotland, organisation and unity under a common head may have been more important than the assertion of popular rights. Be that as it may, in 1584, only two years after his death, the Scots Parliament condemned his Dialogue and History as untrue, and commanded all possessors of copies to deliver them up, that they might be purged of "the offensive and extraordinary matters" which they contained. The "De Jure Regni" was again prohibited in Scotland, in 1664, even in manuscript; and in 1683, the whole of Buchanan's political works had the honour of being burned by the University of Oxford, in company with those of Milton, Languet, and others, as "pernicious books, and damnable doctrines, destructive to the sacred persons of Princes, their state and government, and of all human society." And thus the seed which Buchanan had sown, and Milton had watered—for the allegation that Milton borrowed from Buchanan is probably true, and equally honourable to both—lay trampled into the earth, and seemingly lifeless, till it tillered out, and blossomed, and bore fruit to a good purpose, in the Revolution of 1688.

To Buchanan's clear head and stout heart, Scotland owes, as England owes likewise, much of her modern liberty. But Scotland's debt to him, it seems to me, is even greater on the count of morality, public and private. What the morality of the Scotch upper classes was like, in Buchanan's early days, is too notorious; and there remains proof enough—in the writings, for instance, of Sir David Lindsay—that the morality of the populace, which looked up to the nobles as its example and its guide, was not a whit better. As anarchy increased, immorality was likely to increase likewise; and Scotland was in serious danger of falling into such a state as that into which Poland fell, to its ruin, within a hundred and fifty years after; in which the savagery of feudalism, without its order or its chivalry, would be varnished over by a thin coating of French "civilisation," and, as in the case of Bothwell, the vices of the court of Paris should be added to those of the Northern freebooter. To deliver Scotland from that ruin, it was needed that she should be united into one people, strong, not in mere political, but in moral ideas; strong by the clear sense of right and wrong, by the belief in the government and the judgments of a living God. And the tone which Buchanan, like Knox, adopted concerning the great crimes of their day, helped notably that national salvation. It gathered together, organised, strengthened, the scattered and wavering elements of public morality. It assured the hearts of all men who loved the right and hated the wrong; and taught a whole nation to call acts by their just names, whoever might be the doers of them. It appealed to the common conscience of men. It proclaimed a universal and God-given morality, a bar at which all, from the lowest to the highest, must alike be judged.

The tone was stern: but there was need of sternness. Moral life and death were in the balance. If the Scots people were to be told that the crimes which roused their indignation were excusable, or beyond punishment, or to be hushed up and slipped over in any way, there was an end of morality among them. Every man, from the greatest to the least, would go and do likewise, according to his powers of evil. That method was being tried in France, and in Spain likewise, during those very years. Notorious crimes were hushed up under pretence of loyalty; excused as political necessities; smiled away as natural and pardonable weaknesses. The result was the utter demoralisation, both of France and Spain. Knox and Buchanan, the one from the standpoint of an old Hebrew prophet, the other rather from that of a Juvenal or a Tacitus, tried the other method, and called acts by their just names, appealing alike to conscience and to God. The result was virtue and piety, and that manly independence of soul which is thought compatible with hearty loyalty, in a country labouring under heavy disadvantages, long divided almost into two hostile camps, two rival races.

And the good influence was soon manifest, not only in those who sided with Buchanan and his friends, but in those who most opposed them. The Roman Catholic preachers, who at first asserted Mary's right to impunity, while they allowed her guilt, grew silent for shame, and set themselves to assert her entire innocence; while the Scots who have followed their example have, to their honour, taken up the same ground. They have fought Buchanan on the ground of fact, not on the ground of morality: they have alleged—as they had a fair right to do—the probability of intrigue and forgery in an age so profligate: the improbability that a Queen so gifted by nature and by fortune, and confessedly for a long while so strong and so spotless, should as it were by a sudden insanity have proved so untrue to herself. Their noblest and purest sympathies have been enlisted—and who can blame them?—in loyalty to a Queen, chivalry to a woman, pity for the unfortunate and—as they conceived—the innocent; but whether they have been right or wrong in their view of facts, the Scotch partisans of Mary have always—as far as I know—been right in their view of morals; they have never deigned to admit Mary's guilt, and then to palliate it by those sentimental, or rather sensual, theories of human nature, too common in a certain school of French literature, too common, alas! in a certain school of modern English novels. They have not said, "She did it; but after all, was the deed so very inexcusable?" They have said, "The deed was inexcusable: but she did not do it." And so the Scotch admirers of Mary, who have numbered among them many a pure and noble, as well as many a gifted spirit, have kept at least themselves unstained; and have shown, whether consciously or not, that they too share in that sturdy Scotch moral sense which has been so much strengthened—as I believe—by the plain speech of good old George Buchanan.

THE END.